Sir Charles Gould

*from 1792, Sir Charles Morgan, Bart. of Tredegar*
by Thomas Gainsborough

THE STORY OF LIFE ASSURANCE
IN THE EXPERIENCE OF
THE EQUITABLE LIFE ASSURANCE SOCIETY
1762–1962

EQUITABLE
ASSURANCES

BY

MAURICE EDWARD OGBORN

F I A, F S S

LONDON
GEORGE ALLEN AND UNWIN LTD
RUSKIN HOUSE  MUSEUM STREET

PRINTED IN GREAT BRITAIN
*in 12 point Fournier type*
BY UNWIN BROTHERS LIMITED
WOKING AND LONDON

# FOREWORD

BY J. H. GUNLAKE, CBE

PRESIDENT OF THE INSTITUTE OF ACTUARIES

MISFORTUNE, being dreadful to man, is so far apt to engage his attention as sometimes to incline him to an irrational supposition that what is not bad news is not real news, or that what is not calamity cannot be history. Many, therefore, who have reflected upon the campaigns fought by Wolfe and Clive, or brooded upon the convulsions wrought in Europe by the Seven Years' War, may be unaware—until they read this book—that whilst all these things were going on James Dodson, mathematician of the City of London, was quietly pondering certain ideas which, when they had won acceptance and been implemented, fostered and improved by others, have also not been without their vast consequences. Yet it is not for their magnitude alone that these consequences should excite our interest. If we are impressed (as we are) by the fact that the institutions that have been created after the pattern set in 1762 have affected the lives of countless thousands in all parts of the world, we should accord an even greater share of our wonder to the beneficial nature of that widespread influence; and if we recall that in the mid-course of its two centuries of progress this astonishing movement was disfigured by the appearance of a few Montague Tiggs, we should recollect, with the help of this book, that this came about because some who sought to emulate the success of the Old Equitable paid too little heed to the scientific principles in which its advisers never wavered, and to the prudent sagacity with which all attempts to disregard those principles were resisted by its managers. The pioneer, in fact, not only merits our admiration for having shown the way, but also exacts from us a measure of awe for its own vigorous survival for 200 years afterwards. Surely, it may adapt the words of the younger Pitt, and fairly

7

claim to have created itself by its exertions and the modern life assurance world by its example.

To actuaries, in particular, the tale told in these pages will always be of absorbing interest. Dodson, it is true, was not the first to think in our ways; as the author records, with the mortality studies of Graunt and Halley, and the annuity calculations of Halley and de Witt, actuarial science began to stir some hundred years before the Equitable. It is true also that our scientific methods—though not our essential principles—are in many ways very different from those of William Morgan. And it is true, further, that actuarial science concerns itself nowadays with much that lies outside the friendly society and life assurance fields. But few actuaries, I think, will be able to read unmoved the story of the first premium scale to be drawn up, the first valuation to be made, the first reversionary bonus to be allotted, the first surrender value to be calculated. And when members of my profession see in these pages the record of the long years of determination to preserve inviolate whatever funds were needful for the fulfilment of contracts, of the patient striving for equity between members and between generations, and of the unceasing quest for greater knowledge and understanding for the achievement of these things, they will know that they are looking deep into their own hearts.

For all of these reasons it gives me both pleasure and pride to have had the opportunity of contributing this Foreword. If I add, as a personal reason, my long-standing friendships with the author and with Sir William Elderton, it is not only because this is the way in which I have learned that they are indeed very proud of the 'Old Equitable'. But so, if it comes to that, are we all.

*January* 1962

# PREFACE

FOR more than 100 years, the history of The Equitable Life Assurance Society was the history of life assurance in the United Kingdom. 'If that be not strictly true, it is yet much nearer the truth than the uninformed could imagine,' wrote Cornelius Walford. The reader of this book will, I think, acknowledge the truth of what he said.

Most of the book has been based upon my own research among the original papers over many years. The records left by J. G. Anderson (who did much research among the archives before the war) were, of course, invaluable and I freely acknowledge much help from many persons connected with the office—too many to mention individually. In writing the book I have endeavoured to bring out the contrasts of character of some of the pioneers as well as the background of life assurance in its early days.

The Society's archives in the muniment room have been supplemented by research especially at the Guildhall Library, where the officials have given much advice and where indeed part of the book was written; also by research at the British Museum, the Royal Society, the National Portrait Gallery, Dr Williams's Library, the Institute of Actuaries and the Chartered Insurance Institute; and by information supplied by the Science Museum. I have used the papers of Edward Rowe Mores in the Bodleian Library at Oxford; and the Tredegar papers in the National Library of Wales at Aberystwyth. Richard Price's papers are rather scattered—on both sides of the Atlantic.

I have corresponded with many friends over the years and the course of research has taken me to such various places as the Corporation of Trinity House, the Merchant Taylors' Company, the Grocers' Company, the Surrey Archaeological Society at Guildford, as well as to the valleys of South Wales, the Yorkshire dales and the suburbs of North London. All the help I have been given I gratefully acknowledge. The manuscript was read by Dr Arthur John of the London School of Economics, who has helped to correct the economic background, and by two friends. One also read the proofs.

The Equitable's solicitors were, in fact, founded before the Society. Their early correspondence books are stored by the Misses Warren of Shere in Surrey.

The present Lord Tredegar and his agent have been helpful over a number of matters. It is of especial interest that some of the furniture from Tredegar Park can now been seen in the National Museum of Wales, St Fagan's, Cardiff. The museum is set in attractive gardens and the grounds contain reconstructions of several old farmhouses from various parts of Wales and a Unitarian chapel in the style of a barn adapted for worship. This is the type of chapel which would have been familiar to Richard Price and William Morgan. The interior of the chapel at Newington Green was in much the same style. If this book should awaken interest in Richard Price, the reader might well go on pilgrimage to St Fagan's as well as Bridgend and Newington Green.

The garden (which was formerly the churchyard of St Nicholas Acons) in Nicholas Lane in the City of London, with the plaque marking the birthplace of scientific life assurance, will always be of interest to life assurance men from all parts of the world.

M.E.O.

# EXPLANATION OF DODSON'S SCHEME

*(See graph on following page)*

DODSON's scheme of life assurance can be explained by considering assurances for the whole continuance of life of a group of men all aged 30 at the time the assurance is taken out. Few of them will die in the early years but the number will rise with advancing age to a maximum which, on the mortality of 1949–52, lies between ages 75 and 80. Since a level premium is charged for each person in the group, the aggregate premiums will exceed the aggregate claims in the early years. However, there will come a time when the claims begin to exceed the premiums and the excess of the premiums over the claims in the early years must be stored so as to meet the excess of claims over the premiums in the later years. The situation is illustrated in the graph, where the shaded areas are equal.

The excess of premiums over claims which is stored in the early years can be invested to earn interest and the interest income can be brought into account in a variety of ways. The simplest way (which is illustrated by the broken line on the graph) is to use it to increase the claims by periodical allotments of bonus—though Dodson, himself, assumed a rate of interest of 3 per cent per annum and reduced the premiums correspondingly. The graph shows how greatly the benefits of life assurance are improved by the earning of interest on the invested funds.

Nowadays, there is a much greater variety of types of assurance than Dodson could ever have envisaged but the structure of life assurance is the same for all classes of assurance and its principles are just as valid today as they were 200 years ago.

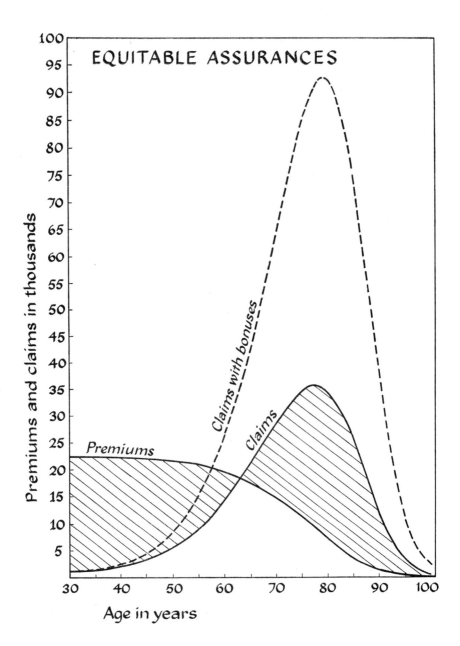

# ABBREVIATIONS

To save undue repetition, (W, and date) is used to indicate 'at a meeting of the Weekly Court of Directors held on the . . .' and other meetings are indicated in a similar way:

W A meeting of the Weekly Court of Directors.

S A meeting of a Summoned Court of Directors, i.e. Special Board Meeting.

G A meeting of the General Court of members of the Society.

C A meeting of a Committee of the Directors.

What is now proved was once only imagin'd.

WILLIAM  BLAKE

# CONTENTS

# ILLUSTRATIONS

## COLOUR PLATES

## ONE-COLOUR PLATES

# CHAPTER I

# THE GENESIS OF LIFE ASSURANCE

THE original establishment of life assurance upon a sound basis was largely the achievement of one office and of the men who served her. This was the Society for Equitable Assurances on Lives and Survivorships, now known as The Equitable Life Assurance Society, and still affectionately called the 'Old Equitable'. The Equitable was the first life assurance society to grant long-term contracts of life assurance for either a stated period or the whole of life, with premiums calculated according to age and type of assurance.

Insurance had been known since the time of the Middle Ages. Its origins can be traced to the rise of Italy as a commercial power and the linking of insurance with seaborne trade. Those who accepted such insurance risks would also occasionally insure a life, but such contracts were only for a year or other short period. Had life assurance remained of that character there would have been no large life offices acting as guardians of a significant proportion of the total savings of the people.

The problem of how best to provide life assurance protection was approached in another way by the establishment of funds which undertook to pay annuities to the widows and orphans of persons in certain occupational groups, e.g. clergymen and civil servants, who might become members of the funds. But until the mathematics of life contingencies had been developed the real cost of such liabilities was imperfectly understood and too little might be collected in contributions to support the hoped-for benefits. One such scheme was established in 1698 by the Mercers' Company, who guaranteed reversionary annuities at the rate of 30 per cent of purchase price. The terms proved to be too generous and in 1738 the annuities had to be reduced by one-third; by 1750, relief had to be obtained from Parliament.

Another experiment was the Society for Assurance of Widows and Orphans, founded in 1699. The scheme was mutual benefaction rather than insurance. There were to be 2,000 subscribers; on the death of any one of them the survivors had to pay 5s each so that the widow might receive £500. A second society was formed in 1703 but the business fell into difficulties and had to be dissolved after about ten years' existence.

By analogy with schemes of mutual help, life assurance may be treated as being an arrangement whereby the premiums contributed by the whole group can be shared among the dependants of those who die; from such a concept it was a short step to the establishment of mutual societies which would pay, in respect of each member's death, a sum dependent on the actual number of deaths and calculated so as to divide the aggregate amount of contributions equally between the claims of those who had died. This step was taken in the first decade of the eighteenth century.

If such a scheme is to be called life assurance, the contributions should be collected in advance, as was arranged by the Amicable Society for a Perpetual Assurance Office, which was granted a charter in 1706. Its purpose was to secure 2,000 subscribers of £6 4s each per annum on the understanding that £10,000 (i.e. £5 per subscriber) would be shared each year between the nominees of those subscribers who had died during the year. The Amicable Society had a long and honourable history; it was eventually taken over by the Norwich Union Life Insurance Society in 1866.

A similar but less substantial scheme started in 1706–7 was unsuccessful and came to an end about 1710. Another such scheme, the Company of London Insurers upon Lives, received a charter in 1709.

So far from being regarded as a disadvantage, the uncertainty implicit in the variation of the payment according to the number of the claims appealed to the gambling instinct prevalent at the time. Many speculative ventures were being promoted and in the 'bubbling year' of 1710 a large number of such societies were started, mainly in association with coffee-houses; these societies used the principle of dividing the sum available among the claims, but the contingencies covered by the insurances were usually marriage, birth of children and so on, though some societies made payments at death. The societies were ephemeral; there is no evidence that they had a continued existence even until the bursting of the bubble in 1720.

In the troubled times of the South Sea Bubble, charters were granted to two corporations, the London Assurance and the Royal Exchange Assurance—in 1720 for the purpose of transacting marine insurance business and in 1721 for fire and life insurance business. The corporations granted life assurance contracts for a year at a time, similar to the contracts that were being granted for fire insurance business. The premium was at a flat rate for a wide range of ages. The corporations were permanent and substantial organizations but the amount of life assurance business transacted was restricted by the limited nature of the assurance cover.

Such experiments produced a variety of forms of life assurance by the end of the first quarter of the eighteenth century but the distinctive features of life assurance transacted on an appropriate actuarial basis had not yet appeared. That life assurance would be practicable with premiums properly calculated on actuarial principles according to age, and the type of the assurance, was first shown by James Dodson (c. 1710–57). These actuarial principles required the study of several different disciplines in order to make a combined attack on the problem.

Central to actuarial science, as also to mathematical statistics, is the theory of probability. Yet the first impulse to the study of probability was given neither by insurance nor by statistics but by gambling. Knucklebones have been used for gaming since prehistoric times and dice may have been evolved from them. The Romans were ardent players with dice and playing with dice was common throughout the Middle Ages. It is fairly easy to see how those who were interested in the fall of dice would come to a practical knowledge of the relative frequencies. Each die may be thrown in six ways and so there are thirty-six ways of throwing two dice and 216 ways of throwing three dice. If three dice are thrown the total of the dice may be any number between 3 and 18. There is only one way (out of 216) to throw a total of 3; there are three ways to throw a total of 4 (i.e. 2, 1, 1 or 1, 2, 1 or 1, 1, 2) and so on. Evidence of an empirical knowledge of relative frequencies can be traced in the surviving records, though no doubt the knowledge was more widespread than would appear from the written evidence. Yet the final step by which the relative frequencies are translated into the pattern of chance events representing a probability law seems not to have entered the minds of men until the seventeenth century.

The rudiments of the theory of probability, as applied to games, are to be found in renaissance Italy but the mathematical theory was slow in developing. The essentials were developed in a correspondence between Pierre de Fermat (1601–65) and Blaise Pascal (1623–62). The Dutch physicist, Christiaan Huygens (1629–93) visited Paris and became interested in the mathematics of dicing. He systematized the mathematical theory in a treatise published in 1657. Huygens also visited England and became a Fellow of the Royal Society. His work was the stimulus to the study of probability in this country.

The nature of man's interest in vital statistics is indicated by the name 'political arithmetic' which was given to the subject now known as demography. The bills of mortality were first used to produce a rudimentary life table by John Graunt (1620–74), a Fellow of the Royal Society, a draper of London and a friend of Sir William Petty. The theory of compound interest requires a relatively simple mathematical technique which had been worked out for such problems as loans and leases. The way in which the chances of death could be combined with allowance for compound interest to produce the value of a life annuity was first shown by Johann de Witt (1625–72). He was the Grand Pensionary, the virtual Prime Minister, of the Netherlands and wished to demonstrate how money could be raised by the Government by the sale of life annuities, which would redeem the loans over the lifetimes of the annuitants.

By the end of the seventeenth century, actuarial principles were beginning to be understood through these various branches of learning. They were fused into a science by the genius of three outstanding men, all Fellows of the Royal Society; some of the distinctive tools of the actuary derive from the work of Sir Isaac Newton (1642–1727), e.g. the *Methodus Differentialis*. Statistics from the bills of mortality for Breslau in the years 1687–91 were used by Edmond Halley (1656–1742) to construct the first mortality table computed from statistics. He gave the mathematical expression for the value of a life annuity and calculated the values for a wide range of ages from the Breslau table of mortality. Abraham de Moivre (1667–1754), a Huguenot refugee and a friend of Newton, produced the first systematic treatment of probability in English and applied the theory of probability to the systematic investigation of problems concerning annuities upon lives. Moivre was the recognized authority on problems concerning chance, annuities and reversionary interests and he seems to have had a considerable practice as a consultant. James Dodson was a pupil and a friend of Moivre and, no doubt, gained his interest in life contingencies from him. It is an interesting question whether the two men ever discussed the mathematics of life assurance but there is no published evidence that they did so and it seems that the work is wholly Dodson's.

Life assurance was born in the middle of the period in England from 1740 to 1780 which has been called Johnson's England. Here, as Trevelyan says, was:

a Society with a mental outlook of its own, self-poised, self-judged, and self-approved, freed from the disturbing passions of the past, and not yet troubled about a very different future which was soon to be brought upon the scene by the Industrial and the French Revolutions.

Agriculture was improved by the investment of capital to such an extent that this period has been called the agricultural revolution. There were big advances in medicine and many of the London hospitals were founded between 1720 and 1745, though their contribution to health was hampered till the causes of infection were better understood. Commercial activity expanded with the establishment of mercantile, industrial and professional families in the new and wealthier England. The flow of traffic was speeded by turnpike roads and canals, where communications had been slow and hampered. The economy was relatively stable during the middle part of the eighteenth century. There was no deliberate debasement of the coinage after the reforms of 1696–8 and prices remained relatively steady. After a gradual fall in the earlier years, prices remained stable from the 1730s to 1760 and then rose gently to 1783. It was only in the last decade of the century that there was a sharp upturn in prices under the pressures of the French Revolution and war.

Those engaged in mercantile, industrial and professional occupations subsisted on incomes or earnings which would be cut short by death. The premature death of husband or father might reduce a family to extreme poverty and distress. There was a need for life assurance protection, which was probably most keenly felt by a provident and thrifty section of the community, though there were many uses for such protection in financial transactions of various kinds.

It appears, then, that life assurance came when it did because the climate was favourable. England was prosperous; the mathematics of life contingencies was at hand; and there was an unsatisfied demand for the protection that life assurance can give.

James Dodson's grandfather was John Dodson, a tailor of Edmonton, whose son John (James's father), became a freeman of Merchant Taylors' Company after seven years' apprenticeship possibly, though not necessarily, as a tailor. James Dodson was admitted to the freedom of Merchant Taylors' Company by patrimony in 1733.

There is no reason to suppose that James Dodson was ever a tailor. Probably he had some inheritance because in his early years he devoted his time to the calculation of antilogarithms, a project which cannot have produced much money, though it brought him recognition. In 1735 he married Elizabeth, either the child or the ward of Sir John Chesshyre, and, some years later, he was living at the 'Hand and Pen' in Warwick Lane, near St Paul's. This was commonly the sign of a writing-master and the evidence suggests that in his early days he supported himself, or perhaps supplemented his income, by the practice of handwriting. The Royal Society has preserved a letter written in 1752 which shows that his handwriting was neat and well-formed, as would be expected of a writing-master.

If he had a practice as a writing-master, the kind of work he may have done was the production of manuscript copies of *The Practice of Interest* by William Jones, FRS (1675–1749) for distribution to the author's friends. The rules in this work, which is only known in such manuscript copies, were quoted by Dodson in the preface to his *Antilogarithmic Canon*, in 1742. It may seem strange that a mathematician should have had to support himself in this way but that may have been due to the times in which he lived.

The flowing English script known as copper-plate was developed by the leading writing-masters towards the end of the seventeenth century and in the early part of the eighteenth. It was well adapted to serve the needs of the growing commercial activity. Thus the practice of handwriting came to be the principal subject of a commercial education, which might also include other commercial subjects such as accounts and mathematics or, at least, arithmetic. Leading writing-masters would have their own schools, the curriculum depending upon the tastes and abilities of the master. There was such a school at the sign of the 'Hand and Pen' in St Paul's Church-yard and it is of interest and significance that there was another school of this kind at the 'Hand and Pen' in Warwick Lane.

The school in Warwick Lane was under a writing-master named George Shelley in the first decade of the eighteenth century. His was one of the most formative influences in the development of copper-plate, his work being elegant and mature. He was a fine scribe and a good teacher. He included arithmetic in his curriculum, for he brought out an edition of Wingate's *Arithmetic* in 1704 and in his portrait he is shown holding this book. In 1710, Shelley was appointed Master of the Writing School in Christ's Hospital, an important appointment where he would have nearly 450 pupils in his care. They would receive an education with a commercial bias such as he had been giving at his own school, which thereupon passed to John Clark, who had the school in Warwick Lane until 1727.

Though there is a gap of some years in the evidence, it seems reasonable to assume that James Dodson had the writing-school at the 'Hand and Pen' in Warwick Lane from, say, the time of his marriage until his removal to Wapping, some time before 1747, where he lived next door to the 'Blue Legge', Bell-dock. Like George Shelley, James Dodson brought out an edition of Wingate's *Arithmetic*; he was responsible for the eighteenth edition in 1751. It was a standard text and would be used in the writing-school at Christ's Hospital.

By 1747, at Bell-dock, Dodson was describing himself as an 'Accomptant, and Teacher of the Mathematics'. It appears that he not only 'examined, constituted and settled' accounts, he was willing to advise businessmen on the forms of account to meet special cir-cumstances and to 'supervise the insertions thereof, until their servants are sufficiently expert therein'. These remarks are quoted from the preface of *The Calculator*, which was a most useful book of tables designed primarily as an aid to mathematical calculations. His heart was in mathematics, whether as calculator or teacher.

In course of time Dodson came to have a considerable practice as a consultant on the values of annuities. His first letter read before the Royal Society contained a plea for more information to be given in the bills of mortality, so that they might be rendered more useful for the purpose of valuing life annuities. A later letter dealt with annuities carrying the right to a proportion of the annuity to the date of death. By 1756, when the Rev. William Brakenridge, DD, had sent to the Royal Society a life table calculated from the London bills of mortality for the ten years 1744 to 1753, Dodson had obtained such a power over the subject of life annuities that he thought it 'almost a duty incumbent upon me to compute the values of them according to your curious table of decrements of life . . .'.

He was becoming better known and in the years at Bell-dock produced his major work, *The Mathematical Repository*, published in three volumes in 1748, 1753 and 1755. The publisher, Edward Nourse, paid him £1 11s 6d for each sheet of calculations (about £25 per volume) for the copyright of the book. The book displayed Dodson's mastery of algebra and his interest in the subject of annuities; it is a classic of actuarial science, though a little out of the main stream. The book secured Dodson's election as a Fellow of the Royal Society.

In 1755 Dodson's abilities as a mathematician were recognized by his appointment as Master of the Royal Mathematical School, a school within Christ's Hospital which had been founded by Charles II to promote the study of mathematics and navigation, especially for the needs of the Royal Navy. In this appointment, it seems likely that he was helped by William Mountaine, who had been mathematical examiner to the Corporation of Trinity House for some ten years and who would doubtless have had some say in the selection of the Master of the Royal Mathematical School, whose boys were examined by the Elder Brethren at the end of the course.

His circumstances having improved, it may be assumed that Dodson's thoughts turned to life assurance. But, in his day, the only forms of life assurance available were the year-to-year assurances granted by the chartered corporations and the small variable death benefit provided by the old Amicable. The story runs that the Amicable had a rule against admitting members aged over forty-five and Dodson, being refused admittance because he was just over that age, turned his thoughts to the proper basis for scientific life assurance. He inserted an advertisement in the *Daily Advertiser* asking those who were interested in the project to meet him at the Queen's Head, Paternoster Row, on March 2, 1756. These meetings led to the formation of the Society for Equitable Assurances on Lives and Survivorships, though Dodson himself did not live to see its formation.

Search has revealed no picture of James Dodson and there is little evidence that would help to fill out his personality. Like many schoolmasters, he was probably good company to anyone with academic interests, for Edward Rowe Mores afterwards declared that he took part in the project to found a life assurance society mainly for the pleasure he got from Dodson's companionship.

Another side to his character is revealed by the manuscripts of Thomas Simpson (1710–61), another Fellow of the Royal Society. In the special collections section of Columbia University Library, there is a letter written on April 4, 1755, by Simpson to a friend, in which Dodson is mentioned. Simpson had reviewed *The Mathematical Repository*, and had mentioned certain mistakes which he thought he had found in the mathematics:

Conformable to your Desire, I take this Opportunity to send you my observations of ye mistakes in Mr. Dodson's Book wherein I have expressed myself without reserve, as I believe you are sensible that I have no design to hurt ye author either in your esteem, or that of ye World; and that (for reasons well known to you) those mistakes will be no farther noticed by me, unless I should find myself under the disagreeable necessity of doing it, in order to clear up Misrepresentations. Tho' (as things are now circumstanced) I reely wish that he had not (by his Treatment of me) given himself room, to look upon me in ye Light of an Enemy.

Simpson[1] was, in fact, right and Dodson was probably too touchy.

A truer picture of Dodson is with his friends, other 'lovers of the mathematics', who used to meet at the Queen's Arms in Newgate Street for an evening's talk on subjects of mutual interest.

The scraps of information that have been collected about Dodson are presented in the family tree, which shows his relationship with his great-grandson, Augustus de Morgan (1806–71), Professor of Mathematics at University College, London.

[1] For Simpson's alleged part in the foundation of life assurance *v.* Appendix I.

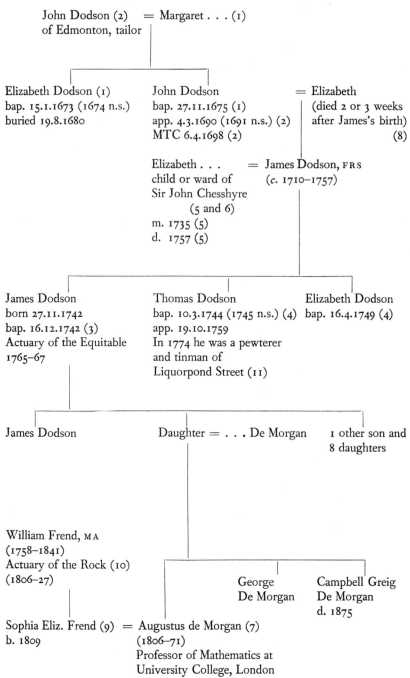

John Dodson (2)  = Margaret . . . (1)
of Edmonton, tailor

Elizabeth Dodson (1)
bap. 15.1.1673 (1674 n.s.)
buried 19.8.1680

John Dodson          = Elizabeth
bap. 27.11.1675 (1)    (died 2 or 3 weeks
app. 4.3.1690 (1691 n.s.) (2)  after James's birth)
MTC 6.4.1698 (2)                        (8)

Elizabeth . . .    = James Dodson, FRS
child or ward of      (c. 1710–1757)
Sir John Chesshyre
      (5 and 6)
m. 1735 (5)
d. 1757 (5)

James Dodson
born 27.11.1742
bap. 16.12.1742 (3)
Actuary of the Equitable
1765–67

Thomas Dodson                    Elizabeth Dodson
bap. 10.3.1744 (1745 n.s.) (4)   bap. 16.4.1749 (4)
app. 19.10.1759
In 1774 he was a pewterer
and tinman of
Liquorpond Street (11)

James Dodson

Daughter = . . . De Morgan    1 other son and
                              8 daughters

William Frend, MA
(1758–1841)
Actuary of the Rock (10)
(1806–27)

George          Campbell Greig
De Morgan       De Morgan
                d. 1875

Sophia Eliz. Frend (9) = Augustus de Morgan (7)
b. 1809                  (1806–71)
                         Professor of Mathematics at
                         University College, London

NOTES (1) Identifications from registers at Edmonton.

(2) Records of Merchant Taylors' Company.

(3) Christ Church baptisms.

(4) Records of Christ's Hospital.

(5) James Dodson's will.

(6) Sir John Chesshyre's will.

(7) *Memoir of Augustus de Morgan* by his widow, pp. 233–4.

(8) Source unconfirmed.

(9) *Threescore years and ten* being reminiscences of the late Sophia Elizabeth de Morgan (1895).

(10) Rock Life Assurance Company, *The deed of settlement, bye-laws, and an address* (1834).

(11) Charter Fund receipt no. 65.

# CHAPTER II

# THE STRUGGLE FOR INCORPORATION
## (1756–1761)

T HE study of life contingencies for the purpose of valuing annuities and reversionary interests evidently turned Dodson's thoughts towards life assurance. In the preface to the third volume of *The Mathematical Repository* he says that he thinks that 'little need be said concerning insurances on lives; as it is a subject not before handled and will shew its own use'.

By the early part of 1756, Dodson had written a treatise, *First Lecture on Insurances*, which remained unpublished.[1] It expounded the principles on which a mutual life assurance society would operate, showing how the premiums should be calculated and how the life assurance fund would work out in a few practical examples.

The *First Lecture* was based on statistics from a pamphlet *Observations on the past Growth and present State of the City of London* by Corbyn Morris, dated March 12, 1750 (1751 n.s.), which gave a summary of the figures recorded in the bills of mortality for the City of London since 1728, when the numbers of burials were first analysed by age. The calculations proceeded from the mean number of burials recorded over the years, 1728–50. As it happened, the weather was especially severe in the years 1740 and 1741, with high food prices and famine; they were years of heavy mortality, ascribed mainly in 1741 to 'fevers etc.' when the burials were between one-fifth and one-fourth more than the mean yearly number. Also, this period of twenty-three years fell within what Dorothy George has called the 'period of cheap gin' which afflicted life in London till the passing of an Act in 1751 effectively restricted the sale of spirits. Thus, the calculations contained considerable margins though the fact was not generally appreciated at the time. There was another margin:

---

[1] Two copies survive in manuscript.

Besides which, as the Bills of Mortality contain the Deaths of all kinds of people healthy and unhealthy and as care will be taken not to insure those Lives which are likely to be soon extinct therefore in all Probability fewer of the Persons Insured will die in Proportion to their Number than of those who are not insured, which will also contribute to the gain of the Corporation since the Premiums are proportioned by the Bills.

The carefully selected lives insured by a life assurance society do, as Dodson thought, experience a lighter mortality than that of the whole population.

The life assurance premiums calculated by Dodson were so much less than was customarily charged for year-to-year assurances that his scheme was mainly attacked on the grounds that the premiums were too low and that the scheme would fail. Possibly to forestall such criticisms he, with a certain bravado, headed his life table:

A table of decrements wherein the hazard of life is esteemed to be as great as any author has conceived it to be, or as can be deduced from any Bills of Mortality hitherto made public.

The *First Lecture on Insurances* was the first investigation into the principles of operation of a life assurance business. Though there have been developments since that time, the general principles elucidated by Dodson are just as valid today as then and form the foundation of the vast life assurance businesses that have grown from such small beginnings.

The meeting called by Dodson (March 2, 1756) at the Queen's Head, Paternoster Row, a tavern with an ancient history, was the first of a series of weekly meetings enabling him to explain his proposals for mutual life assurance and to enlist the support of those interested in them with a view to securing a charter.

Edward Rowe Mores was brought into the project on May 5th at the instance of someone who thought that his range of learning would be useful in the obtaining of a charter; at a guess this would be his step-father, Richard Bridgman. Whether it was Mores's suggestion is unknown, but those interested in the project soon realized that, to launch it, the scheme would have to be put on a more formal basis and funds would have to be raised to finance it. Those who subscribed to the funds would, however, require to be recompensed and it was arranged that they should share a kind of royalty on all the life assurances made by the projected corporation, when it had been established. Each person assuring with the corporation would pay a sum of 10s upon every £100 insured by way of 'entrance money', which would be shared among the subscribers.

Resolutions passed on June 9, 1756, were the basis of an agreement by which the subscribers were formed into a committee 'for the purpose of soliciting a charter' and by June 30th a total of £590 had been raised by forty-one subscribers of 118 shares at £5 a share.

Under the agreement, the intention was that the 'entrance money' should constitute a tontine; the sums becoming available from time to time were to be divided amongst those of the subscribers, or their nominees, who were then surviving, the last survivor taking the whole of the entrance money for the remainder of his or her life. In this way, the appeal for subscriptions was given a speculative flavour that seems foreign to the concept of mutual life assurance, which the subscriptions were intended to promote.

In February 1757, Lord Willoughby of Parham 'condescended to patronize the design and consented that his name might be used in the petition for a charter'. Mores knew him through the Society of Antiquaries and interested him in the project. He had the reputation of having an over-scrupulous conscience and his approval of the scheme should be given due weight when considering the merits of the proposed arrangements.

The petition was presented to the Privy Council on April 20, 1757. It is of interest because it shows the general type of organization and procedure that the promoters had in mind. The petition was signed by eighty-five persons from London, Chichester and Oxford but not all these were to take part in the Corporation. At the start it was to comprise twenty-one persons of whom eighteen were petitioners; the other three persons were added, no doubt, because of their wealth and influence.

The leading ideas of the promoters were:

1.  The contracts would be mutual assurances on the lives of those participating in the scheme.

2.  The main purpose was the protection of dependants against the premature death of the bread-winner.

3.  Incorporation by royal charter was thought to be necessary for the effectual carrying out of the scheme.

4.  The life assurance fund was to be free and open, that is to say life assurances would be freely granted to all who were considered to be assurable.

5.  Those who effected life assurances would have the choice between participating and non-participating contracts.

32

6. Table of the Annual Premiums payable for insuring 100£ during the whole continuance of a single Life of any of the following Ages according to the beforegoing principles

| Age | Annual Premium | Age | Annual Premium | Age | Annual Premium | Age | Annual Premium |
|---|---|---|---|---|---|---|---|
| 14 or under | 2,358 | 28 | 3,404 | 42 | 4,858 | 56 | 7,038 |
| 15 | 2,427 | 29 | 3,501 | 43 | 4,988 | 57 | 7,295 |
| 16 | 2,500 | 30 | 3,612 | 44 | 5,122 | 58 | 7,556 |
| 17 | 2,578 | 31 | 3,698 | 45 | 5,226 | 59 | 7,901 |
| 18 | 2,630 | 32 | 3,801 | 46 | 5,332 | 60 | 8,272 |
| 19 | 2,712 | 33 | 3,880 | 47 | 5,466 | 61 | 8,673 |
| 20 | 2,775 | 34 | 3,976 | 48 | 5,599 | 62 | 9,108 |
| 21 | 2,846 | 35 | 4,076 | 49 | 5,735 | 63 | 9,581 |
| 22 | 2,921 | 36 | 4,180 | 50 | 5,864 | 64 | 10,094 |
| 23 | 3,004 | 37 | 4,287 | 51 | 6,037 | 65 | 10,653 |
| 24 | 3,088 | 38 | 4,399 | 52 | 6,210 | 66 | 11,264 |
| 25 | 3,162 | 39 | 4,493 | 53 | 6,386 | 67 | 11,927 |
| 26 | 3,241 | 40 | 4,611 | 54 | 6,568 | | |
| 27 | 3,324 | 41 | 4,733 | 55 | 6,796 | | |

1. The original table of premiums computed by James Dodson, FRS, in 1756

R. Van Bleeck pinx.    EDWARD ROWE MORES. M.A. & F.A.S    J. Mynde Sc.

2. Edward Rowe Mores, MA, FSA, an engraving

6. In recognition of the royal favour, the corporation would be subject to public supervision.

7. The premiums were to be based on the calculations made by James Dodson, FRS, from the Bills of Mortality of London.

8. Extra premiums were to be charged for hazardous occupations and for females between ages 8 and 50.

9. The premiums were to be proportionate to the sum assured.

10. Assurances would be granted on lives and survivorships.

11. Those who elected to become members would be liable to bear a proportion of any loss or would receive a share of the profit.

12. The investments were to be in 'Government or other sufficient securities'.

13. All persons would assure on like terms with the promoters 'without any private views or advantages whatsoever'.

It may seem surprising that the premiums for non-participating assurances were to be at a higher rate than the premiums for participating assurances but this was logical because the latter carried the liability for a call, should that be necessary.

James Dodson died on November 23, 1757, and it is regrettably true that a somewhat different picture of the last item of the proposals emerges from his will, which reflects the ideas of the subscribers rather than the sentiments of the petition. It seems that the subscribers to the Charter Fund had arranged to charge 15s per cent entrance money on the amount of each assurance; of this sum 10s per cent would, as has been described, go to the subscribers or their nominees for life and 5s per cent was to go to James Dodson or his nominee in consideration of his having made the calculations. No trace of this arrangement appears in the petition and, indeed, it seems inconsistent with the sentiments of its final paragraph. The evidence shows that Dodson had a clear vision of mutual life assurance and a firm grasp of the principles of operation of such a business. He had the energy to translate his ideas into practical affairs. Should he be criticized for wishing to secure some financial benefit from the institution he did so much to found?

The petition at once aroused opposition from those who had already secured charters in this field. Some members of the Amicable Society attended the first meeting in March, with the intention of opposing the proposals, but they withdrew and left the supporters to continue. On May 13, 1757, the general court of the Amicable Society was told 'that attempts are now making for to obtain a new Charter for Insurance on Lives, which . . . may some way infringe upon or break in upon the Rules and Orders of our present Charter'. Caveats had been entered in the offices of the Attorney General and the Solicitor General, and the Clerk of the Patents; King Evans and Stephen Comyn had been retained as Counsel and were authorized 'to take all the proper ways and means' in opposition to the petition.

Next year, on May 11, 1758, the court was told that 'no appointment had been made by the Attorney General for being heard by Counsel for and against the application'. Counsel could not see 'any reasonable foundation' for the opposition but, in the end, the opposition was pressed. By November 16, 1758,

the matter . . . had been learnedly debated (by two eminent Counsel in favour of the Petitioners and two others for each of the London Assurance, the Royal Exchange Assurance and the Amicable Society, in opposition) for three several evenings, and minutes taken thereof by Mr Attorney and Solicitor General of what was alleged and proved on all sides.

They had undertaken to expedite their report; the Court of Directors 'doubted not their having such report . . . by Christmas next'.

The matter was not to be settled so quickly. Eighteen months later, on May 1, 1760, the court was told that the Attorney General and Solicitor General 'had not thought fit to favour the application or to make any Report to his Majesty and Council'. The petition had, in fact, been re-presented with some modifications on March 29, 1760. The number of petitioners had been reduced to eighty-two by the death of Dodson and the death or defection of two others.

The main arguments against the petition seem to have been that a capital fund would be required to back the contracts, and that Dodson's calculations could not be relied upon, the premium scale being too low. Jobbing backwards, it is ironic that the premium scale was thought to be inadequate; it was, in fact, far higher than was required for various reasons, but chiefly because the experience comprised the whole population of London, diseased as well as healthy. To meet the objection the petitioners obtained affidavits from 'Peter Daval, Dr Brackenridge and Mr Mountayne'. The first would be Peter Davall, FRS, Secretary of the Royal Society from 1747 to 1759. The second would be the Rev. Wm. Brackenridge, Rector of St Michael Bassishaw from 1742 to 1762; he was paid five guineas for certifying tables. The third was William Mountaine.

The argument that the project was likely to fail for want of a capital fund was, in effect, a denial of the practicability of mutual life assurance. The very special character of life assurance, whereby the premiums themselves provide the funds to back the long-term contracts for which the premiums are paid, was not understood. The argument was met by a provision for a deposit from each member, the aggregate deposits forming a fund for use should a call be necessary. Doubtless, the promoters felt that the scheme might be more acceptable to cautious authority if provision were made for such deposits. It is amusing to reflect that, in the actual operations of the scheme, deposits were collected for six weeks only; no more was heard of deposits after that.

The Attorney General and the Solicitor General took their time but eventually, on July 14, 1761, they produced their report which (signed C. Yorke and C. Pratt) was adverse to the petitioners:

*First:* Because it appears to us altogether uncertain whether this project will or can succeed in the manner in which it is proposed; and if the success is uncertain, the fund for supporting it, which is to arise from the profits of the undertaking, will be precarious. . . .

*Second:* The success of this scheme must depend upon the truth of certain calculations taken upon tables of life and death, whereby the chance of mortality is attempted to be reduced to a certain standard: this is a mere speculation, never yet tried in practice, and consequently subject, like all other experiments, to various chances in the execution. . . . We are the more apt to doubt the event (i.e. the success of the scheme), because it has been represented to us by the affidavit of Mr Savage, that all the profit which has been received by the Royal Exchange Assurance, from the time of its commencement to the present time, amounts to only a sum of £2,651 4s 6d, the difference between £10,915 2s 2d paid in premiums and the sum of £8,263 17s 8d disbursed in losses, which small profit must have been near exhausted in the charges of management. . . . If the petitioners, then, are so sure of success, there is an easy method of making the experiment, by entering into a voluntary partnership, of which there are several instances now subsisting in this business of insuring; and, if upon a trial these calculations are found to stand the test of practical experiment, the petitioners will then apply with a much better grace for a charter than they can at present, whilst the scheme is built only upon speculative calculations.

*Third:* The Parliament, in erecting the two great companies already mentioned, have sufficiently declared their opinion that such charters ought not to be granted without some benefit accruing to the public . . .; and, as the two great companies paid a very large sum to the public for the privilege of their charters, we cannot advise the Crown to entrench upon their rights on the bare request of any set of men, without a clearer and more certain prospect of public good. . . .

The report was uncharitable in spirit because it recommended the withholding of a charter until the project had succeeded, when presumably there would be little value in the royal favour. The report, also, took a narrow view of the 'public good'. The lawyers were thinking of a money grant to the Exchequer; but the real prize was the establishment of a system of thrift which has been of immeasurable benefit to the public by reason of the protection which life assurance has afforded to dependants and the very substantial contribution which it has made to the national savings.

The petitioners were indeed sure of success. At a general meeting of the promoters on July 15, 1761, the day after the final rejection of the petition, Edward Rowe Mores produced a draft deed of settlement which acted on the hint to proceed by way of a voluntary partnership. In the eighteenth century, many businesses were established as unincorporated partnerships, though the businesses were in fact proprietary in character. However, it is clear that the promoters were aiming at a mutual life assurance office by way of an unincorporated partnership of those members who were willing to effect life assurance policies and who also would contribute to a call, should that be necessary.

The protracted negotiations had been expensive to conduct and a second subscription of £295 was raised by seventeen subscribers of fifty-nine shares at £5 a share. All of these were further subscriptions from original subscribers. A comparison with the list of the subscribers' shares which is contained in Article 59 of the deed of settlement, referred to in the next chapter, discloses a discrepancy since some of the subscribers have the same interests in both lists whereas others have larger interests against their names in the deed of settlement. The explanation lies in the nature of the obligations assumed by persons becoming members of the Society. The petition had proposed that twenty-one of the subscribers should be incorporated as the projected corporation. The petition having failed, it became necessary to form the Society by means of a covenant between the subscribers, or such of them as were willing, that they would insure their lives with the proposed Society and become the nucleus of the membership. Some of the subscribers were unwilling to assume the obligations of membership by insuring their lives and preferred to forfeit their shares of the entrance money: they may have been uneasy at the prospect of failure with the possibility of a substantial call in addition to the loss of their subscriptions. The first step was to ask each subscriber whether he was willing to continue. Out of the original forty-one subscribers seven were unwilling to continue and forfeited their subscriptions of £95 in all.

The numbers of the subscribers had also been reduced by four deaths who forfeited their subscriptions with the exception of James Dodson. No doubt there was the feeling that something should be done for Dodson's family in view of the large part he had taken in the formation of the Society; William Mountaine, also a subscriber, took over Dodson's shares as executor for the benefit of the three children. The dependants of James Brooks seem to have been harshly treated compared with Dodson's. He had intended to participate in the Society but died just before the deed of settlement was executed. He left a wife and four children in great distress, who asked that the subscribers should take their case into consideration, but the shares were treated as being forfeited by death.

Some of the subscriptions had been made by the principal promoters in the names of others, usually persons related to them. These holdings were consolidated in the names of the actual as opposed to the nominal subscribers. Thus Edward Rowe Mores made subscriptions in the names of both the Richard Bridgmans, father and son; although they both, in fact, afterwards became insured with the Society and took part in the direction of the Society, their shares were consolidated with those of Edward Rowe Mores in the deed of settlement, and they did not appear as subscribers.

Some of the other subscribers sold their shares to persons willing to continue. There is no evidence to show why some subscribers were able to sell their shares whereas others forfeited their subscriptions. Also, there is no evidence to show whether the shares were sold at par or at a discount, though it may be assumed that those selling their shares were paid out at par. This is an obscure period and the darkness cannot now be penetrated. It seems difficult to believe that William Mosdell made subscriptions in the names of persons who were apparently unrelated to him. Also, on this evidence Mosdell was credited in the deed of settlement with three shares fewer than he was entitled to. This was described as a mistake, but might be connected with Dodson's three shares which were taken by William Mountaine for the benefit of Dodson's family. A sinister explanation could be put upon some of these transactions and critics later suggested that there was a scramble for shares. This is unlikely though some of the transactions seem to demand explanation.

The final position in the deed of settlement was that there were twenty-one subscribers of 146 shares. The Society has no accounts relating to the subscriptions but in papers published in 1769 there is a printed copy of an account, covering the whole period 1756 to 1763, which is headed 'The subscribers to the Charter Fund with William Mosdell, Treasurer'. This states that all the subscriptions were collected in 1756, which is difficult to believe. The account is subdivided into the periods before and after September 7, 1762, the date of the deed of settlement, when the balance was £165 1s 3d, less £50 paid subsequently to Mosdell for services before that day. The account is not audited and should be treated with some reserve.

By way of recompense for the additional subscriptions, it was arranged (Dodson being dead) that the whole of the entrance money of 15s per £100 should be appropriated to the subscribers, his 5s as well as their 10s.

The twenty-one subscribers who formed the nucleus of the Society were the first members to effect 'equitable assurances', as, of course, they had undertaken to do. Their names, and the names of the subscribers who fell out, are listed in Appendix III.

# CHAPTER III

# MUTUAL LIFE ASSURANCE
# IS BORN (1762)

A SOCIETY has an individuality which is coloured by the characters of the people that form it, for mind and heart determine what thoughts shall be translated into actions and from the actions the structure of society is built. The early history of the Equitable Society, which emerged from the negotiations described in the last chapter, is coloured by the peculiar character of Edward Rowe Mores (1731–78),[1] who in effect acted as midwife to bring to birth the idea that James Dodson had conceived but did not live to see.

Picture a wealthy young man, with exceptional ability in academic studies, yet with a quarrelsome temper. Such a man was Edward Rowe Mores. He had great opportunities, yet somehow fell short of greatness. He was a descendant of the Rowe family, his father's mother being Anne, the daughter of Robert Rowe of Low Leyton in Essex. On the death of his father, Edward Mores (1681–1740), rector of Tunstall in Kent for nearly thirty years, he came into considerable property.

Comparatively late in life, the rector had married Sarah Windsor, the daughter of a City merchant named Shadrach Windsor. Their son, Edward Rowe Mores, was born on January 13, 1730 (1731 n.s.), when his father was forty-nine, and his early years would have been spent at Gore Court which the rector had bought in 1723. His father died in 1740 in Gracechurch Street and in the same year Edward Rowe Mores entered Merchant Taylors' School; he proceeded to Oxford as a gentleman commoner of Queen's College on June 24, 1746, and graduated BA, May 12, 1750, MA, January 15, 1753. In 1749, while he was at Oxford, he produced *Nomina et Insignia*

---

[1] The papers of Edward Rowe Mores are in the Bodleian Library, Oxford. Christopher Ricks is producing an account of him. *v.* note on p. 42.

*gentilitia Nobilium Equitumque*, a work which showed his interests in genealogy and heraldry and gained his admission to the Society of Antiquaries. In 1750 and 1751, he was in Salisbury where he stayed with his cousin Atkins in Catherine Street while he was pursuing his researches. In 1751, he moved to London, where he lived and worked at the Herald's office. Here he became friendly with John Warburton (1682–1759), FSA, FRS, Somerset Herald, and with Andrew Coltee Ducarel, LLD, Commissary of St Catherine's and of the Diocese of Canterbury (d. May 29, 1785, aged 72), who had chambers in Doctors Commons.

Later in the year 1740, after his father's death, his mother married, at All Hallows, London Wall, Richard Bridgman who had a grocer's business in Whitechapel and rose to high office in the Grocers' Company as well as being one of the original directors of the Equitable Society. He had been elected to the Court of Assistants of the Grocers' Company in 1738 and was Master or Senior Warden in 1753–4. As an alderman he was appointed Deputy for his ward in 1756 and was thereafter known as Master Deputy Richard Bridgman.

At the time of the marriage, he was a little over forty years of age and had a daughter named Susan (1730–67) who was of the same age as Edward Rowe Mores. They became devoted to each other. In a letter dated September 2, 1753, John Warburton wrote that 'our friend Mr Mores was married to his old beloved Miss Bridgman on Tuesday last', i.e. on August 28, 1753. Either at this time or earlier, Mores took a house in the College of Heralds or nearby; his address is given as 'at Peters Hill, near the Heralds Office'.

Mores was elected a Fellow of the Society of Antiquaries in 1752 and two years later became a member of a committee for examining that Society's minute books with a view to selecting papers worthy of publication. However, he did not long continue his membership. He refers to disputes in the meetings; '. . . our debates are so frequent and scandalous, and the disorder and confusion which prevails at our meetings so excessive disagreeable . . .' that many of the older members had withdrawn.

In 1759, Mores moved to the estate at Low Leyton, where the rate books usually styled him as Dr Mores. In August of that year he claimed the right of the pew in Leyton Church which his family had held for over fifty years. Next year the old house was demolished and the present Etloe Place[1] was built on plans which Mores was said to have prepared himself. At about this time he used the colophon 'Impress. Leytonae Essexiensum 1759', which suggests that he had his own printing press there. Did Mores build Etloe Place for his wife and then lose her? Susan Bridgman certainly did not live long; she died on January 8, 1767, at the age of thirty-seven. Her loss must have deeply affected Mores, who described her as '*amantissima, fidelissima, dilectissima*'.

Another side of Mores's character is revealed by the letter written by him in 1768 to the matron of the convent where his daughter was to be educated:

> She is a child of ready wit, an acute judgment, and of a temper not unamiable; docile and tractable: but being deprived of her mother (who while living was afflicted with almost continual illness) and being much loved and indulged by me, and entrusted rather beyond what her years might justify, and being in some respects superior to the generality of her age and sex, she refused obedience to all command but mine; who being busied about many things, had not nor have sufficient leisure to superintend and direct her conduct.

That year was marked by disagreeable disputes in the Equitable, when Mores must have been much preoccupied as well as still sad at the loss of his wife. His daughter, Sarah, was about ten to twelve years old and it is little wonder that he felt the task of looking after her was beyond him.

The Society of Antiquaries possesses an engraving by J. Mynde of a portrait of Edward Rowe Mores painted by Pieter van Bleeck (1695–1764). The inscription gives the painter as R. van Bleeck, but Richard died about 1733 and evidently the son, Pieter, is intended. The sitter is shown in a gown with bands, which might be clerical or legal dress. However, Mores did not become either a clergyman or a lawyer, so far as is known, though he is said to have affected clerical dress. The face is of a young man and it may be suggested that the portrait was painted in or soon after 1753, with Mores wearing academic dress. A pencilled note among some papers in the Bodleian states that the engraving was prepared for a work that Mores intended to write on Domesday. The portrait shows a lively, intelligent, forceful man, but with some hardness in his make-up; he looks as if he were too used to getting his own way.

In a contemporary collection of the correspondence of Rev. Edward

---

[1] There is an account of Etloe House, by Frederick Temple.

Lye, MA (d. 1767, aged 73), a well-known authority on the Anglo-Saxon languages, Thomas Percy, the compiler, describes Mores as 'the learned Edward Rowe Mores'. His letters are all in a small, upright, decorated style which gives the impression of a rather special fount of print. A curious handwriting matched a curious character; on the most charitable interpretation of the evidence, he was high-handed in his dealings with the Society.

The archives of Queen's College, Oxford, were made accessible to research by Edward Rowe Mores, who arranged and calendared them so well that it has been said 'his work is, next to the original documents, the most valuable contribution to the history of the college'. Mores had some standing in his old University. He wrote to Lye from Queen's College on September 20, 1761:

I have been here ever since the latter end of July, and begin now to despair of the pleasure of meeting you at Oxford agreeably to your promises. . . . But I have another favour to ask, in which I am seconded by Mr Vice-Chancellor, and through him by Alma Mater herself. . . .

The favour requested was some congratulatory lines in ancient languages on the occasion of the marriage of King George III. There is, however, no poem by Lye in *Epithalamia Oxoniensia* (1761).

John James, the last of the old race of letter-founders, died in June 1772, and Mores purchased 'all the curious parts of that immense collection of punches, matrices and types which had been accumulating from the days of Wynkyn de Worde'. From this material, Mores wrote his best remembered work, *Dissertation on Typographical Founders and Foundries*,[1] published in 1780 by John Nichols, who noted:

The author's whimsical peculiarities in abbreviations and in punctuations deform his pages, and too frequently involve an otherwise clear sentence in obscurity. Mr Mores, it is true, has atoned for this inconvenience, by the manly strength of thought and acuteness of observation with which this little work abounds.

The surprising range of Mores's interests is shown by the contents of his library, which are known to us from the catalogue of the sale soon after his death. The size of the library may be gauged from the fact that the sale was spread over seventeen days. Among the subjects covered were education, theology, biography, classics (two whole days), rare black-letter books, history, antiquities, travel, philosophy,

[1] *v.* edition by Harry Carter and Christopher Ricks (1961).

mathematics, civil, canon and common law, arts and sciences, medicine, surgery, cryptography, history and art of printing, heraldry, English history, ecclesiastical history and topography. Though he need not have read all the books in his library it is difficult to believe that he would have bought the mathematical books unless he wanted them for study.

The mathematical books included Dodson's *Calculator* and *The Mathematical Repository*; Abraham de Moivre's *Doctrine of Chances* and *Annuities upon Lives*; Simpson's works on the same subjects and Price's treatise on reversionary payments. Thus he had the standard works on actuarial science and also West's *Symboleography*, which was a review of mercantile practice, including insurance. There were several books relating to the Equitable and Corbyn Morris's collection of the bills of mortality. The manuscripts included calculations made by Mores for the Society and tables of annuities in three volumes. Could they now be found? It seems beyond doubt that Mores prepared himself for guiding the affairs of the Society by studying the actuarial mathematics of life assurance and the law and practice of insurance.

Towards the close of his life, Mores fell into negligent and dissipated habits. He died at Low Leyton on November 28, 1778, of a mortification in his leg.

The evidence suggests that Mores took the leadership in the projected life assurance society on his own shoulders. He must have had sufficient mathematical ability to appreciate the significance of Dodson's calculations and to apply them in practice; he must have had considerable legal knowledge because he appears to have drafted both the deed of settlement itself and the policies and other instruments required for the use of the Society; he must have had considerable powers of organization because, though comparatively young, he acted in effect as managing director to the nascent business. Perhaps he took too much on himself and would have been wiser to take advice from those competent to give it, for it is clear that his actions sowed the seed of future trouble. Fortunately, the Society was not in the hands of one man.

Mores is stated to have drawn the deed of settlement which was executed on Tuesday, September 7, 1762. That Mores had a considerable hand in the drafting of the deed is apparent from its style and contents, though it is unlikely that he acted without legal advice[1] either on this deed or on the declaration of trust which was agreed in draft at the first meeting of the Court of Directors nine days later and executed on September 27, 1762.

The deed of settlement was enrolled in the Court of King's Bench in Hilary Term, 5 George III, 1765. The delay is intriguing but cannot now be explained.

The main themes of the deed of settlement were the assurances to be issued (Articles 1–13), the obligations of members (14–18), the appointments and duties of the directors, the trustees and the actuary (19–44), meetings of members for elections and other business (45–56), entrance money and its sharing among the subscribers to the Charter Fund (57–64), provision for calls, if required, for dividends out of surplus, and for claims (68–74).

The actuarial ideas were rudimentary. There was provision neither for proper accounts, nor for periodic investigations into the condition of the Society and there was only a brief reference (66) to the investment of the funds which 'shall be laid out in Government or other good and sufficient securities'. The references to calls were vague; the proposals for distribution of surplus were both too explicit and too inequitable to endure.

Provision was made for 'Directors-extraordinary' who would transact business in other places than the City of London but this power was never used. Edward Rowe Mores was appointed a director for life and also 'in some measure to recompense him for the trouble which he hath already undergone' he was to be paid £100 p.a. Mores's papers include a print of the deed in which blanks are left for the insertion of the amounts of the stipends for Mores and Mosdell. Were the amounts to be fixed by a general meeting of subscribers or was there opposition to Mores?

There was a curious restraint (76) against members insuring with any other society for assurances on lives; this was unworkable and was rescinded in 1772.

Hope had not been abandoned that a charter might yet be secured

[1] Over 50 per cent of the subscriptions went in legal expenses, there being a payment of £371 1s 6d on May 28, 1762, to Augustin Greenland, solicitor, and Counsel and Clerk's fees of £11 11s on May 9, 1762. Earlier, in 1760, Mr Barnard, solicitor, had been paid £72 13s, which would be for the original draft and the amended version of the petition.

because it was stipulated (77) that the deed of settlement was to be the plan of the charter, should application be made for one.

Fifteen directors were named in the deed of settlement to constitute the original Court of Directors. Four of these, including the President, did not attend meetings and were not continued in office after the first election in May 1764 (not March as was provided by the deed). These four were:

> The Right Hon. Hugh Lord Willoughby of Parham, FSA, FRS (d. 1765).
> The Hon. Coote Molesworth, MD, FRS (d. 1782 at age 85).
> Sir Robert Ladbroke (1713–73), banker in Lombard Street and Lord Mayor of London, 1747–48.
> Robert Dingley, FRS (d. 1781 at age 72), merchant, treasurer to the Magdalene House (and joint founder of it).

These four distinguished men presumably lent their names to aid the project but did not intend to take an active part in the direction of affairs. The other eleven original directors were:

> Sir Richard Glyn, Bart. (1711–72).
> Sir John Baptist Silvester, MD, FRS (1714–89), physician to the London Hospital, 1746–64.
> Gowin Knight, MA, MB, FRS (1713–72), medical man and scientist who was Principal Librarian of the British Museum from 1756 to his death.
> Edward Rowe Mores, MA, FSA (1731–78).
> Adam Martin, FSA (1707–83), of the Exchequer Office, Barrister of the Inner Temple.
> John Bedford (1715–70), of the Parish of St Andrew, Holborn.
> Rev. William Sclater, MA (1709–?), Rector of Loughton, Essex.
> Master Deputy Richard Bridgman (c. 1699–1764), Master (Senior Warden) of the Grocers' Company 1753–4, Deputy 1756.
> William Bonham (1721–83), merchant, described in Kent's directories as a packer.
> Joseph Sclater (1715–68), druggist in Newgate Street.
> Francis Say (1724–78), citizen and upholder, an upholsterer in Ludgate Hill.[1]

The Trustees elected at the first weekly Court of Directors were Sir Richard Glyn, Sir John Silvester, John Bedford, William Bonham and Joseph Sclater.

The Society's first prospectus was a pamphlet called *A Short Account of the Society for Equitable Assurances on Lives and Survivor-*

---

[1] Many of the years of birth have been obtained by subtracting the age from the year when the assurance was effected and so may be a year out.

*ships* and there is little doubt that it was wholly the work of Mores. On October 5, 1762, barely a month after the deed of settlement had been signed, Mores was asked to prepare an abstract; he hoped to have it ready within a week. Nothing more is heard of it until December 13, 1763, when the 'Society's proposals or books usually given away' were exhausted and 1,000 more were ordered. On September 11, 1764, 500 more 'with alterations' were ordered to be printed. These facts have somehow to be reconciled with the earliest copy in the possession of the Society which bears on the title page the year 1764, and at the end of the *Short Account* the date August 2, 1764, where Mores has added his own initials; is described as being the fifth edition; includes on the title page the assertion 'Established by DEED, Inrolled in His Majesty's Court of King's Bench at Westminster'; and is bound with bye-laws which are obviously a draft with blanks for completion when adopted, the space in the heading assuming adoption in 1763.

The explanation seems to be that the copy is actually a proof of an earlier edition of the *Short Account*, with printed amendments arranged by Mores; that this copy was prepared on the assumption that the bye-laws would soon be adopted and so was bound with them; and that Mores intended to issue this as the fifth edition when the deed had been enrolled and the bye-laws adopted.

The wording of the *Short Account* suggests that it was written in 1762 either before or soon after business had begun to be transacted and the bye-laws would have been drafted at about the same time, though they were never adopted by the Society. At least, there is no record of the adoption of the bye-laws but on October 9, 1765 it was ordered that fifty copies of the Bye-Laws should be immediately printed.

Two circumstances enable these works to be dated more closely. It so happens that there was a mistake in the specimen premiums quoted in the deed of settlement; the premium for an assurance of £100 for one year at the age of fifty was given as £4 4s 8d instead of £4 8s 8d though the mistake seems to have made no practical difference because the early assurances were mainly for the whole continuance of life. Secondly, the entrance money was reduced on October 26, 1762, and the premiums per £100 assurance were increased by 5s, if for one year, and by 1s 6d, if for the whole continuance of life.

Now Mores's copy of the *Short Account*, notwithstanding that it purports to outline the provisions of the deed of settlement, in fact prints without comment the premiums as increased in October 1762 and with the correct figure for age fifty. On the other hand the draft bye-laws include complete tables of premiums at all ages for assurances for one year and for the whole continuance of life and these tables are the correct premiums on the original scale without the increase.

It may be concluded that the deed of settlement, the *Short Account* and the bye-laws were all drafted at about the same time; that the scale of premiums in the bye-laws was copied direct from the original manuscript table; that, when specimen premiums were extracted for the deed of settlement, a mistake was made in copying; and that this mistake was rectified in the *Short Account*.

The Bodleian Library has a copy of the first edition of the *Short Account*, which must have been printed between September 16, 1762 (since it included the names of the trustees elected on that day) and October 26, 1762, when the scales of premium were increased. Probably, when the specimen premiums were altered for these increases the revised copy was called the second edition. The draft bye-laws were not issued with the *Short Account* in the surviving copies.

The *Short Account* gives a fair summary of the relevant provisions of the deed of settlement with one, less than candid, exception— there is no mention of the entrance money and its distribution among original subscribers. The gap was remedied by the draft bye-laws which included a chapter on the subject. The omission from the *Short Account* was inexcusable, unless the draft bye-laws were bound up with it. But were they? It seems unlikely. Later, as might be expected, a sinister explanation was put on the omission.

The *Short Account* includes the earliest description of the events leading to the formation of the Society and an extract will also serve to illustrate the style in which the pamphlet is written; the reference in the third paragraph to 'other less comprehensive societies' is obscure; none are known:

These considerations induced a number of gentlemen, in the beginning of the year 1756, to form a design of establishing a Society for equitable assurances upon lives, with a view to the sole benefit of the Persons Assured, whose interest hath been all along considered as wholly distinct from, not to say incompatible with, that of the Assurers; a society, in which the assured being at the same time mutually assurers one to the other, the interest of one might be the interest of both; in which a life might be assured for a single year, a certain number of years, or for the whole continuance of life; and in which the premiums of assurance should be no more than adequate to the chance of death attending the age of the life to be assured, and to the time the assurance was to continue.

The design was received with approbation, and, with unwearied diligence and application, pursued through numerous difficulties and obstacles, for the space of almost seven years.

During this time other less comprehensive societies, upon plans indeed something different from this, yet originally derived from this, sprung up and flourished.

The promoters, however, of this design, having by perseverance surmounted all obstructions, are at length arrived (at least in this respect) at the completion of their endeavours for the public good, the establishment of A SOCIETY FOR EQUITABLE ASSURANCES ON LIVES AND SURVIVORSHIPS.

The deed of settlement introduced a new word to the English language, or (more correctly) gave a new meaning to a little used, archaic one, by the choice of the title *Actuary* for the chief executive official of the new Society.

The eighteenth century was a period of experiment in various types of business organization. Since it was difficult to secure the benefits of incorporation, the typical business organization was in the legal form of a partnership under a deed of settlement. In the same way that the business affairs of a partnership would be transacted primarily by the partners with the assistance of a secretary and a few clerks, it was customary for the business of a company to be managed by the directors, often through committees, the executive staff acting as a kind of secretariat. Thus it was natural that the head of the executive staff should be called the secretary, not the manager as would be customary nowadays.

The word 'actuary' is derived from the Latin *actuarius*, which was used for a shorthand writer in the specialized sense of the official who was responsible for the official record of the proceedings of the Senate under the Roman Empire. The *Encyclopedia Britannica* (3rd ed., 1797, which might reflect the ideas current in Mores's time) stated that, in the Eastern Empire, *actuarii* were, properly, officers who kept the military accounts, received the corn from the store-keepers and delivered it to the soldiers.

It seems that the reasons for the choice of the curious title of 'actuary' lie in the character and interests of Edward Rowe Mores. He was over-fond of the use of Latin and would have been familiar

or instrument shall be the plan and basis of such charter and all and every the clauses articles provisoes conditions and agreements in this said deed or instrument contained those only excepted

which by reason of the death or removal of any person therein mentioned must necessarily be changed [illegible] shall be the clauses articles provisoes and conditions proposed presented and offered to be inserted therein And if any questions disputes or differences shall at any time or times hereafter happen or arise between the parties executing this present deed or instrument or such other persons as shall at any time or times hereafter become Members of the said Society touching or concerning any matter or thing in this deed or instrument contained or any matter or thing relating thereto or to the management or concerns of the said Society hereby intended to be established that then and in such case the said parties or such other persons shall and will from time to time leave the matters in dispute between them to be decided and determined by the opinion of his Majesty's Attorney-General and Solicitor-General for the time being and the Senior of the Kings counsel practising in his Majesty's Court of Kings-Bench for the time being in manner following that is to say a case containing all the facts and matters in controversy shall be fairly stated in writing and laid before each of them the said Attorney and Solicitor-General for the time being and the Senior of the Kings Counsel practising in the Court of Kings-Bench and the opinion of the major part of them in writing shall be final in determining the same and the contending parties shall respectively submit to the said opinion and the person or persons against whom the said decision or determination shall be made or given shall pay discharge and satisfy all fees costs charges damages and expences which shall have been occasioned by such disputes or differences and by the means of deciding and determining the same in manner before mentioned That these presents and every thing therein contained whether the same be mentioned by way of Covenant Agreement or undertaking or by way of future Constitutions Laws Rules or Ordinances of and for the regulation of the said Society shall be binding and obligatory in every respect to all intents and purposes as well to all and every person and persons whatsoever taking policies and becoming contributors and Members thereby as to all and every person and persons hereunto subscribing and we who have executed these presents do each of us for ourselves covenant promise and agree to and with the others of us and to and with every of them their and every of their executors administrators and assigns that we are and will be firmly held and bounden by these presents and by every thing therein contained in manner above mentioned In Witness whereof we have hereunto severally [illegible] our hands and seals the seventh day of September in the year of our Lord One thousand seven hundred and sixty-two.

[illegible] and delivered every skin being first duly stamped

Wm. Bradley

John Samwell

3. The deed of settlement

THE CORPORATION OF

SITE OF
THE PARSONAGE OF
ST. NICHOLAS ACONS
WHERE SCIENTIFIC
LIFE ASSURANCE
BEGAN IN 1762.

THE CITY OF LONDON

4. Plaque on the site of the Society's first office, in Nicholas Lane

with the use of that title for the official who recorded the decision of a court, a rare survival from Tudor usage. It was used in the courts which met in Doctors Commons. He may have felt that some special title was required for the chief official of the new organization and that 'actuary' would be appropriate, since the principal duties of the new official would be to register the contracts made by the Society. If so, he showed a remarkable prescience. More probably, however, he was merely indulging in an antiquarian whimsy, adopting an archaism to describe an official who was intended to be the Secretary in all but name.

This suggestion appears to be confirmed by the secretarial nature of the duties that were expected of the men who held the post in the early days. A minute (S, January 19, 1769) actually refers to papers being kept in the custody of the Secretary! The business was effectively managed by the Court of Directors and they looked to Mores for actuarial advice. In course of time the Actuary came to a larger responsibility in the management of the Society; other life offices chose the same title to describe their chief officials and in due course the name became attached to the professional men who still mainly, though by no means wholly, use their mathematical abilities in the service of life offices.

# CHAPTER IV

# EARLY DAYS (1762–1766)

THE Society's first office was in Nicholas Lane, which originally ran from Lombard Street to Cannon Street, before King William Street was built, in the parsonage of St Nicholas Acons. The church had been destroyed in the great fire of 1666 and had not been rebuilt but the parsonage was rebuilt, next to the churchyard, and was in the possession of the Rev. Jeremiah Milles, DD, who from 1746 until his death in 1784 was rector of the combined parishes of St Nicholas Acons and St Edmund the King and Martyr in Lombard Street. Milles was also Dean of Exeter Cathedral.

The Society has no record of negotiations with Dr Milles and the house may have been taken informally, by word of mouth, in view of what happened over the rent. Milles belonged to the Society of Antiquaries, being President during the last fifteen or sixteen years of his life. He contributed a letter dated June 17, 1754, to the chapter on the palace of Croydon which Mores wrote for Ducarel, so that Mores would have been acquainted with Milles. Presumably, Mores knew that the parsonage was vacant and arranged a lease of it for the new Society.

The house was on the west side of Nicholas Lane and flanked the churchyard, which is now a garden, on the north. The site is now occupied by the rear part of the Lombard Street office of the Westminster Bank and is opposite, across the garden, the back of another well-known mutual life assurance society, the London Life Association. The City Corporation have erected a plaque to mark the site. The actual inauguration of scientific life assurance took place, however, in the White Lion tavern, Cornhill, where the Directors held their first six weekly meetings, while the house in Nicholas Lane was being got ready.

Though neither picture nor plan of the house is known, something of the lay-out may be discerned from scraps of evidence in the minutes. In the basement there was a cellar which had a window opening on to the street (S, April 6, 1770). Mores had a desk in the 'middle room' (S, December 1, 1768), which was obviously on the ground floor. The outer room would have been used as a general office where the two assistants worked, the middle room by the Actuary. If so, in addition to a double desk belonging to Mores and containing his papers (S, June 14, 1769), it would have contained a desk or table for the Actuary. A passage and stairs (S, October 23, 1769) led to the Court room—which was a large room on a higher level than the ground floor or possibly on the first floor. It was of a sufficient size for two open fireplaces (S, October 23, 1769). The clock would have been bought for this room (S, August 9, 1765). The Society's papers and cash were originally kept in an iron chest with three locks (W, July 26, 1763), which was probably placed in the Court room because a few years later the Actuary was instructed to arrange for a mahogany book-case 'with drawers and other conveniences' in the north-east corner of this room, where the Society's papers could be kept under lock and key in the custody of the Actuary (S, October 20, 1768). The wording suggests that the Court room ran from the front to the back of the house, the east end of the room looking over Nicholas Lane—otherwise there seems little point in the reference to the north-east corner.

Meetings of members of the Society were held in the Court room. The number attending such meetings was usually about sufficient to fill a fair-sized room but on one occasion 105 members came to the meeting, possibly because of the interest aroused by the election of a new actuary (G, April 24, 1767). They must surely have overflowed into the passage and other parts of the house.

The Court of Directors also met in the Court room. The weekly Court was usually in session on Tuesday from 11 o'clock until the close of business at 3 o'clock because business was customarily transacted in person with the Court, not with the Actuary or other official as would now be the case. There were fifteen Directors but not all of them could spare the time every week, neither did those present necessarily stay the whole time; it was necessary merely to arrange for the minimum of five for a quorum. The minutes record no break for lunch though tea and coffee were to be provided when Summoned Courts were convened to meet at 5 o'clock on the afternoon of the same day as the weekly Court (S, October 2, 1766).

By the terms of his appointment, the Actuary resided in the Society's house and presumably had the use of the upper part, with possibly a kitchen in the basement. When a clerk was appointed to assist the Actuary, this assistant was also to 'have a room in the Society's house for his own use to lodge in' (S, August 6, 1765), though this may have been an exceptional arrangement.

The first meeting of the weekly Court of Directors was held on Thursday,[1] September 16, 1762, when the deed of settlement 'was exhibited, fair, uncancelled, and without obliteration'. Dr Gowin Knight was chosen as chairman; trustees were elected and other formal business disposed of, 'and then the Court proceeded upon the business of the Society'. The principal business was the making of new assurances. It is easy to reconstruct the scene with the help of the minutes and the draft bye-laws. The applicant for life assurance had to come to the Society's house on a Tuesday, at an appointed time from 11 o'clock onwards, when the Court of Directors was in session. The applicant was met in the outer room of the office by the Actuary or one of his assistants, who required him to sign a declaration in a printed book of forms. This gave his name, address, occupation and age and information about his state of health. If the assurance was to be on the life of another person, a longer declaration had to be made, setting out the nature of the insurable interest, and the deeds establishing the interest had to be produced.

The applicant was next shown into the Court room, where the directors were meeting, and it may be guessed, took a place reserved for him at the table. The Chairman asked the Actuary to read the declaration just made by the applicant and the directors doubtless took the opportunity to question the applicant about the assurance and his state of health, after which he was requested to withdraw while the Court gave 'due deliberation' to the proposal to assure the life. The question whether the proposed life should be assured was put to the Court in three parts: (a) whether the party shall be permitted to make assurance with the Society, upon and for the whole continuance of his own life? and if the same pass in the negative, then,

[1] Subsequent meetings were held on Tuesdays, as provided by the deed of settlement, beginning on Tuesday, September 21, 1762.

(b) whether, etc., for a number of years certain? and if the same pass in the negative, then, (c) whether, etc., for a single year?

A risk that was unacceptable for the whole of life might well be acceptable for a shorter period. Acceptance had to be by the unanimous vote of the Court since one of the directors might know of objections to the proposed life which it could be improper openly to declare.

If the Court accepted the assurance, the next task was to fix the premium. For the early assurances there are small, unexplained variations in the actual premiums compared with Dodson's tables and the Court seems to have relied upon those directors, such as Mores, who had access to Dodson's calculations, until complete tables were available. The applicant was then recalled into the room, made acquainted with the decision and asked for his assent, whereupon he had to pay the entrance money and the first premium and to sign the covenant entered into by the members of the Society. The Chairman then admitted him into the membership, saying: 'We admit you a member of the Society for Equitable Assurances on Lives and Survivorships, and we wish you a long and happy life'. Surely, the words were accompanied by a smile and a handshake by way of greeting the new member.

Gowin Knight had taken the chair at the early meetings but on December 7, 1762, he produced an instrument, under the hand and seal of Lord Willoughby of Parham, which appears to have nominated Edward Rowe Mores as Vice-President, for Mores took the chair as such at the next weekly Court. For such an important occasion it is curious that the deed, or at least the fact of the appointment, was not recorded in the minutes. As will be seen, the instrument presumably appointed Sir Richard Glyn as the other Vice-President though there is no record of this; he was not attending the weekly Courts.

Mores's first action as Vice-President was to represent from the chair that 'the want of an obligation to secresy [sic] . . . had already occasioned some difficulties, and would if not timely remedied be productive of numberless inconveniences and greatly impede the progress of the Society'. Having regard to the personal nature of the information given by applicants for life assurance, an oath of secrecy seems not unreasonable; it was as follows:

I do swear that I will not disclose or make known to any person whatever, except to a Director, Member, or Officer of the Society, who shall have first taken this oath, the Name or Names of any Person or Persons, who shall be assured or apply to be assured by the Society (my own Name only excepted) nor any matter or thing which shall be transacted in any Court of Directors or General Court of this Society touching or concerning any assurance which shall be made or proposed to be made by the Society. So help me God.

The oath was first taken by Mores, who then administered the oath to the other five directors present, to the Actuary and his two assistants, Richard Jenkenson and John Osgood. The oath was administered to the remaining directors when they next attended the weekly Court.

The Society soon ran into a time of trouble which came to a head in the autumn of 1763 and which was touched off by a shortage of cash. Why this was so can be traced to the questionable relationship between the subscribers to the original charter fund and the other members of the Society. The deed of settlement required each person assuring with the Society to pay an entrance fee of 15s for each £100 of assurance, which fee would go to the subscribers, and a deposit of 20s. These charges were soon felt to be burdensome and unduly restrictive of the business of the Society. The promoters were confident that deposits were unnecessary. Since, however, the calculated premiums contained no specific contribution to a reserve fund nor any provision for expenses, which, it was hoped, would be met out of certain margins in the calculations, it was essential that the premiums should not be encroached upon and that the funds should be built up as rapidly as possible.

The financial situation of the Society was worsened when a general meeting of the subscribers, held on Thursday, September 21, 1762, agreed that the entrance money should be reduced to 5s for each £100 of assurance on the understanding that the difference should be made up to them out of the Society's funds. The Society was to charge 'such advance in premiums' as would enable it to pay to the subscribers 10s (making 15s in all) for each £100 assured for the whole of life or for periods of more than one year and 5s (making 10s in all) for each £100 assured for a single year. On the following Tuesday the premiums for one year's assurance were increased by 5s per £100 and the premiums for assurance for the whole of life were increased by 1s 6d per £100. Though there is no record of the decision, it seems that the same meetings decided to waive the deposits on all subsequent assurances. At one stroke, the Society had lost such protection as was afforded by the deposit and had to encroach upon the first premiums paid by new assurers in order to make up the entrance money to the subscribers; it is true it gained an expectation of a higher premium income thereafter.

What kind of situation should be inferred from the laconic minute of September 6, 1763: the Directors having an occasion of the declaration of trust from the Trustees of the Society, Mr Mosdell the Actuary refused to produce the same? That there was dissatisfaction with the conduct of affairs is plain. Some of the directors may have sought the help of Glyn. The following Tuesday, September 13th, Sir Richard appeared at the weekly Court for the first time and took the chair as Vice-President, presumably as the senior Vice-President since Mores was also present. The result of his first enquiry was dramatic:

> Sir Richard Glyn called for the minutes of the fourteenth of December last, touching the oath of the Members, the iron chest being opened, neither the minutes nor any of the capital stock of the said Society, nor the Deed of Settlement, nor anything belonging to the Society were there found and Sir Richard enquiring where they were was informed that they were at Mr Bonham's house having been carried there by direction of the Court.

William Bonham was one of the trustees and evidently an informal arrangement had been made that he should hold the Society's cash but the arrangement had not been properly authorized. Later, Bonham became bankrupt and on the last day of 1765 he was removed from his trusteeship.

There had been trouble during this first year of operations both about the proper keeping of books and about the cash. An amusing letter (dated Exeter, October 15, 1763) was written by Dr Milles, the landlord of the Society's house, to Edward Rowe Mores:

> I find myself obliged to renew my application to you for the rent of my house, my Clerk informed me that he attended the Trustees for payment by Sir Richard Glyn's order but that he was sent away without receiving the money the reason of which he knows not and therefore I hope you will be so kind as to explain it to me. He further says that being asked whom he considered as my tenant in the house he replied Sir Richard Glyn. I shall hope for your further elucidation of this dark affair.

Since Glyn had moved a month previously that the rent should be paid and the motion 'passed in the negative', it is not surprising that he felt his honour was 'greatly reflected upon'. By the end of the year a committee had been appointed 'to consider the present state of the Society'. On April 10, 1764, it was ordered that moneys were to be lodged every Court day with Messrs. Vere, Glyn and Hallifax, Bankers.

The General Court met twice—on April 26 and May 3, 1764, when new directors were elected. They elected Sir Richard Glyn President. He had the right to nominate the Vice-Presidents and it is significant that he did not ask Mores to continue in that office. The minute is missing, but evidently the new President nominated John Silvester and Robert Wilsonn (a new director) as Vice-Presidents.

Richard Glyn was one of those men whose life was centred in the City of London and whose business acumen built up the prestige of the City. Like his father he was a drysalter (a dealer in dyes and chemicals) in Hatton Garden and took an active part both in the promotion of various enterprises and in the politics of the City of London. He was knighted in 1752 when he was sheriff of the City of London and served as Lord Mayor in 1758–9. He was President of the Bridewell and Bethlehem hospitals from 1755 to his death. He was one of the M.P.s for the City of London from 1758 to 1768, when he was defeated in the election in which John Wilkes intervened. But he found another seat at Coventry, which he represented from 1768 to 1772.

Glyn was the founder of the famous banking firm, now known as Glyn, Mills & Co. The bank, founded in 1753, opened for business on Saturday, January 5, 1754, as Vere, Glyn & Hallifax; with a Glyn always in association, it has flourished for over two hundred years and is now one of the City's most respected institutions. Such a man had the ability and influence to guide a new project. As Fulford[1] says, his portrait by Zoffany shows him as a sturdy and humorous, completely trustworthy man.

With Glyn as President, a firmer hand in control can be sensed. Lord Willoughby of Parham was thanked for the use of his name. The accounts and books were to be put in order and the debts were to be paid. Dodson's original tables had been obtained from William Mountaine (W, January 24, 1764) and six months later his son, James Dodson, was asked to copy them.

The *Short Account* was evidently too long for it was decided (W,

[1] *Glyn's 1753–1953*, by Roger Fulford.

October 2, 1764) to produce a shorter pamphlet, written in a more popular way.

The Actuary was ordered to comply with the memorandum which had been prepared by Isaiah Millington about the keeping of the books. Possibly William Mosdell was by now a sick man. Mores is stated to have offered himself as Actuary on November 21, 1764. In December Mosdell died. Little is known of him but he had some mathematical ability because his daughter was paid twenty guineas for some survivorship calculations he had made.

His successor had to be elected by the General Court, an unusual procedure which took place on July 5, 1765. There were three candidates—James Dodson, Robert Ellis and Harry Minors Long. James Dodson was known to the members as being the son of the founder. Long had been helping with the minutes. Three directors favoured Ellis, the other candidate. The first step was to announce to the meeting the opinion of the directors, which had been ascertained by ballot, James Dodson getting nine votes and Robert Ellis three. The General Court then proceeded to a ballot and James Dodson was declared to be elected.[1]

It had been expected that Mores would take some considerable share in the direction of the Society's affairs and his emolument of £100 a year was in part 'for the trouble which he . . . may undergo hereafter'. By way of clarifying the situation, an arrangement was made with him (S, November 28, 1765) that he would (a) prepare all printed matter required by the Society; (b) draw any special policies and see to the printing of the general policy forms; (c) calculate premiums that were not in the tables; and (d) answer enquiries from distant parts that might require special calculations.

An offer that he would calculate the reserves on claims and other policies going off the books was not accepted. The arrangement shows that, effectively, the actuarial oversight of the Society was in the hands of Mores, though possibly it was intended to limit the part he might have played in other matters. It was not finally ratified until September 3, 1767.

Mores's work under this arrangement is illustrated by a printed list of the policies and other instruments of the Society, which is bound with Mores's papers in the Bodleian library. The list is of all the general policies prepared for the different circumstances of various

[1] The figures were: Dodson 26 votes, Ellis 3 and Long 22.

assurances together with special policies for complicated cases. Unfortunately the book of policy forms to which the list refers has disappeared. The printed list is dated February 11, 1764 and the list has been corrected by hand to December 31, 1767.

At this time a momentous decision was taken which has coloured the whole character of the Society. On November 7, 1765, a Mr Syprut appeared before the Court to ask whether the directors would pay him commission. Decision was deferred for a fortnight but then the motion 'passed in the negative' (S, November 21, 1765). The Society has been faithful to this decision ever since and it remains one of a few offices with this special characteristic. Much of the Society's business is introduced by members of the Society themselves, who thus benefit the whole body of members by the expansion of the Society's activities in an economical way.

Jacob Syprut was the promoter of the 'Society for Annuities encreasing to the Survivors'. He lived in Bury Street in the parish of St Mary Axe and, as was the custom, used to transact his business at the Caroline coffee-house in Birchin Lane, where he could be found from 11 a.m. to 2 p.m. His scheme was a variant of the tontine schemes that were popular at the time. The object was to raise subscriptions in 'centuries', i.e. 100 subscriptions of £100 each, totalling £10,000. The interest on this capital would be divided among the survivors from time to time and when the number of members in any 'century' had been reduced by deaths to ten or fewer the capital was to be divided among the survivors. The subscribers were divided into six classes according to age, each class covering a range of ten ages, with one group for ages fifty and over.

Syprut's society was actually established in 1769 but drafts of the deed of settlement and the declaration of trust (prepared in 1768) are bound with Mores's papers relating to the Equitable. It is said that Mores drafted these deeds also, and they do bear some resemblance to the Equitable deeds, but Mores may have kept them merely as a matter of concern over possible competition. The four trustees for the annuity scheme include two who were Equitable directors, i.e. Roger Staples and John Woodhouse.

Both the difficulties of transacting life assurance and the flavour of business in those days can be illustrated by the story of one assurance

made by the Society. On January 29, 1765, a certain Edward Cartwright of Queen's Square, Westminster, appeared before the Court,
being desirous of assuring the sum of £200 for the period of seven
years upon the life of William Jenkin of the parish of Clench Wharton,
in the county of Norfolk, aged 65 years. Cartwright declared 'that
his (Jenkin's) state of health now is and generally has been very
good, that he hath had the small-pox, that he is not given to drink
or other intemperance . . .'. Cartwright had paid Jenkin £536 on
October 10, 1764, for an interest in certain property in Clench
Wharton, which was occupied by William Jenkin and a certain John
Edwards and which was held by William Jenkin for a term of sixty
years from October 9, 1764, 'if the said William shall so long live'. In
view of Jenkin's age the property was virtually held for life and this
was deemed to be a sufficient insurable interest. The Court agreed
to accept the assurance of £200, but for a period of five years only,
at an annual premium of £17 4s 6d which was the usual premium
by Dodson's tables for that period of assurance (with the addition of
5s per cent). Edward Cartwright agreed the terms and paid the first
premium with an additional 10s for entrance money.

On May 14, 1766, Mr John Staples was requested to go to Lynn
to enquire about the state of health of William Jenkin. Whether
Jenkin was already dead is uncertain but, on June 12, 1766, Edward
Cartwright appeared before the Court to report the death and claim
the £200 assured. He was told that the Court had made some enquiry
of Jenkin's state of health and found that he was in a bad state of
health at the time the assurance was made; they could not pay the
sum assured. John Staples was instructed to write to an attorney at
Lynn to collect what evidence he could. Stirred by this experience
the Court, at the same meeting, decided that, thereafter, no insurance
should be made upon any person until proper enquiry had been made
about the way of life and the health of the person proposed to be
insured unless the person were known to one of the directors. Also,
immediately on notice of the demise of any member of the Society,
the Actuary was to endeavour to learn how and in what manner the
person died.

Edward Cartwright took legal advice and the following letter
(sent 'by order of the Court of Directors', September 2, 1766, and
signed by James Dodson, to Cartwright's attorney, who was named
Bassett) explains the Society's attitude:

It was owing to an enquiry made by the Directors that Mr Cartwright was refused his claim: a claim which they as trustees for a numerous Society could not admit without a deviation from those principles of justice and equity upon which they are established. It is with regret that the Directors ever find themselves obliged even to hesitate at a demand made upon the Society—much more so to refuse payment of such demand and it would be pleasing to them could they satisfy the demand now made by Mr Cartwright without a breach of the trust reposed in them by their constituents. But the life of Mr Jenkin was by no means agreeable to the warranty upon which the assurance was made.

That was not the end of the matter. On October 2, 1766, Edward Cartwright and his attorney produced certain certificates of the state of health of William Jenkin 'which not being satisfactory the Court agreed to make further enquiry'. Perhaps the further enquiries were inconclusive. At any rate, the Court agreed (S, January 30, 1767) to compromise on the claim up to £250 and the claim appears to have been settled on February 3rd for £235. Since the assurance was for £200 only, the sum actually paid must have included some expenses. One outcome of this case was the decision to charge an additional premium of one-half per cent for non-appearance, unless the life proposed were known to at least one of the directors.

# CHAPTER V

# THE DISPUTE WITH THE SUBSCRIBERS
## (1766–1769)

THE uneasy relationship between the original subscribers and the other members of the Society was bound to come to a head sooner or later. The members of the original Court of Directors were aware of the appropriation of the entrance money to the subscribers, but when other members came to be elected to the Court they may well have been ignorant of the circumstances—unless they had been told or had asked questions about the entrance money at the time they joined the Society. One of these new directors, William Waller (of Tooke's Court, in the parish of St Andrew, Holborn) who was first elected in 1765, set himself to destroy the interests of the subscribers, who had formed the nucleus of the Society and undertaken the obligations of membership, including the liability to contribute to a call, should that be necessary. It was easy to belittle their efforts and to criticize their claim for compensation by sharing the entrance money, which was in essence a kind of royalty on all assurances granted by the Society. The original subscriptions, in shares of £5 each, were somewhat akin to subscriptions to share capital but the agreement of June 9, 1756 made clear that the subscribers were to have no proprietary interest, other than in the entrance money. The corporation was to be a mutual society 'for the more free and equitable insurances of lives'.

The subscribers might have been able to persuade most of the new members of the justice of their claim to some recompense had the circumstances been fully disclosed when assurances were effected. Mores, however, seems to have intended to keep silent on this question. The application of the entrance money was not mentioned in the *Short Account*; new members who asked to see the deed of settlement were shown an engrossed copy which was in a shortened form, excluding all reference to the subscribers' interest in the entrance money. This silence merely had the effect of magnifying the suspicions of Waller and his associates; they inferred that there was something sinister about the oath of secrecy; they alleged that the premiums had been set at too low a level so as to benefit the subscribers at the expense of the Society; and Waller asserted that the subscribers had taken £110,000 in entrance money in some five years of operations, whereas that was the approximate total of the assurances in force! A signal volley, by way of prelude to the battle, was fired on the question whether the deed of settlement could be altered.

Experience might indicate the need for changes in the constitution of the Society, but could changes be made? Had the General Court the power to alter, change or annul any of the laws, statutes and ordinances contained in the deed of settlement?—or merely those that the General Court itself had made? The committee which was asked to draw up a case for counsel (Charles Yorke, the Attorney General) reported, instead, on May 31, 1765, that they were of the opinion that strict adherence to the deed of settlement was indispensably necessary to the very existence of the Society and that its credit might be greatly prejudiced by the slightest attempt to alter it. The mere drawing of the case could be considered, at least, as a reflection upon the Society and might prove a foundation for future mischief. This vigorous protest was evidently inspired by Mores, for the sentiments are scarcely in character with the later actions of Waller, and the third member of the committee, Adam Martin, drew the case in the end.

The core of the problem is in two sections of the deed of settlement:

> That the said General Courts being so Assembled shall have power to make Statutes & Bye-Laws Rules Orders & Ordinances for the good Order of the said Society, and the same at their pleasure to Annul and Alter; But that no Repeal of any Statute Bye-Law Rule Order or Ordinance be binding, untill the same shall have received the approbation of three Successive General Courts or Meetings of the said Society, whither Quarterly or Extraordinary; . . . That the Deed and everything therein contained shall be binding and obligatory in every respect to all Intents and purposes to the Parties who have Executed the said Deed.

The Attorney General, on May 22, 1766, gave his opinion briefly but cogently against the suggestion that the deed of settlement could not be altered:

> In such a Society the alteration of times and circumstances may make it expedient to Vary many Rules and provisions, which were right in the first institution. . . . I do not see any words in the Covenants sufficient to Control the power of the General Court, as to the subject matter of their Bye-Laws.

The warmth of the discussions about the 'separate interest' of the subscribers in the entrance money tended to hold up the discussion of other matters and retarded the growth of the Society. Indeed, one of the directors felt that it was inconsistent with the character of men of honour to continue the transaction of new assurances while the dispute was still unsettled. His written protest is included with the minutes (W, March 10, 1767); though unsigned, it may reasonably be ascribed to William Waller. He was usually present at the weekly meetings but he, alone of those who were accustomed to come, did not attend between December 23, 1766 and March 10, 1767. He wrote:

> As I consider that the dispute about the Charter Fund has drawn Dr Silvester out of the Society—has made Sir Richard Glyn and Roger Staples, Esq., refuse to execute any Policies—and I myself have absented myself from the Tuesday meetings not thinking it justifiable to draw in persons to make insurances with us while a dispute which I think threatens the dissolution of the Society is now farther from being settled than when it began—As I consider that several members of the Charter Fund are disposing of their shares which must involve the Society in lawsuits with the purchasers whilst this Fund is industriously concealed from every new member, and the disputes about it much more so—As I consider that the members of the Charter Fund always compose a great majority of the Court of Directors—I think myself bound in honour and conscience to protest against admitting any new members into the Society, 'till the dangerous disputes about the Charter Fund are settled'—As it can answer no end but enriching that Fund at the expense of such new members.

It was felt that the subscribers should give up their claim to the entrance money in return for some fixed compensation. The first offer was a payment for each share of either £10 down or £1 10s p.a. for life or £36 within one year after the death of the subscriber (S, November 13, 1766). Mores suggested £30 a year (for life?) after 15 years. The subscribers did not like any of the alternatives but were willing to accept £2 per annum for twenty-one years in respect of each share. After six months' negotiations, the directors decided to offer a compromise of £2 per annum for fourteen years in respect of each share. The consent of the members was obtained (G, May 5, 1767) by means of a report of the Court of Directors which embodied the offer. The subscribers met on May 8, 1767, and all except two signed an agreement accepting the offer.

The report was designed to explain how the situation had arisen and put the subscribers' case in a favourable light. It referred to the 'torrent of opposition' to the establishment of the Society and called the entrance money 'a tributary acknowledgment upon those who should seek benefit from the success of the subscribers'. Later, it came out that no draft of this report had been considered by the Court of Directors; the report had been neither approved by it nor signed by the Chairman. Mores admitted that he had drawn the report in the coffee-house on the morning of the General Court! It would not be surprising if the newer directors felt they had been tricked.

This was not the first time such a thing had happened. The report submitted to the first General Court on April 26, 1764, is said to have been endorsed by Mosdell, 'The paper called by Mr Mores etc. the report of the Court of Directors, April 26, 1764'. Unfortunately, the minutes no longer exist but the implied doubt is clear. Mores must have had the confidence of the majority of the directors but the disaffected ones were naturally suspicious of his good faith.

The first year's payment under the agreement was paid in half-yearly instalments in 1767 to a total of £140 each; the remaining £6 was the share of John Cleveland, a director who had bought some of the subscribers' shares; he was not an original subscriber. Neither he nor Mores signed the agreement, but Mores accepted it in fact because he took the payment of £2 a share. However, two half-yearly payments only were made under this agreement.

James Dodson, the Actuary of the Society, resigned his office (W, February 10, 1767) in order to take an appointment with the Customs Office. He was young, under 25 years of age, and may have felt the post too much for him, a feeling that would be heightened by the heat of the dissensions. At least the candidates for the vacant office were all older men. They had to appear before the weekly Court in order to assure their lives:

| February 10, 1767 | Phillip Pitt, Gent., of the Parish of St Mary Magellan, Middx, aged 29 years. |
| March 10, 1767 | Nicholas Crowdson, Gent., of Portugal Street, in the Parish of St Clement Danes, aged 42 years. |

# This present Instrument or Policy of Assurance

Witnesseth, that Whereas *[name]* hath become a Member of the SOCIETY FOR EQUITABLE ASSURANCES ON LIVES AND SURVIVORSHIPS, according to a certain Deed of Settlement bearing date the *Seventh* day of *September* in the year of our Lord One Thousand Seven Hundred and Sixty-two, inrolled in his Majesty's Court of King's-Bench at *Westminster*; and hath made Assurance with the said Society in the Sum of *[ ]* ... but now upon the natural Life of *[ ]* ... not exceeding the age of *[ ]* ...

5. An early policy granted by the Society

6. Sir Richard Glyn, Bart., by Zoffany

March 17, 1767    John Edwards, Merchant of Long Acre, in the Parish of
                  St Martin-in-the-Fields, aged 37 years.

March 24, 1767    John Robertson, Gent., of the Parish of St Botulph,
                  Aldersgate, aged 55 years.

The election took place at a General Court on Friday, April 24, 1767, when 105 members were present, a record number for those days and an indication of the interest taken in the elections. Were the candidates in any sense nominees of rival factions in the membership of the Society? We do not know. When the ballot was closed at 2 o'clock the voting was found to be:

| | | |
|---|---|---:|
| John Edwards .. | .. | 54 |
| Nicholas Crowdson | .. | 28 |
| John Robertson | .. | 20 |
| Phillip Pitt .. | .. | 3 |
| | | 105 |

'whereupon Mr John Edwards was declared duly elected Actuary of this Society'.

Mores's critics really had not grasped the principles on which a life assurance society operates; their criticisms tended to expose their ignorance, e.g. in arguing that the premiums had been set at too low a level. Mores retorted that the subscribers had known him more than six years, during which time he had transacted everything, and 'there were sufficient circumstances to induce them to believe that he was at least upon a level with a schoolmaster, a teacher of boys'—a slighting reference to his former friend, James Dodson, which was unworthy of him; his pride had been stung.

It was probably Waller who told Mores that he was 'a collegian and an antiquary, and might be able to make up a bursar's roll or an account for the Society of Antiquaries, but that he knew nothing of merchandise or double-entry, and therefore the clerk, though a stranger, was better qualified for the business than himself who had founded the Society'.

The directors felt that the agreement of May 8, 1767, should be embodied in a deed and William Waller was (S, March 10, 1768) asked to call on Joseph Cruttenden (a member who was an attorney and clerk to the Corporation of Surgeons from 1745 to 1780) with

E                                    65

a view to preparing a draft deed for counsel's consideration. Unfortunately, this merely fanned the flame of further dissension for, within a few weeks, Cruttenden himself was elected a director, and he and Waller led a renewed attack on the subscribers. The main battle was joined.

Payment of the agreed annuities to the subscribers was stopped. In June, a committee was appointed to examine all the facts in the dispute; their report ran to thirteen folios. On August 25th, payment of the £100 a year secured to Mores by the deed of settlement, and unkindly called an 'annuity', was deferred. On October 20th, Mores was ordered to deliver up all his papers, a copy of the order being sent to him at the Caroline Coffee-house.

On the appointed day, November 8th, Mores brought with him a characteristic letter. After the meeting had started, he handed the letter across the table, probably with some insolent comment, and walked out of the room. His name (he having withdrawn without leave of the Court) was ordered to be placed under the line, i.e. struck out from the list of those present who shared the fee for attendance. The letter, addressed to Edwards the Actuary, ran:

I received from a Porter your letter sent by orders of the Directors. Did they order you to send it unsealed too?—for answer to it, Mr Mores hath not in his custody or power any papers or writings belonging to the Society.

His reply was considered unsatisfactory; his desk was sealed and he was ordered to bring the key of the desk on Wednesday, December 7th. The desk was finally opened a week later and a list made of the contents, the Actuary being given custody of the papers.

Meanwhile, John Madocks had given his opinion as counsel that a Court of Equity would not uphold the claims of the subscribers. However, the facts stated in the case put to Counsel were hotly contested; the debate continued with more warmth than ever and other business, apart from the granting of new assurances, was at a standstill.

In February 1769, Mores was given a copy of the case, so that he could prepare a full answer, which he did by adding twenty-nine notes in the margin. John Edwards found himself between cross-fires in the dispute, a most difficult position. Though he had custody of the papers, he lent the case with Mores's answer to the two disgruntled directors, Cruttenden and Waller, and as a consequence was censured by the other directors for his 'notorious breach of trust' in direct contempt of the Court.

The bare bones of the minutes are clothed in resonant flesh by the report of the directors approved (S, April 15, 1769) for submission to the General Court. It is simple, direct and vigorous—surely the stamp of the personality of Richard Glyn himself:

The year past has been a year of very disagreeable trouble to the old Directors of the Society for immediately after the last election one of the Directors of the preceding year availing himself of the new choice and of the unacquaintedness of the newly elected Directors with the affairs of the Society by applying himself to them separately in a disingenuous and clandestine manner, and by a blameable misrepresentation of facts and circumstances engaged them in an attempt to perplex and confound all things. Hence have arisen disputes and differences which have been carried on in a very illiberal and rancorous manner on the part of the said Director and his adherents aiming to subvert the Deed of Settlement and the constitution of the Society.

And here we do not mean to allude only to those affronts and insults which have passed *viva voce* at the Meetings of the Directors. This Director and his adherents have gone farther: they have committed their Sentiments to paper and in certain writings which they call protests have delivered themselves in so extraordinary a manner as to justify the severest censure of their behaviour, a behaviour but rarely met with amongst those who make any pretentions to education or decency.

But to give the best account we can of the cause of these animosities, it is to be known that towards the latter end of the year 1767 a Society was set on foot by the name of the Laudable Society of Annuitants for the Benefit of Age, a society as we imagine founded on no true principles of calculation.

To defeat the views of the projector of this Society Mr Mores devised a Scheme which would in all probability have brought to the Equitable the greatest part of those who were engaged in the Laudable. His design was approved of: and two of the Directors of this Society were delegated by the Court of Directors to desire him to proceed in that design; to calculate the necessary premiums; and to prepare a new account of this Society, and in that Account to give a general Specimen of the premiums taken by the Society for every Species of Assurance made by them.

Mr Mores undertook the work, at the same time observing to the two Directors that as such a specimen would discover the manner in which he formed the premiums, and as the one Director had openly declared that if he could discover Mr Mores's method he would advertise for some Hackney accomptant who should compose tables of Premiums upon Mr Mores's plan, and as the preparatives for establishing the premiums now desired would be preparatives for forming all the tables wanted by the Society Mr Mores having gone through the first trouble would expect to complete the whole. The two Directors assured him that nothing else was desired or intended but that he should complete the whole and that no such disingenuous use should be made of his calculations.

67

But when the calculations and the new Account of the Society were finished by Mr Mores the one Director notwithstanding what had passed before insisted to have both the calculations and the new account without any reserve whatever, even though by his practices he had prevailed that Mr Mores's Scheme should not be adopted, and that great part of the business of the Society should be stopped under a pretence that the Directors were not impowered to make such Assurances and these assurances are those which are most advantageous to the Society.

Mr Mores therefore kept back his papers and the one Director, impatient of any contradiction, whether he be right or whether he be wrong, hath ever since with his associates continued resolutely bent to oppose Mr Mores; forcing him to litigation and defence, and to a legal remedy for the recovery of the annuity due to him under the Deed of Settlement of the Society cavilling at every branch and every the most minute circumstance of the practice of the Society for no other reason than because it was planned by Mr Mores; and every thing done by him shall be wrong and in consequence of this opposition no Account has been published of the Society for almost two years.

But the malevolence of this Director is not solely confined to Mr Mores: it extends to the rest of the Old Directors likewise, and to every one who does not think like Mr Waller—the Affair of Entrance Money, that lasting topic of the loquatiousness of New Directors, settled by himself has by himself been un-settled again. A Case has been stated by him and his adherents founded upon false facts and virulent Scandal. All attempts to represent matters truly have been most strenuously opposed by them, and by an Opinion obtained upon a Case so falsely stated they insist that the defending parties ought to be bound by which means they also are put to a legal remedy for recovering that which is due to them under the Deed of Settlement of the Society.

The false case and the answer to it are both upon the Table but as they may be thought too prolix for the perusal or hearing of this Court it may be not unnecessary to state in few words the sum and substance of them here.

By the original proposals for establishing the Society it is stipulated that every person making assurance with the Society shall at the time of making such assurance pay the sum of 15s on every £100 assured. This sum of 15s is known by the name of Entrance money, and by the Deed of Settlement is appropriated to the Subscribers at whose expense the Society was established.

But the original Directors perceiving soon after the establishment of the Society that the expence entailed by the Deed of Settlement upon the admission of a Member was an impediment to the progress of the Society did with the Assent and appro-bation of those who were at that time Members of the Society determine that instead of the Entrance fee of 15s no more than 5s should be paid for every £100 assured at the time of entrance into the Society and that the deficiency should be made good to the Society by the addition of an increment to the premium of assurance which increment, though small, is yet such that the Society are gainers by the alteration and this proceeding of theirs was amongst others approved and confirmed by a General Court of the Society holden April 26, 1764.

Nevertheless when New Directors came into a Share of the management of the Society they began out of a principle of jealousy to grumble at the emolument received by the Subscribers, saying that it was a separate interest—that they saw no particular merit in the Subscribers, nor any reason why they should be rewarded more than themselves.

And upon this Subject have the minds of some New Directors been employed ever since the first election of Directors in the year 1764 to May 8, 1767, when a proposal made by the one Director aforementioned was assented to by the Subscribers for the sake of peace and the Welfare of the Society by which proposal they were to give up their right to the Entrance money in consideration of an Annuity of 40s to be paid to them by the Society for every of their Shares during the term of 14 years, but this proposal has never been carried into complete performance through the means of that very same Director who made it; and who now affects to say that the Subscribers are not entitled to any thing.

But this is a frivolous matter, foreign from the real Interest of the Society and suited only to the harangues of those persons who know not in what the real Interest of the Society consists.

Yet as good is oft times produced out of evil; and the bad designs of individuals made subservient to the benefit of the body politic so may it be in the case of this Society which is capable of being advanced to an height unthought of by those who first attempted the establishment of it and as in the course of these odious disputes a doubt has arisen in the minds of some whether in strict conformity to the Deed of Settlement unassisted by the further authority of a General Court some assurances made by the Directors may safely be made without that Assistance, We recommend to this Court that they be pleased to ordain and Order

That the Directors be enabled and empowered to make assurances of any sort in any instance wherein the Claim to become due by virtue of such Assurance shall depend upon the contingency of Life or Death to happen at a time to come and more particularly

That they be enabled and empowered to Assure Reversionary annuities for the Continuance of one Life after the failure of another and

That they be enabled and impowered to Assure either a Gross Sum or an Annuity to be paid to children after they shall have attained an Age assigned and

That they be enabled and empowered to Assure either a gross sum or an annuity to grown persons if a life on which the Assurance is made shall be Subsisting at a time to come

Which three species of Assurance are greatly sought after; and will (more especially the two latter) be attended with considerable advantage to the Public and to the Society.

We do not Scruple to own that it was the intent and has been the constant endeavour of us who first embarked in this design to monopolize the business of Assurance upon Lives, and so cause the whole to centre in this Society and this may easily be brought about if the General Court will so far interfere as to prevent any obstacle to our endeavours from New Directors who cannot by the bare force of election to the Directorship be instantly endowed with that knowledge which is the result of the practice and experience of almost 14 years.

The rhetoric of the report may awaken our sympathy for the old directors, as against their critics, but rhetoric needs to be tested by reason, for the critics may have reason on their side though they may pursue their ends in objectionable and even in unfair ways. John Madocks had said that the appropriation of the entrance money . . . 'is a provision unreasonable, not agreeable to the professions of the deed; *recompense* must mean a just and adequate recompense, proportioned to the sums advanced, the interests of those sums and the hazards of repayment, not an unbounded recompense'. After seeing Mores's notes on the case, Madocks gave as his further Opinion 'I cannot find anything in the state of the case, as represented by either party, that can make the recompense provided for the charter fund proprietors (i.e. the subscribers) consistent with the principle on which the Society is founded, or with the declarations and professions of the deed . . .'.

When the report of the directors came before the General Court on April 28, 1769, Glyn, as President, tactfully proposed that the meeting should be adjourned to the Salutation Tavern in Nicholas Lane. Reassembled in more agreeable surroundings, the meeting opened with the reading of the report. However, the move was unavailing. The report was swept aside and resolutions were forced through for the appointment of yet another committee. Glyn had deserved well of the members for his conduct of affairs through difficult years, but democracy can be an ungrateful master. At the election on May 8th, Glyn was defeated, receiving only 16 votes out of 55 members present. So he passed out of the Society's affairs, without any recorded word of thanks for the great service he had rendered. Three years later he had to face the financial crisis when his bank had to stop payment for a few weeks and in a few more months he was dead.

# CHAPTER VI

# THE NEW REGIME (1769-1772)

THE defeat of the old directors left the Society in the hands of the critics. They were men who had concerned themselves much more with the disposal of the entrance money than with the actual business of life assurance that the Society was promoting. One of them, John Spencer Colepeper, was elected President and he nominated Joseph Cruttenden and Samuel Crosley as his Vice-Presidents.

John Spencer Colepeper was descended in the only surviving male line from an ancient family whose demesnes (according to Hasted) spread over the whole face of the county of Kent, more especially in the western parts of it. The name was variously spelt Culpeper or Colepeper and occurs as far back as the time of King John in the early thirteenth century. Catherine Howard's mother was a Culpeper and her misfortunes as the queen of Henry VIII were due to her childhood friendship with her kinsman Thomas Culpeper of Hollingbourne. At her execution she said: 'I die a queen, but I would rather die the wife of Culpeper'.

John Spencer Colepeper inherited the family seat of Greenway Court in the Parish of Hollingbourne, which had been bought by his great-great-grandfather, Francis Culpeper, in Elizabeth's reign. The house was situated close at the foot of the chalk hills, nearly a mile eastward of Hollingbourne Church.

Greenway Court came to him through his grandfather, Sir Thomas Colepeper, whose elder brother inherited Leeds Castle in the next parish. The eldest son of Sir Thomas was William Colepeper (d. 1726), the poet and politician. Since he is known to have had three sons, it is likely that John Spencer Colepeper was one of them and inherited Greenway Court as son, rather than as nephew. William Colepeper was chairman of the quarter-sessions at Maidstone on

April 29, 1701, when the famous petition was signed which was presented to Parliament on May 9th and which in temperate language humbly implored 'that your Loyal Addresses may be turned into Bills of Supply, and that His most sacred Majesty . . . may be enabled powerfully to assist his Allies before it be too late'. The Tory majority voted the petition 'scandalous, insolent and seditious' and ordered the imprisonment of the five who presented it, including William Culpeper of Hollingbourne and Thomas Culpeper. But the citizens of London gave them a public dinner at the Mercers' Hall on their release.

John Spencer Colepeper was born at Hollingbourne on April 4, 1712, but nothing is known of his early life save that he had a legal training. He was the Receiver (an officer appointed to receive the rents and pay the bills) of the Charterhouse from February 16, 1739, until May 1, 1779, and lived there for most of this time. He first went to the Middle Temple but he transferred to the Inner Temple on February 7, 1735 (1736 n.s.) and was called to the Bar on July 2, 1742. His chambers from 1736 to 1742 were up two pairs of stairs on the left hand in the staircase on the south side of Hare Court, but he did not afterwards take fresh chambers. Perhaps it is significant that he also had chambers in Staple Inn if, as seems certain, he was the person of that name who was admitted to Staple Inn on June 13, 1740. He married in 1743 and took up residence in the Charterhouse. The only light on his legal career is that his name was one of three given to Cliffords Inn on May 3, 1755, for the choice of Reader, which suggests that he was still a practising barrister. He was a wealthy young man for, apart from his direct inheritance, he was also heir to his aunt who died early in 1741.

A clerical member of the family, Thomas Colepeper, officiated in St Paul's Cathedral, when John Spencer Colepeper married Ruth Webb of St Clement Dane on December 21, 1743. They had only three years of married life; Ruth died in childbirth. Their son, a second John Spencer Colepeper, was born on December 18, 1746 but the mother was dead when the child was baptized on Christmas Day. Just over five years later, on April 4, 1752, his fortieth birthday, Colepeper married Mary Webb, a relative of his first wife who was employed in the Charterhouse; perhaps she had come to take care of the child. Mary Colepeper bore two children, Robert Spencer on Sunday, February 11, 1753, and Mary on Tuesday, October 8, 1754, but the son did not survive long.

Her husband's career ended in disgrace, for he was removed from his Receivership when he failed to pay tradesmen's accounts out of the rents received from tenants. His resignation as a trustee and director of the Society was reported on July 7, 1779, and shortly afterwards he went to live in Boulogne in France (W, November 17, 1779); he died there on June 28, 1788.

Besides coming to a final settlement on the dispute with the subscribers, the new directors had to overhaul the provisions of the deed of settlement and put the practice of the Society on a sounder footing. The review was completed by the following summer and a series of bye-laws amending the provisions of the deed of settlement were adopted in the years 1770 to 1772. Some of these merely amounted to tidying up; other are of interest to mention.

Though the deed provided that every person making an assurance with the Society would become a member, those who assured the lives of others were disfranchised by a later provision which restricted votes to persons assuring their own lives for at least £100. This was not the worst because (possibly by a piece of bad drafting) the right to share in any surplus was restricted to members assuring their own lives notwithstanding that all members of every class had to contribute to a call should that be necessary. The situation was remedied by placing persons assuring the lives of others on the same footing as those assuring their own lives.

When the person whose life was to be assured could not appear before the Court it had been the practice to charge an additional premium for non-appearance. This charge was amended to an addition of 15s per cent to the entrance money, making a total of £1 per cent in such cases.

The directors took specific power to accept the surrender of a policy and later—so as to make the situation quite clear—'to purchase the same upon such terms as shall seem to them reasonable and equitable'.

There had been doubt about the types of assurance that could be granted; these were to include (a) assurances to provide annuities instead of gross sums (i.e. survivorship annuities), (b) endowments on the lives of children either for gross sums or annuities on survival to a certain age, (c) endowments on the lives of grown persons either for gross sums or annuities on survival to a certain age, and (d) immediate annuities. In connection with the last named, the bye-laws laid down the maximum amount of annuity that could be paid. For a life aged under 45 the maximum rate was 6 per cent per annum of the purchase money; at higher ages there were larger maxima with an over-all maximum of 10 per cent per annum at ages over seventy.

On June 27, 1770, a member's note of hand carrying interest at 4 per cent per annum was accepted from one of the older members who was unable to pay his premium—the first instance of a loan on a policy. However, it was subsequently decided that this was a special case and was not to be regarded as a precedent. It was many years before it became a regular practice to lend money on the Society's policies.

An amusing little incident at this time is worth mentioning, both for the humour with which Henry Colley made his request, and for the action taken by the directors, which foreshadowed modern practice.

Colley, a linendraper of Barnstaple in Devon, had effected an assurance at the age of 45 years to provide an annuity of £12 for the remainder of his life, if he should survive seven years. The agreed annual premium was £10 5s for seven years. In passing it may be mentioned that the comparable premium using modern mortality would be about £24; the high mortality of those days worked both ways—life assurance was costly but survival benefits were cheap. After paying premiums for three years, Henry Colley found himself unable to pay any more and wrote on November 24, 1769:

As the time is approaching for the payment of my annual premium and I having thro' many unforseen accidents had other calls for my money am willing either to dispose of my interest of the £30 15s. already paid with an elapse of near 3 years out of seven or fix my annuity by a new policy for an annuity of six pounds a year only at the expiration of the 7 years. Your professed plan for the good of mankind encourages me to hope for the indulgence of a candid answer. What you will give for the one or expect for the other?

P.S. *Pray answer soon.*

He followed this up on December 5th:

I wrote to you about ten days or a fortnight since requesting the favour of a speedy answer—which as I have not recd any am doubtful that my letter miscarried, the contents of which was to acquaint you that thro' many unavoidable and unforeseen losses and accidents I was totally rendered incapable to continue my annual subscription and premium of £10 5s.—therefore must again implore the exertion of your avowed principles of accomodating your practice to the exigencies of your members, by either purchasing my interest in your Society or permitting me to surrender my policy and exchange it for the one half which is six pounds annuity only after expiration of the seven years. This is so reasonable a request that altho' my greatness of distance from you preventeth me from a personal application yet I cannot I will not think you so cruel to deviate so far from your own established principles of Equity to avail yourself so far as to take advantage of my necessities and deprive me of a property which without your indulgence is out of my power to keep. My desire then was to know (which I here crave leave to repeat) what you would give for the one or do expect for the other.

The directors offered either to pay £25 for the surrender of the policy, compared with £30 15s paid in premiums, or to issue a new policy for one-half the benefits (i.e. £6 annuity) if Henry Colley would pay the expenses of the new policy and a further six months' premium of £5 2s 6d, so that he would have paid three and one-half years' premiums in all, being one-half of the agreed total—the first known instance of a 'proportionate paid-up policy'.

Counsel had advised that a Court of Equity would set aside the claims of the subscribers and it was at first proposed to prosecute a suit against them (S, August 31, 1769). Mores's so-called annuity was to be annulled and he was to be sued in equity. The members decided to seek the opinion of the Attorney General, the Solicitor General and a Senior King's Counsel, and a committee was appointed to negotiate with the subscribers. Two weeks later, 'it appearing that nothing had been done', Charles Gould was added to the committee; he proved to be the man who was destined to lead the Society from the trough to prosperity within the space of a few years.

On October 23rd, Charles Gould and his committee wrote a conciliatory letter to the subscribers, which produced no result. The committee wished 'their endeavours had met with the success their hopes flattered them with' but they saw no prospects of settling affairs with the powers entrusted to them. From this time onwards, there was a firmness in the settlement of the dispute that, reading between the lines, was probably attributable to Charles Gould.

The General Court (November 3, 1769) proposed arbitration by five independent persons, two nominated by each side with a fifth chosen by the nominees. If the arbitrators disagreed, the decision of a majority of any three would be binding. Sir Richard Glyn and the subscribers met at the George and Vulture Tavern on November 10th; they all agreed to the proposal with the exception of Mores and Cleveland. The General Court was willing to proceed to arbitration without Mores, leaving Cleveland to be dealt with separately as a special case, but the other subscribers would not permit arbitration to proceed unless the decision was binding on Cleveland, too.

The dispute was in danger of reaching an impasse and in these circumstances the General Court (November 29, 1769) made a firm offer of 25s per annum for thirteen years from December 1767 in respect of each share. The offer was accepted by the subscribers, except Cleveland, and it was hoped that the differences had been settled and harmony restored to the Society. However, Cruttenden and Waller still protested against this settlement and it was a little while longer before they could be silenced.

When the directors met from 9 o'clock to 11 on the morning of April 20, 1770, to consider their report for the General Court at 11 o'clock that morning, they learned that the Law Officers agreed with John Madocks and no doubt Cruttenden and Waller were able to sway their fellow directors into a decision to pay no more, either to the subscribers or to Mores. However, wiser counsels prevailed at the General Court and the agreement with the subscribers was honoured. Mores was removed from his office as a director for life and, though he put up for election on May 7th, he was defeated, receiving only fifteen votes.

The settlement was embodied in two deeds, dated June 19, 1770, which gave a 'mutual general release' to each party to the dispute. Each side released the other from all claims in respect of entrance money and 'all and all manner of action and actions suit and suits cause and causes of action and suit debts dues duties reckonings accounts sum and sums of money quarrels controversies trespasses damages and demands whatsoever which the said Society or Community and all every or any of the members proprietors contributors adventurers . . . ever had or now have or hereafter may or can have challenge claim and demand or be entitled to . . .'. So an unhappy period was brought to an end.

The subscribers had received shares of the entrance money between 1762 and 1767 which approximately repaid the original subscriptions.

As a result of the settlement, they received for each share an annuity of 25s in respect of the twelve years 1768 to 1779 making with the £2 for 1767, and the entrance money before that time, a total of about £22 in all; looking back, this seems a generous settlement compared with the £5 originally paid per share.

In the general spirit of goodwill engendered by the settlement, the General Court decided to make a gift of £300 to the children of James Dodson, by way of acknowledgment of the use that his tables had proved to be in the Society's business. Mountaine received the gift on their behalf.

In the final stages of the dispute Edward Rowe Mores showed a dignity which softens the harsh impression left by his earlier acts. It had been intended to sue him but it seems likely that the suit was not prosecuted, because on May 22, 1771 he wrote asking for arbitration; but the directors replied that they did not feel able themselves to grant the request because the matter had been under consideration by the General Court and they thought that Mores should seek redress from the General Court. This reply seems rather obstructive because they might surely, had they wished, have brought the request before the General Court. Mores retorted by asking that the rule with regard to arbitration should be waived, but the directors told Mores (S, November 30, 1771) that they were not authorized to suspend or waive any clause of the deed of settlement and, consequently, could not waive the rule for arbitration. Since no more is heard of the question it seems likely that Mores decided that his claim was not worth pursuing.

There is tantalizingly little in the records about the men who gave the Society the required mathematical advice, especially when Mores was not available. One of these was William Mountaine, FRS, who, though he is a shadowy figure in the records, was a man of considerable substance and attainments. He had a long-standing friendship with James Dodson, whose contemporary he was, and he seems to have played a considerable part in the affairs of the Society, though behind the scenes for he never was a director.

William Mountaine was a Yorkshireman whose early life was spent in the countryside near Ripley. Looking back to his early years near Summer Bridge in the Nidderdale, he remembered with gratitude the help he had received 'from sundry worthy persons in that district when I first launched out into the world'. He was interested in Burnt Yates Endowed School, Ripley,[1] which had been established in 1760, and he left his library to the school together with his charts and instruments of various kinds, including his telescopes. Mountaine came to London early in life and lived in Southwark, at first in the parish of St Olave and afterwards in Gainsford Street in the parish of St John's, where he had considerable property. He was of sufficient standing to be married by a special licence in St Paul's Cathedral where he married Mary Norman of the same parish of St Olave, Southwark, on October 26, 1732. Was James Dodson present at the wedding? We do not know when their friendship commenced, though it clearly dated from their early days in London.

Like his friend, Mountaine was a teacher and in 1745 he had pupils or a school at Shad Thames, by St Saviour's dock, near where he lived in Southwark. He taught mathematics, especially in its naval applications.

The first collaboration of the two friends concerned the application of mathematics to navigation. The earliest world chart of magnetic declination had been published in 1701 by Edmond Halley. There is a secular change in the magnetic declination which the two friends decided to study; in 1744 they collected observations from various sources and produced a new chart of magnetic variation on the lines of Halley's chart. They presented their chart to the Royal Society in the following year and published the results in a pamphlet in 1746.

Such a revised chart would be needed every ten to twelve years and, on March 20, 1755, Mountaine and Dodson wrote a letter to the Royal Society, seeking publicity for a request that observations should be sent to them before March 25, 1756. They had a good response and were able to give the results of upwards of 50,000 observations in six periods covering the years 1700 to 1756. It had been hoped that the new observations might serve to test the theories regarding magnetic variation that had been propounded by 'learned and ingenious gentlemen' but the two friends were 'determined . . . to publish nothing which shall not be warranted by the observations'.

The set of tables were given in a letter which was read to the Royal Society on November 10, 1757, only thirteen days before James Dodson's death.

[1] There is an account of this school in *Researches and Studies*, No. 2, May 1950, of the University of Leeds Institute of Education.

Since that time it has become clear that there is a variation in other magnetic elements, as well as in the declination, and information about this variation is still being obtained from fixed observatories. While many more observations are now available, the behaviour of the magnetic force emanating from within the earth is still not satisfactorily explained.

Mountaine was mathematical examiner to the Corporation of Trinity House from 1745 to the time of his death. From quite early days, the conduct of practical and theoretical examinations for the Royal Navy had been one of the most important duties of the Elder Brethren and a part of the examinations was mathematical. Another duty was the examination of candidates for appointment as schoolmasters, a class of naval instructor created by an Order in Council on April 21, 1702, for the purpose of teaching the art of navigation to embryo officers. For all these duties the Elder Brethren would have relied upon the mathematical examiner.

Some five years before Mountaine's appointment, in the time of John Weston, several commanders had complained that their apprentices were ignorant 'in some points which are usually taught in schools and useful in practice' and the syllabus was revised. When John Weston died, Mountaine applied for the post; there were three applicants and, on July 7, 1744, James Rossam was chosen. However, he fell ill in the early autumn; the November examinations had to be postponed and by the end of the year he was dead. Mountaine was elected Assistant Mathematical Teacher on January 5, 1744 (1745 n.s.) to succeed him. Though this was the official title, the holder of the post was required to conduct examinations, not to teach. The duties were part-time. There would be yearly or half-yearly examinations of the mathematical boys of Christ's Hospital; and of other candidates as required. The duties were heavier in time of war when the salary would be increased by way of compensation, as happened in 1708 to 1714, in 1745 to 1748, and again in 1756.

Mountaine was elected a Fellow of the Royal Society on March 14, 1750 (1751 n.s.). It is interesting that his sponsors included Gowin Knight, who acted as chairman of the Court of Directors at the first few meetings, and James Hodgson, the Master of the Royal Mathematical School at the time.

The syllabus of the course for schoolmasters in the Royal Navy covered the same subjects as were treated in *The Mariner's New*

*Kalendar*, a standard work in use in many editions throughout the eighteenth century. Mountaine produced the revised edition of 1757. He also wrote a dissertation on maps and charts in 1758, and a defence of Mercator's projection in 1763. How much of his time was given to teaching it is difficult to say. He was a member of the Society of Schoolmasters and would have regarded teaching as his profession, but it seems unlikely that teaching filled all his days; he had the means to live the life of a leisured gentleman with mathematical and scientific interests though his published work does not show the originality of his friend, James Dodson.

Like many persons with scientific interests at that time, Mountaine was skilful with his hands. He made a chart of the South Seas on vellum and mounted upon cedar in a gilt frame, and he probably made some of the instruments he used. Some of these instruments would have been for use in his teaching, for example his seventeen globes. Others—his magnets, compasses and Gunter Scale—would have been used partly for teaching and partly for his own work. He had a large library and no doubt many of the instruments would have been kept in it, but it would be interesting to know where he put his 9-foot refracting telescope. Had he a room which could be used as an observatory or would it be used in the garden or yard?

Mountaine was one of the original subscribers to the Charter Fund and after Dodson's death he had custody of Dodson's papers and probably gave the Society such actuarial advice as was needed. At least, when the Society had been formed and he proposed to assure his life the proposal was accepted at the usual premium for his age, 'notwithstanding he has been many years subject to the gout in a violent degree', in consideration of his having been a contributor to the establishment of the Society. There is the merest hint that he was consulted from time to time, for why else should he have taken the oath of secrecy on May 17, 1763? Possibly he was asked to go to meetings when his mathematical abilities were required or when Dodson's papers had to be consulted.

John Edwards, soon after his election as Actuary in 1767, turned to Mountaine for advice and help. Mountaine had computed premiums for survivorships on two lives for combinations of ages which were multiples of five: 'the rest might easily be proportionated', so saving the expense of full tables. Dodson had given two tables, one based upon the 'mean hazard' and another upon the 'greatest hazard';

7. William Mountaine, FRS, by an unknown painter in the style of Highmore

8. Richard Price, DD, FRS, by Benjamin West

Edwards was wondering whether he could use the survivorship rules for both tables or only for the 'mean hazard' as used by Dodson. Mountaine's letter of October 17, 1768, leaves the impression that Mores was urging the use of the 'greatest hazard'. One of the directors, Josiah Wallis, thought that the 'genuine method' of making such calculations was one given by Simpson in his *Select Exercises*. Mountaine had at first agreed with Mores about the use of the tables based upon the 'greatest hazard' but when calculations of both tables had been compared with Simpson's he changed his view. 'These considerations arising from the great differences, stagger my former sentiments.' However, the premiums derived from Simpson's figures and Dodson's mean hazard agreed reasonably well; 'we shall see no very great difference between them'. The Society might 'with safety and prudence' make use of either. 'Both those calculators were eminent in this branch and . . . . were personally (and well) known to me.' At this time, Mountaine was confined to his room, probably with gout; he asks for 'consideration of much pain and shortness of time'. Otherwise he would have come with Mr Sclater to give his opinions in person.

Following upon a gift to the hospital, Mountaine was elected a Governor of St Thomas's Hospital in 1772 and attended the Courts of the Governors in the years 1773 to 1778. He was also a Justice of the Peace for Surrey. Shortly before he died, he presented to the Elder Brethren a copy of a book he had written *A description of the lines drawn on Gunter's scale, as improved by Mr Robertson*. He died on the morning of Sunday, May 2, 1779, at his home in St John's, Southwark.

The early holders of the office of Actuary did not solve the problem of what accounts should be kept though advice had been taken from Isaiah Millington. No doubt some books were kept but no statement was produced to a General Court until after the election of John Edwards as Actuary. He seems to have set himself to put the business of the Society in order. There was evidently no opportunity of producing accounts going back to the start of the Society but a fortnight after his election, possibly under the direction of Mores, Edwards produced a statement showing the position reached at December 31, 1766. This showed the cash in hand, the investments, and the business in force.[1]

---

[1] *v.* Table on p. 83.

A year later, Edwards produced a cash account for the year 1767 as well as 'a State of the Society on December 31, 1767', which was in the same form as the previous year with the addition of the claims notified but unpaid at December 31st. In those days claims were payable six months after proof of death (or six months after the end of the first year, if death should occur in that year) as a precaution to protect the Society's funds, so that the unpaid claims were substantial and included, of course, a few that were disputed.

It is revealing that no accounts for the year 1768 appear in the minutes of the General Court. They were appended to the report of the Court of Directors but, as has been mentioned, the President and his supporters were defeated at the elections in 1769. If the report was put to the members, there is no record of it and the accounts were not considered by the General Court. In the following year, the accounts for 1769 were produced without comment on the lack of accounts for 1768. The series continued in similar form for 1770 and 1771. However, as time passed and Edwards gained a fuller understanding of the business, it became clear to him that something more was needed. The statement of assurances in force and accumulated funds did nothing to show whether the funds were sufficient to meet the contractual liabilities under the assurances.

Early in 1772 the directors were holding special meetings on Saturdays so as to clear up such problems. A new method of keeping the accounts and valuing the assurances was discussed on February 22, 1772 and 'compleated' a week later. The accounts for 1772 were made up on the new method and the 'State of the Society on December 31, 1772', includes a new column headed 'Rent value'. This was the first attempt at valuing the liabilities but, unfortunately, the term 'rent value' is undefined and it is impossible now to say exactly what was done. The 3 per cent stocks were valued at $86\frac{1}{2}$, about market price, and the computation shows a balance of £4,190 after deducting the aggregate 'rent value' and other liabilities from the value of the assets. The accounts for 1773 followed a similar pattern but the figures are not given in full, probably because Edwards had died at the end of that year.

When considering the figures in the table, the change in the value of money should be remembered, as also the practical limitation on numbers by the requirement that the assured had to appear in person before the weekly Court when the assurance was made. The figures clearly reflect the disruption of affairs by the course of the dispute and show an actual contraction of business in force in the years 1768, 1769 and 1770. The figures of business in force at December 31, 1767 were not attained again until December 31, 1771, by amount and December 31, 1772, by number. The worst year was 1770 when the new assurances fell to ninety-nine for an aggregate of £25,160 only.

THE STATE OF THE SOCIETY ON DECEMBER 31ST OF EACH YEAR

| Year | Assurances in force | | | Accumulated funds | | Out-standing claims |
| | Number | Amount | Premium income | Nominal amount of 3 per cent stocks | Cash | |
| --- | --- | --- | --- | --- | --- | --- |
| | | £ | £ | £ | £ | £ |
| 1766 | 450 14 | 119,404 556* | 3,021 | 8,000 | 515 | ? |
| 1767 | 556 19 | 145,060 478* | 5,807 | 10,000 | 1,196 | 3,660 |
| 1768 | 538 26 | 144,228 1,127* | 6,358 | 12,000 | 956 | 1,840 |
| 1769 | 506 20 | 140,496 530* | 6,147 | 17,500 | 660 | 3,050 |
| 1770 | 471 19 | 126,210 510* | 5,720 | 17,500 | 865 | 920 |
| 1771 | 522 20 | 151,208 620* | 7,037 | 23,875 | 763 | 3,220 |
| 1772 | 567 20 | 174,282 694* | 7,558 | 29,875 | 313 | 2,910 |
| | | * Annuities | | | | |

The figures also illustrate the tremendous turnover in business because in the five-year period from 1768 to 1772 the new assurances were 770 for an aggregate of £227,776 and twelve annuities for £913 per annum; the wastage must have been approximately the same. A large proportion of the assurances were temporary assurances for short periods. Also many members must have dropped their policies because of the dispute.

Though the period seems to be one of stagnation of business, the new assurances barely keeping pace with the wastage, there are healthy signs in the way the premium income kept up, reflecting a better type of business, and in the growth of the invested funds.

At this critical time in the Society's affairs, the directors were anxious that their decisions should be based on as full and complete evidence as could be obtained and they sought advice from several people. It is at this point that a most unusual person enters the story —Richard Price, DD, FRS.

# CHAPTER VII

# RICHARD PRICE (1723–1791)

T HE character, life and achievements of Richard Price[1] had a consistency which is given to few men and his gentle influence was felt in the affairs of the Equitable Society as in his other activities. There could scarcely be a greater contrast than with Edward Rowe Mores.

The intellectual and spiritual background of Richard Price derived from the Act of Uniformity of 1662, when clergymen who could not, for conscience' sake, subscribe to the Articles of the Church of England, were ejected from their livings and began to minister in barns and farmhouses to those of their flock who followed them. Such clergymen might be supported by a few wealthy families and often took up teaching as a means of supporting themselves. One of these clergymen was Samuel Jones, vicar of Llangynwyd in Glamorgan who, after his ejection, ministered to congregations meeting in Brynllywarch, a farmhouse belonging to his father-in-law, and in neighbouring farmhouses. These congregations afterwards built meeting-houses in Bridgend and Bettws. Among the influential families to whom he ministered were the Prices of Tynton. Two sons of this family were so influenced by him that they followed him into the ministry; the elder brother, Rees Price succeeded him at Brynllywarch and the younger brother, Samuel Price, became co-pastor with Isaac Watts in St Mary Axe, Bury Street, London. Rees Price inherited the family estate of Tynton, which he managed.

Richard Price was born at Tynton on February 23, 1723, the son of Rees Price by a second marriage. The early influences on him were the severe Calvinism of the father and the gentle character of his beautiful and delightful mother, Catherine Richards, the daughter of the doctor at Bridgend. Richard Price had considerable intellectual

[1] There are biographies of Richard Price by Roland Thomas and Charles B. Cone.

capacity which was developed by a good education. As a dissenter, the universities were closed to him but he received his higher education at a dissenting academy in Chancefield, Talgarth, Breconshire, one of those run by dissenting clergymen for the benefit of children of dissenters.

A dominating influence in Richard Price's life was his passion (if such it may be called) for reason. So he was led to a unitarian faith which was displeasing to his father and his uncle, but which was the expression in his spiritual life of his attachment to reason. Years later, Price said that he owed much to David Hume whose writings 'put me upon examining the ground upon which I stood, and taught me not hastily to take anything for granted'.

Rees Price died in 1739 leaving a widow and six children. In such circumstances, it must have been an unbending character that could, on principle, leave almost all his estate to the favourite son by his first marriage and leave his widow and young family ill-provided for. Catherine and her children had to leave Tynton and move into a smaller house in Bridgend, but Richard was able to complete his studies at Talgarth. Despite a frail constitution, Price more than once walked the forty miles of mountain country between Talgarth and his home.

His mother survived her husband by less than a year. Richard had to make his own way in the world and decided that he would seek the help of his uncle in London. His elder brother lent him a horse for the first twenty miles on the road to Bristol, where he got a place on a broad-wheeled waggon coming up to London. A year of study in unwholesome surroundings near the Monument undermined his health and he had to return to his sisters for a holiday to recuperate.

From 1740 to 1744, Richard Price studied at the dissenting academy founded by a Mr Coward, which was then situated in Tenter Alley, Moorfields. The principal tutor, John Eames, FRS, was a good mathematician and was a friend of Newton. Thus it came about that Richard got an education of university standard, especially in mathematics and theology, possibly a better education than he would have received at the universities.

For the next twelve years, he was family chaplain to a Mr Streatfield of Stoke Newington, a form of patronage which left him with time for study and which gave him a means of support while he was becoming known amongst the various congregations to whom he ministered from time to time. A fruit of this leisure was a major work on philosophy, *A review of the principal questions and difficulties in morals*. It was a worthy companion to the better known works of the time. As against David Hume, it was written to defend the intellectual view of ethical thought. Price held that right and wrong are perceived by the understanding, by which he meant intuitive reason. Price gave to rectitude a primary place which anticipates Kant's 'categorical imperative' by some thirty years. The vigour of his prose may be seen from the following passage, quoted by Thomas:

> Rectitude, then, or Virtue, is a Law. And it is the first and supreme law, to which all other laws owe their force, on which they depend, and in virtue of which alone they oblige. It is an universal Law. The whole creation is ruled by it; under it men and all rational beings subsist. It is the source and guide of all the actions of the Deity himself, and on it his throne and government are founded. It is an unalterable and indispensable Law. The repeal, suspension, or even relaxation of it, once for a moment, in any part of the universe, cannot be conceived without a contradiction. Other laws have had a date; a time when they were enacted and became of force. They are confined to particular places, rest on precarious foundations, may lose their vigour, grow obsolete with time, and become useless and neglected. Nothing like this can be true of this law. It has no date. It never was made nor enacted. It is prior to all things. It is self-valid and self-originated; and must for ever retain its usefulness and vigour, without the possibility of diminution or abatement. It is coeval with eternity; as unalterable as necessary, everlasting truth; as independent as the existence of God; and as sacred and awful as his nature and perfections. The authority it possesses is native and essential to it, underived and absolute. It is superior to all other authority, and the basis and parent of all other authority. It is indeed self-evident that, properly speaking, there is no other authority; nothing else that can claim our obedience, or that ought to guide and rule heaven and earth. It is, in short, the one authority in nature, the same in all times and in all places; or, in one word, the Divine authority.

Streatfield died in 1756 and left Price a handsome legacy. Samuel Price died in the same year and left his nephew a house in Leadenhall Street. The change of circumstances and fortune enabled Richard to marry—he married Sarah Blundell on June 16, 1757—and in the following year, when he became morning and afternoon preacher at the meeting house at Newington Green, he moved to Stoke Newington. Some handsome, some old houses stood round the village green. At that time, it was the dwelling-place of many dissenters and the congregation would include a considerable proportion of people of radical thought; when she was a girl, Mary Wollstonecraft Godwin sat in a pew next to the Rogers family. Whether through the congregation or otherwise, Price also became friendly with many well-known men in science, mathematics and economics. In all fields, Price's devotion to reason made him an advocate of reform and of freedom of thought.

A weekly supping club was established, which met in turn in the houses of Richard Price, Thomas Rogers, the banker, and a Mr Burgh. Price became firm friends with Thomas Rogers's family of lively and intelligent children. He was interested in science and it is easy to imagine the charm that his laboratory would have had for them. He was a most delightful companion for boys, energetic and fond of frolic.

A glimpse of him at this time is given by Samuel Rogers, who was born at Stoke Newington on July 30, 1763:

> Price was our neighbour (at Newington Green) and would often drop in, to spend the evening with us, in his dressing-gown; he would talk and read the Bible to us till he sent us to bed in a frame of mind as heavenly as his own. He lived much in the society of Lord Lansdowne and other people of rank; and his manners were extremely polished. In the pulpit he was great indeed,—making his hearers forget the *preacher* and think only of the *subject*.

Price, according to Rogers, was:

> Slim in person and rather below the common size, but possessed of great muscular strength and remarkable activity. With strong features and a very intelligent eye, his countenance was the mirror of his mind and, when lighted up by conversation, his features were peculiarly pleasing.

In the year 1761, Price was elected a member of Dr Daniel Williams's Trust which showed the measure of the recognition given to him in his ministry. His earliest notes on public finance date from this year as does his work on the mathematical doctrine of probability, which led on to his interest in life assurance. It would be interesting to know whether he had previously studied, say, *The Doctrine of Chances* and *Annuities upon Lives* by Abraham de Moivre.

Another dissenting minister, and a good mathematician, Thomas Bayes, FRS, of Tunbridge Wells, who was Price's senior by twenty-one years, died in 1761 and his papers came to Price; he saw their importance and prepared them for submission to the Royal Society. It seems likely that Bayes and Price knew each other well since they moved in a similar circle, though the evidence is scanty. Price calls Bayes 'our deceased friend' and Bayes left a legacy to Price in his will. One of those who recommended Thomas Bayes for election to the Royal Society in 1742 was John Eames, who at the time was Price's tutor. John Eames (*c.* 1685–1744) was on the staff of Coward's Academy for about thirty years, his subjects being classics and science until in 1734 he became the tutor in theology. It seems a likely guess that Bayes as well as Price was educated at this academy and learned his mathematics from Eames.

Bayes's papers included an essay which, according to Barnard, must rank as one of the most famous memoirs in the history of science; the problem it discusses is still the subject of keen controversy. It is characteristic of Price that his own part should have been kept in the background and the whole credit given to Bayes:

> His design at first in thinking on the subject was, to find out a method by which we might judge concerning the probability that an event has to happen, in given circumstances, upon supposition that we know nothing concerning it but that, under the same circumstances, it has happened a certain number of times, and failed a certain number of other times.

Bayes left two solutions, being dissatisfied with the first of them. Price chose the more satisfactory solution, wrote an introductory letter, completed the essay and added an appendix dealing with numerical examples. Price wrote:

> The problem . . . is by no means merely a curious speculation in the doctrine of chances . . . it is certain that we cannot determine, at least not to any nicety, in what degree repeated experiments confirm a conclusion, without the particular discussion of the before-mentioned problem; which, therefore, is necessary to be considered by any one who would give a clear account of the strength of *analogical* or *inductive reasoning;* concerning which, at present, we seem to know little more than that it does sometimes in fact convince us, and at other times not.

The mathematician is interested in Bayes's theorem as being one of the modes of inductive inference from statistics. It is difficult for the modern mind to enter sympathetically into the problems that interested the eighteenth century. Bayes and Price were philosophers as well as mathematicians and their purpose was:

> To show what reason we have for believing that there are in the constitution of things fixt laws according to which events happen, and that, therefore, the frame of the world must be the effect of the wisdom and power of an intelligent cause; and thus to confirm the argument taken from final causes for the existence of the Deity.

Price was elected a Fellow of the Royal Society on December 5,

1765. The Marischal College, Aberdeen, conferred on him the degree of Doctor of Divinity on August 7, 1767.

The earliest contacts between Price and the Equitable Society are recorded in copies of his correspondence between August 1768 and March 1771. Someone had proposed an assurance which involved complicated survivorships on three lives, females aged 64 and 62 and a male aged 60. The Actuary, John Edwards, would have felt unable to consult Mores because of the dispute then raging. A Mr Curties—either the proposer or a go-between—took the problem to Price, who gave the solutions. Price was doubtful if he had correctly understood the queries. However, 'if the proposer will endeavour to be more intelligible, I shall be glad to express my esteem for Mr Curties by giving him any further answer what he shall desire'.

The contact was made in the summer of 1768 when Edwards was most in need of help with his survivorship calculations and Price gave the results of his own calculations for comparison. In October 1768, William Mountaine warmly commended him to the Society:

Mr Price is a member of the Royal Society—has been such about three years, I believe, but I have not the pleasure of his personal acquaintance, having not been able to attend there of late, as I used formerly to do; however I know him by character and some things that he has published, and from thence I do believe him to be an ingenious, and strictly honest man, so that what he gives under his hand, I dare say may be depended upon.

Price had already had experience of the subject, since the investigation which he sent to Edwards had been drawn up some years previously for someone else:

I have more on the same subject, but it enters so far into Algebra as not to be so intelligible. . . . I have considered the printed accounts of your Society, which you were so good as to give me, and I cannot help thinking that it is a Society that may be of great service if proper care is taken.

Price counselled that the Society, ought to have tables of values for all ages and every different term of years in order to guard against 'careless or unskilful calculations'. Later, in November 1768, Colepeper and Edwards called on him at Newington Green, and Price writes that he is obliged to Edwards for 'the two volumes on the Greek Testament'.

Price modestly says: 'I know I am liable to mistake' and suggests that the Society should not trust to any one calculator. Two months later, he writes:

> I am sensible that the Society cannot be supposed to be judges of these demonstrations and it would be unreasonable to expect they should take my words—I therefore wish they would consult other mathematicians.

He asks to be excused from further applications because he has heard of the disagreements in the Society. On June 9, 1769, Price writes again:

> The question . . . is not a subject of calculation for there are no rules by which the chance can be determined that a person now unmarried shall hereafter marry and have a son who shall live to be of age.

Price's power over questions dependent on human life gained public recognition by the reading of his essay—in the form of a letter to Benjamin Franklin—*Observations on the Expectations of Lives*, to the Royal Society on April 27, 1769. The essay would have gathered up the fruits of research over a number of years and Price may have been encouraged to make the results public by his contacts with the Equitable in the previous year. The essay was followed by a second in May 1770, *Observations on the proper Method of calculating the Values of Reversions depending on Survivorships*.

The consultations with Price became more formal when the directors (S, August 22, 1770) asked for his assistance in the calculation of tables of survivorships, endowments and deferred annuities on children's lives and similar contracts on adult lives. Some months later, they made him a present of some 'mathematical instruments' at a cost of £51 4s. Were these the telescope, microscope and electrical machine mentioned by Clayden in the *Early Life of Samuel Rogers?*

Price's interest in questions of life contingencies had been awakened by the many different projects for societies to provide annuities in widowhood or in old age. Such schemes had been known for a long time; the scheme started by the Mercers' Company in 1698 had had a long, though chequered, history; a scheme for ministers and professors in Scotland had been established by an Act of 1748, and for the London clergy in 1765. In the period 1765 to 1770, there happened to be a sudden outburst of activity in the promotion of such projects, mostly on insecure foundations.

Price says that he was first consulted about a society which had been planned by lawyers but which, as a result of his advice, was ultimately laid aside. The London Annuity Society was formed on January 1, 1765, and the Laudable Society of Annuitants in the following year. These were followed by others, e.g. the Equitable Society of Annuitants, the London Union Society for the comfortable support of aged members, and the Amicable Society of Annuitants. The *Gentleman's Magazine* for 1770 printed the proposals of one such Society and also a letter demonstrating the insufficiency of the proposed contributions. In 1771 Price was consulted about a proposed scheme for the General Body of Protestant Dissenting Ministers (Baptist, Congregational and Presbyterian).

> There are, indeed, multitudes of societies in London for the relief of old age, where much greater advantages are promised for smaller payments, but the plans of these societies are extremely insufficient and it is now well-known that they are laying the foundation of much future disappointment and calamity.

The trouble with such societies is that their insufficiency may be concealed in the early years by the comparatively few claims made upon them but, if the contributions are insufficient, the funds must eventually run out and the longer that time is delayed the more hardship is likely to be caused. The promoters of the projects were probably ignorant of the true cost of the benefits they were promising. It needed a mathematician to demonstrate the real situation and Price accepted the challenge.

In 1771, Price published his *Observations on Reversionary Payments*, which went through seven editions in the next forty years and remained a standard text in actuarial science for about a century; in Benjamin Franklin's opinion, it was 'the foremost production of human understanding that this century has afforded us'.

This book had a profound influence on the annuity societies, material evidence of which is the handsome silver coffee-pot presented by the London Annuity Society to Price in 1790. The book includes a brief reference to friendly societies, which shows Price's concern for them, and suggests a plan that might give them a more stable foundation than many had at that time. He also included a chapter on public credit and the national debt, a subject which had stirred him for most of the 1760s. This is a subject on which views of economists have changed considerably in recent years but to be fair to Price his general thesis must be borne in mind—that too little of the current burden was being borne by his own generation and too much being left to posterity. He criticized the raising of supplies for public service by borrowing money at interest without 'putting its debts into a regular and certain course of payment'. He meant that it was wasteful to raise money by selling 3 per cent stocks at a discount, creating a vast nominal debt; the stock ought to carry a more realistic rate of interest and provide for repayment by means of a sinking fund. The annual service of the loan would be more but the burden on the future would be reduced.

A sinking fund had been established in 1716 but the fund had been used to balance the ordinary budget and had been 'generally alienated' from its true purpose: 'I find it difficult to speak with calmness. But I must restrain myself. *Calculation*, and not *censure*, is my business in this work'.

Membership of the Royal Society would have gained Price many friendships through the regular meetings for discussion of scientific topics. He was a member, too, of the 'Honest Whigs', a club for dissenting ministers and other professional men, possibly appealing to those trained in the dissenting academies. Benjamin Franklin was a member and so was Boswell, despite the incongruity! The club met in St Paul's Coffee-house, and later in the London Coffee-house on Ludgate Hill, famed for quiet, social dinners and good wine. Most of the evening was spent in talk, with wine and punch upon the table, and some smoking. 'Conversation goes on pretty formally, sometimes sensibly, sometimes furiously.' At nine, supper would be laid on a side-board for members to help themselves to toasted cheese and apple-puffs, porter and beer. The cost was about 18d a head. The political temper of the club was radical: on Thursday, September 21, 1769, 'much was said this night against the Parliament'.

Just how limited the franchise was it is difficult now to realize. Price noted that in Great Britain out of about six million inhabitants, '5,723 persons, most of them the lowest of the people, elect one-half of the House of Commons'. Place-seeking, and the corruption that went with it, were customary features of eighteenth-century parliaments. The extension of the franchise would, Price thought, enable virtuous men to exercise a greater influence on politics than formerly and so would lead to better government. Price's ideas about political freedom were rooted in his moral philosophy. His advocacy of civil liberty was directed, not so much to government by the majority, expressing the 'will of the people', as to government by consent, emphasizing the worth of the individual soul and respect for honest, even if minority, opinions.

Events were leading Price on to a wider stage. He had gained many American friends and in correspondence with them he saw the way the situation was tending and learned the colonial point of view. The question was a particular case of the problem of the reform of Parliament; distance added weight to the arguments for no taxation without representation. The religious beliefs of many of the settlers were those associated with radical opinions in politics.

Early in 1776, Price published his *Observations on the Nature of Civil Liberty, the Principles of Government, and the Justice and Policy of the War with America*. The effect was tremendous. The book was received with enthusiasm in America; at home, it stirred up a pamphlet war whose vehemence surprised the mild author of the original tract. The modern reader may well be surprised by the farsightedness of the good Dr Price. In it he suggested a general confederacy of the states of Europe by the appointment of a Senate consisting of representatives from all the different states. The Senate would manage the common concerns of the united states of Europe and would judge and decide between the states in disputes. It would also have the force of the states to support its decisions. Another suggestion looks remarkably like the concept of the British Empire embodied in the Statute of Westminster of 1931, i.e. an association of self-governing communities under the Crown, though Price—with his ideas coloured by eighteenth-century practice—thought of the monarch as being the supreme executive power rather than the titular head:

> In a word, an Empire is a collection of states or communities united by some common bond or tie. If these states have each of them free constitutions of government, and, with respect to taxation and internal legislation, are independent of the other states, but united by compacts, or alliance, or subjection to a Great Council, representing the whole, or to one monarch entrusted with the supreme executive power: In these circumstances, the Empire will be an Empire of freemen.

These views, expounded with simplicity and candour, had an explosive effect which brought forth a spate of replies, some argumentative, some abusive. They ensured that from thenceforth Price would be a public figure. He happened one day to be at the Bar of the House of Lords, when the Duke of Cumberland came up and said to him, 'I read your essay on civil liberty till I was blind'. Lord Ashburton, who was standing near, replied: 'It is remarkable that your Royal Highness should have been blinded by a book which has opened the eyes of all mankind'.

The war with America aroused in Price and his friends a state of alarm which must be taken into account when his views on population are considered. His early experiences in London would have coloured his views. It was common for the burials in the towns to be considerably more numerous than the christenings—a feature of society which would have been painfully real to a minister of religion who shared the human joys and sorrows of these family occasions; though the explanation of the excess lay partly in omissions from the christenings and partly in burials of persons born elsewhere, yet when due allowance has been made for such factors, there is no doubt that the mortality in the towns was much higher than in the country. The population question aroused in Price the instincts of the reformer:

The encouragement of population, therefore, ought to be one of the first objects of policy in every state; and some of the worst enemies of population are the luxury, the licentiousness, and debility produced and propagated by the great towns.

The war with America led to a great increase of expenditure which swelled the national debt to alarming proportions. Round about him Price saw a false prosperity with an increase of luxury that he thought would be ruinous to the kingdom. The window tax returns showed a change from cottages to larger houses, yet at the same time there was a decrease in the number of births and burials and a decrease in the yield of the duties on ale and beer. In an essay dated May 20, 1779, Price interpreted all this as evidence that the population was decreasing fast and so a smaller population was likely to be burdened with a larger debt. In this Price was wrong because the population was in fact expanding, but it is unfair to the memory of Price merely to remember his views on population without allowing for the circumstances which gave rise to them. Remember, too, that in 1779 England entered into a sharp trade depression which lasted until 1783. As it happened the discovery of vaccination by Jenner (which was published at the end of the century, some years after Price's death) was a main factor in the rapid increase of the population in the next century. This made Price's views look more absurd than they were in fact at the time.

The germ of modern ideas of social security can be seen in the

95

projects of Price and his friends for mitigating the lot of the poor by schemes for self-help against indigence in old-age and ill-health. Francis Maseres, who became a baron of the Exchequer in 1773, and Richard Price devised a scheme whereby contributions to parish funds would provide old-age pensions, backed if necessary by the local poor-rate. Price calculated the required tables of contributions and a bill was introduced into Parliament in 1772; it passed the House of Commons but was rejected by the House of Lords.

A similar object could be achieved by the establishment of friendly societies and a pamphlet commending them (produced by John Acland in 1786) started a discussion which led to the appointment of a committee of the House of Commons. The committee requested Price to compute a series of tables of contributions whereby the labouring poor might assure weekly payments in sickness and old age. These tables were embodied in a Bill of 1789 which met with the same fate as the previous Bill. The tables, however, did not die with the Bill. The movement to encourage friendly societies came to fruition in the Act of 1793, which required tables of contributions of friendly societies to be certified by the Justices of the Peace. For this purpose, Price's tables were the only standard of reference for many years, being finally superseded by the extensive tables of actual experience collected in 1825.

In his later years, Price corresponded with a wide circle of friends, among them many of the leading figures of America, France, and other countries. On March 14, 1776, the freedom of the City of London was conferred on him, the freedom to be presented in a gold box of the value of £50. On October 6, 1778, Congress resolved to invite Dr Price to settle in America, so that they might receive his assistance in regulating their finances. A deputation waited on him but he felt he was too old to make such a great change in his life. On April 24, 1781, the Yale Corporation voted to confer the LLD upon two distinguished men—George Washington and Richard Price.

Boswell was dining with a friend named John Lee (a lawyer and a politician) when after dinner Price happened to come in. 'He and I began to stagger as to Pitt . . .' (Wednesday, July 6, 1785). Notwithstanding the differences between them, Boswell enjoyed his talks with Dr Price and a rather pathetic note (Friday, October 12, 1787) reveals much of the two men:

Sadly depressed. Walked to Hackney and visited Dr Price. He obliged me

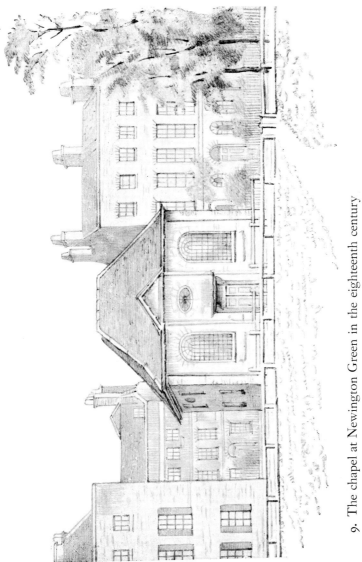

9. The chapel at Newington Green in the eighteenth century

Pub.ᵈ Dec.ʳ 3 1790 by H Humphrey N.° 18 Old Bond Street.

Smelling out a Rat; _____ or ___ The Atheistical-Revolutionist disturbed in his Midnight Calculations.
— "Vide A troubled _____ conscience"

with the rate of an annuity on money sunk. Vexed that I did not relish his conversation. Dined at Sir Joshua Reynolds. . . . Revived somewhat.

Price's eminence can be seen by his *Observations on the Importance of the American Revolution and the Means of making it a Benefit to the World* which was published in London in 1784 and which tendered advice to the new government of the United States. It was well received in America. With the outbreak of the French Revolution it was to Price that liberal-minded people turned for leadership. George Cadogan Morgan, a nephew of Price, happened to be in France when the Revolution broke out. He reached Paris on July 9, 1789, and his letters gave the first news of the fall of the Bastille on July 14th. On November 4, 1789, meetings were held by the 'Society for Commemorating the Revolution (of 1688) in Great Britain' and Price gave an address subsequently published as *A Discourse on the Love of our Country*; it called forth Burke's *Reflections on the Revolution in France*, which in turn provoked Tom Paine's answer, *The Rights of Man*. Price welcomed the Revolution in a state of exaltation:

What an eventful period is this! I am thankful that I have lived to it; and I could almost say, 'Lord now lettest thou thy servant depart in peace, for mine eyes have seen thy salvation'. I have lived to see a diffusion of knowledge, which has undermined superstition and error.—I have lived to see the rights of man better understood than ever; and nations panting for liberty, which seemed to have lost the idea of it. I have lived to see thirty millions of people, indignant and resolute, spurning at slavery, and demanding liberty with an irresistible voice.

Lest the reader hastily judge Price in the light of what came after, remember that Price died in 1791 before the Revolution turned to a blood-bath.

Price was a mild and gentle man whose strength of character led him into a position of great authority, yet without any trace of self-seeking. In some ways he was remarkably far-sighted and in others remarkably wrong-headed, but with it all honest and candid.

# CHAPTER VIII

# THE FOUNDATIONS OF PROSPERITY
## (1773–1782)

CHARLES GOULD had proved himself useful in the dispute and in other ways. When the Society happened to be short of cash, he lent money to tide over the Society's affairs for short periods, e.g. £650 borrowed from him on August 28, 1770, was repaid early in the following year and £300 borrowed in September 1771 was repaid six months afterwards. No doubt his abilities and strength of character marked him out for leadership and, on May 11, 1773, the Court of Directors unanimously elected him President of the Society.

Charles Gould's first major task was the provision of new premises. Just before he was elected President, it had been decided to hire premises 'for the more convenient accommodating the Society' at a rent not exceeding £200 a year, compared with the £75 a year being paid for the parsonage house in Nicholas Lane. At his first meeting as President (G, June 3, 1773), the power to rent premises was extended to the purchase of premises up to the same maximum equivalent rent.

Within four months, Charles Gould was able to report the purchase of a 'house known as the Swan Tavern situated near the foot of Blackfryers Bridge'. The price agreed with William Miller of the Old Bailey, stone-mason, was £2,000 for the 99-year lease, three years expired, held from the City Corporation at a yearly ground rent of £45 18s.

The building of Blackfriars Bridge by the City Corporation was suggested as a celebration of the 'year of victories', i.e. 1759, the decisive year of the seven years' war. The bridge was a memorial to William Pitt, Earl of Chatham, and was originally known by his name, though it soon began to be called Blackfriars Bridge. The bridge took nine years (1760–9) to erect. Robert Mylne won the competition for its design with one for elliptical arches—as compared with the traditional semi-circular arch used by other leading architects. Mylne, a young man then coming to the fullness of his powers, made his name by his work on the bridge. From that time onwards he had a considerable practice as an engineer and architect in the City of London. He designed and built a number of houses in New Bridge Street, Blackfriars, including his own house, and it is reasonable to assume that he was also responsible for Chatham Place which was a square at the end of New Bridge Street where it joined the bridge. His drawings show the types of house and office he planned for this area. The Society's house was the corner house where New Bridge Street opened out into Chatham Place, on the east side of the street. The directors had seen the house and it seemed to them 'to be commodiously situated and to afford room for transacting the business of the Society'. It was indeed a good situation in a new part of the City and was a convenient point on the route to the new suburbs in South London. Later, it seems, coaches stopped there.

Charles Gould took the leading part in the negotiations. On October 3, 1773, the day after the directors' meeting, he wrote to Edwards from Royston:

I signed an Agreement before I left Town for the House, but could not obtain from Mr Miller more than an allowance of £20 towards painting and whitewashing, nor would he undertake for delivering up with the House any Fixtures, which were not his own Property. . . . In order the more strongly to incite him to procure us speedy possession I have stipulated that he shall make good our rent for the house in Nicholas Lane from Michaelmas day last to the day of his putting us into possession. I hope what I have agreed will meet with the approbation of my Brother Directors: I wish I could have rendered them better service.

A man's qualities of leadership are often shown by his choice of men to serve under him. In his first few years as President, Gould showed his qualities by some exceptionally good choices. His first duty as President was to nominate two directors to serve as Vice-Presidents and he chose John Pocock and Thomas Manningham, MD. John Pocock was a young man of thirty—born on February 19, 1742 (1743 n.s.). From 1766 to 1769 he was living in Knightsbridge but about 1770 he moved to Dean Street, Fetter Lane. His occupation, if any, is unknown but since his signature was in a copper-plate handwriting, with flourishes like Dodson's, it may be surmised at least that he had had a commercial education based on writing, arithmetic and accounts.

It so happened that, towards the end of 1773, while the Society was in course of getting its new premises, John Edwards died. There was no one suitable to act as Actuary temporarily until a formal appointment could be made and Gould took charge of the papers, keys and cash for the time being. The contract with William Miller was signed early in 1774 and it was arranged that business should be transferred to New Bridge Street on April 7, 1774. Meanwhile a General Court of members of the Society was held there on Thursday, February 17, 1774, partly to elect a new Actuary and partly, no doubt, to give the members an early opportunity of viewing the Society's new home.

With Gould as chairman, the General Court dealt firmly with the problem of the Actuaryship. The person appointed as Actuary should 'give security for the faithful discharge of his duty and particularly for the duly accounting for . . . all moneys which shall come to his hands for the use of the Society'; he had to give bonds of £2,000 himself and a total of a further £2,000 by other sureties. The Actuary was required to reside in the Society's house and was granted a stated salary of £150 per annum payable quarterly. The election on that occasion was to be determined by a show of hands, and John Pocock was elected. Although a Vice-President, he had evidently been asked to stay outside the Court room until the election had been made, for he was then called in and told of his appointment; he accepted with thanks. On being elected Actuary, he resigned his offices as Vice-President and Director and gave as his sureties, James Mountfort of Staple Inn and James Eyton of Spread Eagle Court, Finch Lane.

An additional officer, called an Assistant Actuary, was to be appointed and allowed a salary of £100 per annum. The matter of the Assistant Actuary was remitted to the Court of Directors and the next meeting of the General Court was postponed one month, to April 7, 1774, so as to give time for the purchase of the new house, the completion of the removal and the preparation of the annual accounts. The Court of Directors appointed William Morgan as Assistant Actuary who gave his two uncles as sureties, the Rev.

Richard Price of Newington Green and Samuel Price of Park, Glamorganshire.

Unfortunately, John Pocock died on January 24, 1775. On the following day, Gould reported that he had obtained from Mrs Pocock the Society's papers, keys and cash and invited the directors to a special meeting of the Court, on Friday, January 27, 1755, in his own home, which would facilitate a private discussion of the un-expected vacancy. In the short while that Morgan had been employed by the Society, his abilities had been observed by the directors and they thought that 'his general demeanor in the discharge of his duty as Assistant Actuary point him out as a very fit candidate for the vacant office of Actuary'. No other candidate was put forward and, at the next General Court, on a show of hands, William Morgan was elected Actuary of the Society. So began an unparalleled period of service which within his own lifetime established the Society as one of the wealthiest corporations in the world.

Morgan was the son of William Morgan, a doctor of Bridgend who had married Richard Price's sister. The son intended to follow his father's profession and came to London for his training, which was then often gained by apprenticeship to an apothecary, who might be a medical man rather than a druggist. The life was strenuous and the bed a hard one—under the counter. His own account of his first job (when he was nineteen) was:

Went to Mr Smith at Limehouse, July 11, 1769. Left him, October 11th, in a pet, at my quarter's end.

His master was a disagreeable man—

My Welsh temper could stand it no longer; I turned upon him and laid him in the kennel.

There is no record of an apprenticeship. He went to another apothecary and entered St Thomas's hospital as one of the 'Pupils and Dressers' on May 28, 1770. The date suggests that he had not completed his training when his father died in 1772. The story is told that Morgan returned to Bridgend and attempted to carry out the wish that he should succeed to his father's practice, but that his youth and his club foot made his position difficult. It is perhaps rather more likely that Morgan felt his career lay away from Bridgend and that Edwards's illness in the autumn of 1773 made an opening for him. Price asked him whether he knew mathematics—'No, uncle, but I can learn'. Morgan could have spent the winter of 1773–4 in the study of life assurance mathematics, a useful preparation for his appointment as Assistant Actuary in the spring. The year under Pocock was sufficient to show Morgan's mathematical ability and his medical training would have been a material help in the business of life assurance.

Morgan's promotion left a vacancy in the post of Assistant Actuary. The choice fell on Thomas Cooper, who was a student in an academy at Hoxton, which would be Coward's Academy, where Richard Price had been educated, and which moved to Hoxton in 1762. Cooper was born in November or December 1751, being some eighteen months younger than William Morgan, and so was twenty-three at the time of his appointment, which seems rather above the average age for a student. He would be leaving the academy just as William Godwin (1756–1836) entered it.

At the first election in the Society's new house, one of the new directors chosen was William Bray, of Great Russell Street, Blooms-bury, the historian of Surrey. He was the principal of a firm of lawyers who were in Great Russell Street for over 150 years and who have been the Society's legal advisers throughout. At the time of his election, he and Dr Price exchanged visits for dinner; they could use the opportunity to talk about the Society's affairs, Price thus playing a useful part behind the scenes.

The weekly duty of considering the admission of new members made the directors conscious of 'the danger to which the Society is exposed from the admission of bad lives', and a letter from Dr Price on this subject spurred them into action (S, April 2, 1776). They recommended the appointment of some confidential medical person as 'Assistant to the Court of Directors'; a reasonable compensation for his trouble would not exceed one hundred guineas per annum. The elections were impending and the question was held over for the new Court, which agreed, but when the proposal came before the members in General Court, the resolution 'passed in the negative' (G, October 3, 1776). Probably, the members were satisfied with the way the Society's affairs were going and were less conscious of the dangers. It seems odd that the members should have rejected the considered opinion of the Court of Directors on such a question but the decision was respected and no medical officer was appointed for many years. Morgan himself had had a medical training and there were always several medical men in the Court of Directors, though not necessarily available at the weekly Courts.

When the year 1775 opened, the Society had been transacting business for more than twelve years and though, under Edwards, it had evolved a sufficient system of records, it had not been able to devise a method of arranging its accounts so that the financial state of the Society could, in Price's phrase, be 'digested'. Probably the directors were aware of this lack and hinted as much to him. At any rate when they met in the President's home on January 27, 1775, they had some outspoken observations by Dr Price to consider. 'Nothing can be rightly infer'd from the present method of stating the Accounts of the Society' he said, and explained how the funds of a life assurance office must go on increasing for many years in order to meet the claims in later life, even though there were no increase in the number of lives who were assured.

It becomes the Society, therefore, to be very cautious: and if its number is kept up, its capital (i.e. the funds of the Society) ought to go on increasing for at least sixty to seventy years. Nor will it be proper to divide any part of the Stock as directed in Art. 21 of the *Short Account*. . . . For should it appear that the annual payments added to the interest of its growing Stock, are more than sufficient to support the growing annual claims . . . the right measure will be either to increase the claims or sink the payments (i.e. reduce the premiums), and not to enter upon the Stock.

He suggested three methods of approach to the problem: (1) A comparison of the actual mortality experience with the expected mortality by the tables used in the calculation of the premiums. (2) 'The shortest method of trying the state of the Society is by comparing the amount of the premiums paid with the amount of the claims'. Some part of the premiums on assurances for the whole duration of single lives would be required to build up the reserves; one-third of the premiums might be taken for this purpose leaving two-thirds for the cost of the current risk, with which the claims ought to be compared. (3) A comparison of the Stock (i.e. funds) of the Society with the value placed upon the liabilities by a 'specimen of a method of determining the surplus stock of the Society'. The specimen is the familiar valuation balance sheet.

Price thought it might be found that in the four years 1770–73 the premiums had been double the claims and the profit on mortality had averaged £2,250 per annum. The funds at Christmas 1773 amounted to nearly £33,000; the value of the liabilities might be found to be £12,000 on single lives and perhaps £10,000 on other assurances and on annuities, leaving a surplus stock of about £11,000. If these estimates should 'on a future examination prove to be the truth', he suggested (1) that half the annual profit should be used to defray the expenses of management, (2) that a part of these expenses should be divided into salaries for the directors, their number to be reduced, and larger salaries to the President and Vice-Presidents, (3) that either the claims should be increased or the payments reduced a tenth—which would accelerate the increase of the Society, and (4) that £4,000 or £5,000 should be 'established as a reserved stock . . . never to be entered upon except in seasons of particular mortality . . . the interest . . . to be added . . . to the principal, till it shall rise to such a sum as may be deemed a sufficient security to the Society in all events'.

Richard Price's observations were the first to show how the business of a life office should be arranged and valued.

William Morgan's first big task was to prepare estimates of the premiums and claims 'agreeable to the specimens stated by Dr Price' and it was nine months before the estimates were ready (W, November 1, 1775). They showed that Price's figures were indeed 'near the truth' and a month later Morgan was asked to make a full valuation of the liabilities. There were 922 contracts in force on January 1, 1776, and each of them had to be separately valued, involving several thousand calculations. The whole work was completed within a little over four months (S, April 24, 1776). When the full results were reported to the members they gave William Morgan a gratuity of one hundred guineas 'for his diligence in preparing the estimates'; the directors had called it 'extraordinary diligence'.

This was the first valuation of an actual life assurance business. The results were considerably better even than Price had thought— he had had to judge the position from somewhat sketchy information. The assets on January 1, 1776, were worth £41,928 (taking the 3 per cent stocks at $86\frac{1}{2}$), the liabilities were put at £16,786 and the surplus was £25,142. Thus approximately 60 per cent of the assets could be regarded as being surplus. Such an amazingly good result required time to digest its implications. The Society was faced with a problem which had never been tackled before and it was only proper that the approach to the problem should be a cautious one. The deed of settlement enjoined that any surplus should be divided amongst the members but Price advised against such a course and his view prevailed. It seemed 'prudent to reserve a much larger sum than the present surplus stock of the Society as a security against extraordinary events or a season of uncommon mortality'.

The Society had been making an additional charge for the larger assurances, the limit beyond which the excess was charged being raised from time to time. In view of the prosperous state of the Society the members thought that this additional charge might be discontinued. This was a comparatively small first step and the members as well as the directors were thinking about what should be done. When the accounts for the year 1776 were being considered by the General Court some months later, a member proposed that all premiums should be reduced. The whole question was considered in a series of four meetings of the General Court in the summer of 1777. With the consent of the member, some modifications were made in his resolution to put the proposal in more detailed form and it was finally agreed that a reduction, of an amount to be fixed by the directors, should be made in all premiums and that credit should be given to each existing member for his overpayments by set-off against the next payment of premium after November 1, 1777. The reduction the directors recommended was 10 per cent of the premiums.

The credit for past overpayments was, in effect, equivalent to a cash bonus because, if the allowance exceeded the next premium, the excess was to be paid in cash and, if the member died before the next premium became due, the allowance was to be made to the persons claiming under the assurance.

In the early days, the Society's spare cash had naturally been invested in Government Stock, which in practice meant the 3 per cent stocks, such as Consols then were. In 1778 the directors began to look more widely afield. The Society's funds were, of course, growing but probably the impetus to change came from the stress of war. The American War of Independence had been in progress for some three years. Early in the year 1778 France recognized the new American Republic and in July joined in the struggle by declaring war on Great Britain. There was a sharp fall in the prices of the public funds and Government borrowing had to be greatly extended to meet the costs

of war. This gave the Society the opportunity to diversify the investments.

The *Short Account* stated that the usual practice was to invest the
moneys of the Society altogether in the public funds. The members,
however, agreed (G, September 3, 1778) that the Court of Directors
nevertheless had 'full and free liberty', agreeable to the original deed
of settlement, to invest either in Government or in other 'good and
sufficient securities' at their discretion.

Soon afterwards, William Bray brought forward three propositions;
for the purchase of ground rents in Marylebone at $17\frac{1}{2}$ years'
purchase (thus yielding about $5\frac{3}{4}$ per cent interest), for a loan
of £2,000 at 5 per cent, secured on the foregoing ground rents, and
for a loan of £1,500 at 5 per cent, secured on freehold property in
Essex.

The directors had doubts 'not only of the expediency but of the
power given them by the deed of settlement to make any absolute
purchase' but were interested in the mortgage on freehold property
(S, November 4, 1778). However, a week later the Court decided to
continue to invest in Government stock, rather than in mortgages,
since 'purchases may be made in the public funds at so low a rate'.

The Society's own house in New Bridge Street had been taken on
a lease. The Committee for building and completing the Blackfriars
Bridge Scheme offered the freehold of the house to the Society at
thirty years' purchase, which would have cost about £1,400 since
the ground rent was £45 18s. When the offer was reported to the
members (G, December 3, 1778), they resolved to buy the freehold.
Nothing, however, seems to have been done.[1] Probably, the directors
had second thoughts about investing their money at a rate of interest
as low as $3\frac{1}{3}$ per cent, which would have been, in effect, the yield on
the transaction. They may well have been deterred, too, by doubts
whether the Society ought to own a freehold. Though these doubts
may seem strange, the directors would have been regarding the
Society's assets as belonging to a self-liquidating fund, the surplus
income in the early years of each batch of assurances being invested
so as to meet the excess outgo on claims in the later years. However,
on a long view, what a very valuable property would have been
secured.

---

[1] Fifty years later, it was stated that the proposed purchase, on terms which had been
agreed, was abandoned because of some defect of title (S, April 16, 1828).

The exigencies of war demanded new finance and the Government raised the money on terms that Dr Price thought were extravagant. In each of the three years 1777–79, stock was issued in two parts, one a stock carrying interest for an unlimited time, and the other an annuity which was effectively additional interest for a limited time. Thus in 1779, there was a combined issue of 3 per cent stock at 60 and a 'short annuity' of £3 15s per cent for 29 years at a price of 11¼ years' purchase, giving a total price for the loan of a little over 100. In effect, the Government was offering 6¾ per cent for 29 years and 3 per cent thereafter, which works out at about 6 per cent over-all, an arrangement suggested by Dr Price in 1771. The directors began to put some of the Society's money into these 'Short Annuities'.

The fluctuations in price to which Government and other quoted securities are subject have always been felt to be an inconvenience. The effect of such fluctuations can be mitigated, e.g. when prices rise, by maintaining the assets at 'book prices' instead of market prices and, when prices fall, by changing the basis on which the liabilities are valued but, in the early days, such sophisticated arguments would have carried little appeal, even had the situation been better understood. Thus it was natural that a feeling should grow in favour of investment in mortgages, which are free from complications of market fluctuations. A start was made with a loan of £8,000 at 5 per cent interest to Sir Thomas Gascoigne of Partington, Yorkshire, upon the security of estates at Garforth, near Leeds, whose net annual value was £591. If the loan was restricted to two-thirds of value, the estate must have been valued as being worth at least £12,000, i.e. on the basis of a yield of 5 per cent or less (W, August 11, 1779). Within less than three years the total invested in mortgages had risen to £36,000, which was some 30 per cent of the total assets and seemed sufficient for the time being. A similar thought was in the minds of members. Gould was absent from the next General Court, when a member secured the adoption of a resolution which would have confined the investments to Government securities (G, June 6, 1782). Gould's character is shown by his action in getting the resolution amended at the next meeting so as to leave investment policy to the discretion of the directors.

When William Morgan had had a few years' experience of the business of life assurance, his uncle encouraged him to write a book on the subject, which he did in 1779. Dr Price used the opportunity for the giving of good advice to the Society. In an introduction to the book, he warmly commended the Society and its 'strict mathematical principles'.

There is not any other Society now existing of the same kind; and its business has been increasing so fast, that it is already become an object of vast importance to the public, and is likely soon to become of much more importance.

Price approved the caution shown when the results of the valuation of the year 1776 had been known. 'It was proper to give the plan of the Society a longer trial.' There might be 'seasons of extraordinary mortality'. He gave only qualified approval to the reduction of one-tenth in the premiums for he disagreed with the return of 'the whole overplus':

Different opinions have been entertained of this measure; but the truth is, that (however safe and just the prosperous state of the Society then rendered it) it is in itself a measure of the most pernicious tendency. . . . A repetition . . . might hurt the Society essentially, by withdrawing from it that security which it has been providing for many years, and bringing it back to infancy and weakness.

These last words give the key to his fears. He believed that the Society was 'capable of being made an object of great consequence not only to this, but to other kingdoms . . .' and offered some suggestions. First, he thought that the Society should be:

Furnished with a set of tables . . . more correct and elegant than it now uses . . . tables founded on observations . . . not among the bulk of the people in London, where life is particularly short but among mankind in general. . . .

He suggested tables deduced from the bills of mortality at Northampton or Norwich as being nearly the mean between the mortality in great towns and in country parishes and villages. But he specially recommended a table derived from the mortality of Chester, 'an old and healthy town . . .'. Its Register (of mortality) was, he said, more minute and correct than any other and the only one . . . that 'gives the difference between the chances of living among males and females . . .'. If the premiums were thought to be too low, he suggested making an addition of 10 or 15 per cent.

Secondly, the business of the Society required tables of the values of two joint lives at all ages 'agreeably to the best observations, and true to three places of decimals'; also tables of three lives would be an advantage.

Thirdly, he reminded the Society of the care necessary 'to prevent the intrusion of bad lives' for the Society 'must be ruined, should it ever become, not a resource for the living and healthy, but a refuge for the sick and dying'. He wanted a medical assistant to be appointed, but that proposal had already been rejected by the members.

Last, he referred to 'the danger of employing unskilful calculators . . .' and spoke of the 'long and laborious computations, which none but able mathematicians can make . . .'. Thinking of possible future vacancies among the staff, he stressed 'the importance of both ability and probity'.

Some months after these suggestions were published the members themselves brought the issue to a head by asking the Court of Directors to consider whether the premiums could be reduced and whether a further dividend or return of premiums could be made (G, June 1, 1780). Various calculations had to be made, which occupied six months, but the directors were then able to report that 'the contributions required from the present members are more than sufficient for the perfect security of the Society'. However, the making of any further dividend or return of premium would be a measure 'highly inexpedient' and 'detrimental to the interests of the Society'.

A comparison of the mortality in the previous twelve years with the mortality of the Northampton table constructed by Price showed that that table would be well-fitted for the business of the Society 'adding such small charge to those computations as shall be thought necessary to render the Society perfectly secure'. The Northampton table showed rather higher mortality than the Chester table.

While the premiums for new assurances could be reduced, there was the troublesome question of the existing assurances. In order to place the old members on an equal footing with new assurers, claims arising from existing assurances should be increased 'in proportion to the time which the claimants have been assured'. The recommended addition was $1\frac{1}{2}$ per cent of the sum assured for each year's premium paid, the maximum rate being $28\frac{1}{2}$ per cent[1] for an assurance which had subsisted the whole nineteen years of the Society's existence—'a measure which . . . will not be attended with hazard nor excite an opinion unfavourable to the credit of the Society'.

The solution followed the lines of a suggestion made by one of the members, named William Batten, about two years earlier. Though

[1] A later table shows a maximum of 30 per cent.

the proposition 'passed in the negative', it contained the germ of the idea of reversionary bonuses and may have been Batten's own idea or one that was being discussed by others, including Price. William Batten, a Wiltshireman, aged fifty-eight, was an officer in the Custom House when he effected his assurance in 1765.

The members approved the recommendations and so reversionary bonuses were born. It will be seen they arose simply as compensation to the existing members in lieu of a refund of premiums. There was an attempt by one of the members to upset the decisions for the disposal of the surplus, because on December 12, 1781 the directors and trustees were told that notice had been given of a resolution calling for a further dividend or refund of a rateable part of the premiums paid. They reviewed the arguments for and against this course and also those in favour of the resolution that had been adopted. It seems they were influenced against making any refund partly by the comparatively low price of the public funds at the time; they came down decisively against any cash refund and decided 'by every means in their power to dissuade an attempt so injudicious and hazardous'. The member cannot have had much backing because no reference to the matter appears in the minutes of the General Court and he did not in fact move any resolution. Probably, he was told privately of the views of the directors and was persuaded of the rightness of their decision.

The table of mortality which the directors had selected was derived from the bills of mortality for the parish of All Saints in Northampton from 1735 to 1770, a period of thirty-six years, including both males and females. Though both the statistics and method of construction could be criticized, Price put such checks on his calculations as he could and in particular he made (what later critics have tended to overlook) a close comparison with the results of a census of the parish made in 1746. He wished to spare no pains to give the Society a broad basis for its calculations and he calculated a fresh table including a further ten years' deaths, thus covering altogether the 46 years from 1735–1780. This was the table which was used for all purposes for over half a century.

William Morgan and his assistant Thomas Cooper spent most of the year 1781 in the calculation of the various values of annuities and assurances so that as complete a set as possible would be available. The first four tables, including annuity values on two lives for all combinations of ages, were completed by April 12, 1781. The next four tables, including values of assurances for periods up to ten years and for the whole continuance of life as well as assurances on two lives for combinations of every fifth age, were completed by May 14, 1781. The ninth table, which was a complete table of survivorship assurances, i.e. of one life beyond another, for every combination of two ages, took over five months; Morgan began the calculations on May 31, 1781, and with what relief did he put 'Finis, November 3, 1781, W. Morgan'! Next month, the salaries of the Actuary (£150 per annum) and the Assistant Actuary (£100 per annum) were doubled and the increase was back-dated.

When the complete tables were ready, the Court of Directors, acting perhaps with an excess of caution, decided to increase the premiums by 15 per cent 'for defraying the salaries of officers and for making the security still more full and abundant' (G, December 5, 1781). The expenses were small and there is the merest hint that Gould thought the charge excessive, for the report to the members opened with the guarded phrase 'The President . . . was instructed to recommend . . .'. In 1783, in the fourth edition of *Observations on Reversionary Payments*, Price called the 15 per cent charge 'exorbitant'.

In reply to a letter from Gould, Price wrote (December 17, 1781):

I feel very sensibly the favourable manner in which you . . . are pleased to receive my endeavours. . . . No one can rejoice more than I do in the prosperous state of the Society, or wish more to promote its usefulness and stability. The new Tables . . . will contribute greatly to this end; and, together with the advantage it enjoys in being honoured with so excellent a President, will probably soon raise it to the highest credit, and render it an object of particular importance to this Kingdom.

Looking back, it is clear that the years 1780 and 1781 were decisive years when the very structure of life assurance was formed. The old ideas were stripped away and a new fabric built. The members must have had some, perhaps dim, apprehension of the greatness of the occasion and they wished to make it memorable. The General Court wanted Price 'to accept some present from the Society as a lasting testimony of their respect'. Gould endeavoured to discover what present would be acceptable, but was unsuccessful. He was unable to be present at the General Court on January 17, 1782 but sent a letter giving tactful guidance: 'I will see if I cannot prevail with the

Doctor to accept one hundred guineas, or whatever sum the Society shall be pleased to appoint'. The sum was agreed and was paid on January 23, 1782.

At the same meeting on December 20, 1781, the General Court resolved to ask Sir Charles Gould to accept a service of plate of £500 value as 'a testimony of their gratitude and the high approbation they wish to express for his conduct in the direction and management of their affairs, which are now in so flourishing a situation'.

A month later, on January 17, 1782, the General Court resolved that, as 'a further testimony of the gratitude and respect of the Society to Sir Charles Gould, the President, as well as in some measure to perpetuate the memory of the great services and honour he has done them', he should suffer his picture to be painted and hung up in the great Court Room of the Society. The members wished that the painting should be the work of an eminent artist and decided to invite Thomas Gainsborough to do it. They chose well.

Gould chose a gold cup,[1] which was made by Gabriel Wirgman (1734–91) for Pickett and Rundell, the silversmiths of Ludgate Hill, who were paid £528 3s for it on October 30, 1782.

Gabriel Wirgman was a member of an interesting family who were descended from Peter Virgander, a Swedish clergyman. He entered his mark at Goldsmiths' Hall in 1773, and at the time the cup was made was working in Denmark Street, Soho. The William Pickett who was asked to 'wait upon Sir Charles Gould' was himself Lord Mayor of London in 1789. His firm had been at the sign of the Golden Salmon, 32 Ludgate Hill, for some thirty years; from 1805 to 1839, at the same address, it was styled Rundell, Bridge and Rundell, the celebrated firm of silversmiths.

The cup is a handsome piece of work in 22-carat gold. It stands 17 inches high and weighs 100 ounces. On one side it is inscribed with a record of the presentation. On the other side there is a symbolic picture in an oval frame, which contains two figures in classical dress and at their feet, at the back of the picture, a nest with three chicks being fed by the mother bird. This is the pelican which was the seal device used by the trustees of the Society from the earliest days. The standing figure is holding scales and represents justice, presumably

---

[1] There is an account of the cup in *The Connoisseur*, April 1957, pp. 165–7. See illustration opposite.

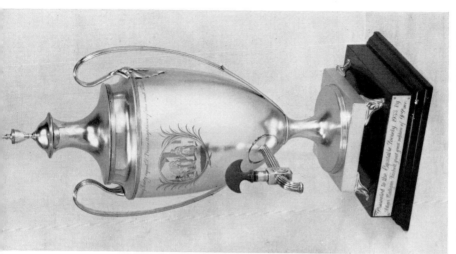

11(a). Gold cup presented to Sir Charles Gould by The Equitable in 1782

11(b). Silver urn presented to Richard Price by the London Annuity Society, and given to The Equitable by Arthur Cadogan Vachell

12. St Paul's and Blackfriars Bridge, showing the office in Chatham Place (marked by an arrow)

*[from an engraving, in the Guildhall Library, of a watercolour by Black*

in the sense of equity or fairness, though it could refer to Gould's position as Judge Advocate-General. The seated figure holds a rod with serpent, which represents authority and wisdom, and a mirror, whose symbolism is obscure; it could have some reference to reflection or divination. At the foot, the cup bears Gould's arms. It was purchased by the Society in February 1957 from the collection of the third Viscount Tredegar, a descendant of Sir Charles Gould.

Gainsborough's portrait[1] is one of his best of a male figure. The stance is unassuming but dignified. The thickness of the paint enhances the rich colouring. The treatment of the detail, e.g. of the waistcoat and the sword-handle, is executed with a minute care. Gould is shown as a firm, kindly man with a sense of humour which was probably more lively than could be portrayed. The frame was carved by William Flaxman. This would be the William Flaxman (c. 1753– c. 1795) who was the elder brother of the sculptor, John Flaxman, and was himself a modeller and exhibitor. The frame is evidence of his wood-carving. Gainsborough was paid a fee of one hundred guineas on September 24, 1782. The frame cost a further fourteen guineas and curtains for the picture, made by Quinton Kay, upholder, cost £8 10s 6d, giving a total of £128 4s 6d. The picture still adorns the Board Room of the Society and is one of its most proud possessions.

[1] Reproduced as frontispiece.

# CHAPTER IX

# A TIME FOR BUILDING (1783–1800)

THE Society's funds were growing fast and it was evident that the surplus was accumulating rapidly. Why this was so needs a little explanation.

When the Society was being formed the main argument against the subscribers' proposals was that the premiums were set at too low a level and that the project would fail. Though the argument was fallacious, it was difficult to counter, partly because the principles on which a life office operates were so little understood and partly because the available mortality statistics were unreliable. Under the influence of Richard Price, the Society's actual mortality experience was studied and a rough computation made of the amount of the surplus from the favourable mortality experience. In those days, this was the greater part of the surplus and it was substantial.

The position was even better than would be thought from this circumstance. In the early days, a great part of the new assurances were temporary assurances which by their nature lasted for a few years only at most. These assurances had expired (if they had not become claims) and gone off the books long before the question of distribution of surplus could be considered. The same would be true of many assurances of more permanent kinds, which were dropped for one reason or another long before they had run their course. Consequently, a considerable part of the surplus was created by the premiums of former members who no longer shared in the surplus. The effect was a kind of 'gearing' of the profits of those members who were assured for the whole continuance of life. Had there been a loss on mortality, they would have had most to lose; since there was, in fact, a profit on mortality, they took the benefit.

The other principal item of surplus was the excess interest earned over and above what had been assumed in the premium scale. This item was of little importance at first when the funds were small but grew in significance with the growth in the funds.

Some five years after the last distribution of surplus, the members began to feel that there should be another reduction in premiums or an increase in the claims. However, the distribution in 1781, when the Northampton table had been introduced, had been made merely on the year-to-year analysis of experience without any detailed calculation of the values of the assets and liabilities; ten years had elapsed since the valuation of 1776. It seemed desirable to make a full valuation of all the policies and the Court 'gave it in charge of the Actuary, taking to his aid the Assistant Actuary, and such other confidential person as he should think proper'. The wording shows that the directors had gained confidence in the abilities of their Actuary, William Morgan. The reference to 'such other confidential person' may, possibly, be an authority for William Morgan to consult Price, should he feel it desirable to do so; the question was left to his discretion.

There were over 2,000 policies in force and each policy required four calculations. The work is contained in a folio volume, which shows that the computations were made individually, policy by policy, taking first the January renewals, then the February renewals and so on. The work was begun on June 12, 1786, and the main part of it was finished about November of the same year. The whole work was not finished until June 12, 1787, exactly one year to the day since it was started.

The position disclosed by the valuation was amazingly good. The assets were valued at £197,274, taking the 3 per cent stocks at 70. About 40 per cent of this was required for the liabilities.[1] The figures show that in 1786, as in 1776, about 60 per cent of the assets could be regarded as being surplus.

Morgan's analysis of the experience over the twenty-year period from 1768 to 1787 showed that the source of the bulk of this surplus was the comparatively low mortality that had been experienced; more than half was profit on temporary assurances, which had nearly all expired and gone off the books well before the valuation.

---

[1] The actual value placed upon the liabilities was £32,838 but this figure was artificially low. The true value was £72,974, on the assumption that the future premiums receivable would be the net premiums, excluding the 15 per cent addition made in 1781.

The 15 per cent added to the premiums was removed from January 1, 1786 and claims were to be increased by 1 per cent for each year's premium paid before that date (G, December 7, 1786). The distribution followed the general pattern established five years earlier—a reduction in the future premiums with a reversionary bonus to compensate for past overpayments.

The growth of the Society's membership began to cause concern because, in a mutual society, decisions were effectively in the hands of the members, acting in the General Court. And the members could be swayed by unworthy considerations, if a group of them were determined to benefit themselves at the expense of the future, so endangering the stability of the Society. The Court of Directors proposed:

> . . . for the more effectually guarding against any improvident distribution of the surplus stock of the Society, and for precluding any alarm, which the idea of such measure being at any time unadvisedly taken, might excite; that in future no return . . . nor any further reduction in the rate of premium, nor any augmented allowance upon claims . . . nor . . . any dividend . . . (be made) unless four-fifths of the directors for the time being shall concur in the measure.

This would have given the Court of Directors effective control. The resolution passed one General Court but not the second.

The remarkable growth under Gould's leadership can be illustrated by a few figures[1] which are given in five-year periods so chosen as to show the effects of the reductions of premiums in 1781 and 1786. There was an immediate jump in new business after each of these reductions. The new assurances granted were at a peak in 1791, when the number of new assurances was the highest in any year until recent times, though the amount was substantially exceeded after 1802.

In each five-year period up to 1791, the number and amount of new assurances were greater than the number and amount remaining in force at the end of the five-year period. For example, the period 1782–6 started with 1,268 policies in force, 2,777 new policies were granted making a total of 4,045, out of which 2,311 remained in force at the end of the period; that is to say, 1,734 policies had become claims or expired or were not renewed.

The surplus was allowed to accumulate for a further five years

[1] *v.* Diagram on opposite page.

after the distribution of 1786 but towards the end of 1791 the time seemed ripe for another distribution. Though no individual calculations had been made, the yearly estimates were available and the

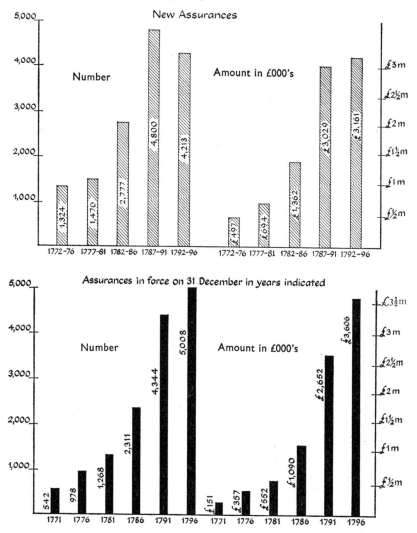

Court of Directors recommended 'a further . . . allowance to claimants after the rate of 1 per cent for every year's payment . . . prior to January 1st next (i.e. January 1, 1792)'. The recommendation was not reached without some argument but the Court of Directors wholly accepted Dr Price's views that a cash distribution or a reduction of premiums 'might deeply affect the credit of the Society and endanger its stability'.

The distribution of 1791 is interesting because it was not accompanied by a reduction in premiums and so marks a transitional stage to the now customary periodical declaration of bonus. However, the distribution was regarded as being compensation for past overpayments of premiums and so was given once again in proportion to the number of premiums paid.

When the resolution was put up for confirmation there was a record attendance of 127 members and some of them unsuccessfully sought to double the rate from 1 per cent to 2 per cent. Possibly this experience determined William Morgan to make some kind of approximate valuation, which he did in the course of the year 1792. Later, in 1800, he specifically said that the only occasions when he made 'a separate computation of the value of each policy of assurance' were 1776, 1786 and 1800. When the computations were ready, early in 1793, the Court of Directors recommended an additional allowance to claimants at the rate of 2 per cent for each premium prior to January 1, 1793. But the dangers of being misled by the rapid growth of the Society's funds were so apparent to William Morgan that he decided he must give the members a strong warning. At the meeting when the recommendations were announced, he 'addressed the Court in an impressive speech', which was afterwards printed and sent to all members of the Society (G, March 7, 1793).

Morgan opened with a personal reference to his own association with the Society for nearly twenty years, describing the Equitable as 'certainly the most extensive and important of all the institutions of the same kind in this or any other country'. He went on to speak of the investigation of 1776, the introduction of the Northampton table in 1781, and the further investigation of 1786:

The Society . . . appears to have uniformly founded its determinations on the sure principles of computation; and I trust that neither its increasing capital, nor any other apparent sign of accumulating wealth, will ever tempt it to deviate from a course so wise and salutary.

He referred to the rapid accumulation of the Society's 'capital', i.e. funds:

But there is danger of being misled by this accumulation into an extravagant opinion respecting the circumstances of the Society; and it is to guard against that pernicious error, that I have been principally induced to address myself to the members. . . .

Morgan pointed his argument with an illustration, taking 1,000 members at the age of thirty years. Assurances of £100 on each life for one year would cost £1,666, which, with its interest for the year, would merely suffice to pay the claims at the end of the year; if the assurances were for the whole continuance of life the total annual premiums would be £2,666, or £1,000 more than if the assurances were made for one year only. This sum of £1,000 ought to be laid by towards paying the claims when they exceed the annual premiums. The excess of premiums over claims would be a little less than £1,000 in the second year and would continue to diminish in the following years;[1] in about thirty years the claims would equal the annual premiums, and thereafter would exceed them. This supposed that no new assurances were made but, if the number of members were always kept up to 1,000, the excess of premiums over claims would accumulate for more than sixty years before the claims and the premiums became equal:

In the Equitable Society the assurances are made upon lives of all ages from 8 to 67 years; their number, instead of being limited, is continually increasing. . . . Is it then at all surprising that its capital increases with great rapidity? It would indeed be an alarming circumstance if the contrary were true.

After reciting the magnitude of what had already been done, he spoke encouragingly of the future:

If the Society confines itself within the limits now proposed, it will not only be perfectly secure, but still continue, though with a retarded progression, to increase its surplus. I hope the time will never come when the annual profits of the Society shall entirely cease. It is necessary for its credit and security that these should continue.

The additions to claims should go no farther than that the members may 'derive a due share of advantage without endangering the expectations and property of those that shall succeed them', and he added that it would always be advisable 'to continue the present terms of assurance unreduced . . . the preservation of its capital (i.e. the Society's funds), sacred and inviolate, is indispensable'.

After this strong warning, it must have been with some considerable apprehension that, within less than three years, Morgan faced demands

[1] cp. chart on p. 12.

for a further distribution. The yearly analysis of the experience was available as a guide and the Court of Directors decided to recommend another addition of 1 per cent for each year's premium paid before January 1, 1796. The Court felt it necessary to warn members against the 'captivating splendour of a very large capital' and recommended that thereafter notice should be required of any proposal for a further distribution and that no such resolution should be effective unless four-fifths of the members present at the General Court 'shall be consenting thereto'.

Morgan felt constrained to speak again (G, December 3, 1795) on some of the dangers which the Society was facing:

The measures which have hitherto been pursued by this Society in regard to the disposition of their surplus stock have in general been temperate, and secure; and were it certain that the same moderation would always guide them in their future determinations, it would be unnecessary to offer any observations which might induce them to change their plan. But . . . this, like all other Societies, is composed of a transient body which is perpetually changing, and . . . however well-disposed the present members may be to persevere in that temperate course which has raised this Society to its present eminence, yet . . . other members may succeed with very different ideas and intentions. It is indeed hardly possible to contemplate the accumulating stock of the Society without apprehension. The annual addition of thousands to a capital which already exceeds the best part of a million, though absolutely necessary to discharge the immense demands which must hereafter come upon the Society, will naturally lead the uninformed to entertain very extravagant and dangerous opinions of its opulence. The continued accession of new assurances, which unavoidably produces a continued addition to the annual savings of the Society, will also serve to increase the delusion and the danger; and if there should be the same accession for a few years longer, the capital must increase to such a sum as will not only mislead the ignorant, but probably have the more alarming effect of awakening the passions of the covetous and self-interested. I do not know that a much better method can be devised of making all the members to participate in the profits of the Society, without endangering its security, than that which has been repeatedly adopted during the last fourteen years. By increasing the claims, not only the object of the assurance is promoted in the best manner, but the surplus stock of the Society is diminished so gradually as to excite no immediate alarm by the sudden reduction of that capital on which its welfare and safety depend. But, on the other hand, it must be confessed that though this measure, when employed with discretion, is both safe and eligible, yet that the very circumstance of its being so gradual and remote in its operations may, by producing its too frequent repetition, render it ultimately more ruinous in its consequences than any other.

He gave a numerical example which typified the Society's own situation—a Society with 4,000 members of all ages from 15 to 75 years assured for £1,000 each (which was about the average amount) and showed how considerable was the effect of distributions at the rate of 1 per cent for each year of assurance when repeated every five years, and how much greater the effect if it were to be repeated every four years or every three years. After twenty years there would be 2,155 survivors assured for £2,155,000. The aggregate additions to the survivors' assurances would be £1,099,050 if the distributions had been made every five years, £1,314,550 if every four years, and £1,747,600 (after twenty-one years) if every three years. In the period of fourteen years from 1782 to 1795 there had been four distributions, an average of three and one-half years (Morgan called it four in twelve years), and the rate had sometimes exceeded 1 per cent:

> Were therefore these additions to be often repeated at this rate, it is evident
> . . . that in a few years they would amount to such a sum as would exhaust not
> only the surplus stock but even the whole capital (i.e. funds) of the Society.

Evidently, Morgan was under pressure to reduce the premiums, but this would be 'depriving the Society of one of the chief sources of its wealth'. He explained that a reduction would be inequitable because new members at the reduced premiums would share equally with the older members, whose payments would have created the surplus. Also, the older members benefited far more by an increase in their assurances than by a reduction in their payments:

> I only wish to moderate the expectations of the members of this Society, and
> to convince them that, while the measure of reducing the premiums is neither
> safe, equitable, nor advantageous. the other measure of increasing the claims is
> liable, by the remoteness of its operations, to be too often repeated, and hence
> to be ultimately productive of the most fatal consequences.

Within another two years, the members were eager for another distribution of surplus. The request was refused and was not pressed to the General Court (S, November 20, 1797). The last investigation into the real state of the Society's finances had been made in 1786 and Morgan felt that there should be another investigation before any further distribution of surplus; the decision to do this was taken on the day before Christmas in the year 1798. It was hoped that the results would be known within a year but there were more than 5,000 contracts in force and more than 20,000 calculations to be made. This 'immense labour' was not completed until April 1800.

William Morgan was now faced with the greatest problems of his career. It was clear to him that the Society could not go on in a haphazard way, with distributions of surplus whenever the members or the directors felt the time was ripe. Distributions had been made at far too frequent intervals for the healthy development of the Society and some regular, and reasonably long, period must be set. As the Society grew in size, the increasing labour of full investigations into the Society's finances made it essential to keep fairly long intervals between each investigation. The financial results tended to be irregular from year to year and a suitable period was needed for averaging the profits. The Society's stability and credit required great restraint in the distribution of surplus. A large part had always been carried forward undistributed, so that at any given time the surplus had arisen much more from the older policies than the newer policies —an argument for giving the older policies a larger allocation of surplus than the newer policies.

Morgan first made up his mind that ten years must elapse between each valuation of the Society and hoped he could persuade the members that no distribution of surplus should be made without such an investigation, i.e. future distributions would be made every ten years. Next he had to consider whether surplus should continue to be used to increase the sums assured or whether it would be better applied in some other way such as a reduction in premiums or a cash refund. He felt strongly that additions to the sums assured were preferable both from the point of view of the Society and from the point of view of the member, as well as being more equitable between members of different generations. Thirdly, he had to consider what would be the proper proportion of surplus to distribute at each valuation and what to carry forward. In the past a small part only had been distributed and obviously the Society had to be more generous in its allocations. But how much more? There were no signposts to guide him and he chose proportions of two-thirds to be distributed and one-third to be reserved; it would have appeared a reasonable and cautious decision.

So far he would have been led by purely practical considerations to the concept of valuations at ten-year intervals, the reservation of one-third of the surplus and the allocation of surplus by way of bonus additions to the sums assured. The last step was the most difficult of all—how should the bonuses be calculated to suit these circumstances?

It had been customary, for other reasons, to allot bonus additions on each occasion in proportion to the number of years' premiums paid, i.e. in proportion to the whole time that the policy had been in force. Morgan was able to satisfy himself that this system would give equitable results provided that on each occasion a substantial pro-portion such as one-third of the surplus was reserved and carried forward. There is no record of the calculations by which he satisfied himself on this question but various calculations have been made to check the theory and, of course, the system did work well in practice.

Morgan might satisfy himself but it was a major task to carry others with him in the adoption of measures of self-restraint. He was helped by the splendid results disclosed by the valuation which he was able to make known in April 1800. The assets were valued at £1,041,219, taking the 3 per cents at 61 and the 4 per cents at 80. The value of the liabilities came out at £557,165 leaving a surplus of £484,054, which was about 46 per cent of the assets. This is a smaller percentage than the 60 per cent shown in 1776 and 1786 but there had since been substantial bonus additions which had increased the liabilities and reduced the surplus; these fully account for the smaller percentage.

Morgan probably thought it undesirable to distribute the full two-thirds of the surplus in 1800, in view of the three comparatively recent additions in 1791, 1793 and 1795; he recommended a bonus of 2 per cent of the sum assured for each year's premium paid before May 1, 1800. This cost £258,946 which is not much more than one-half of the surplus and left nearly one-half undistributed; the Court tactfully said it 'will leave something more than one-third'.

Both the magnitude and the changing character of the business can be seen from the valuation statistics. There were 5,124 contracts in force assuring sums of £3,904,685 and annuities of £12,383. These figures had been increased by bonus additions to £4,183,947 and £12,964 respectively. About 72 per cent of the contracts were assurances for the whole continuance of a single life.

Morgan addressed the members in a magnificent speech which succeeded in persuading the members to adopt the measures he recommended (G, April 24, 1800). The earlier part was devoted to the principles on which the computations were made and a review of the past which included a statement of the mortality experience; it remained for many years the only published mortality experience of a life office and extensive tables were afterwards calculated from these few figures.

From the period in which I was first chosen to my present situation, the accounts have been so arranged as to enable me, in every year, to determine, with sufficient precision, in what degree the decrements of life among the Members, compared with those in the table of observations from which the premiums are computed, have, or have not, been favourable to the Society; and the following statement contains the result of an annual experience of thirty years:

| | | | | | |
|---|---|---|---|---|---|
| From the age of | 10 to 20 | they have been as | | | 1 to 2 |
| ,, ,, | 20 to 30 | ,, | ,, | | 1 to 2 |
| ,, ,, | 30 to 40 | ,, | ,, | | 3 to 5 |
| ,, ,, | 40 to 50 | ,, | ,, | | 3 to 5 |
| ,, ,, | 50 to 60 | ,, | ,, | | 5 to 7 |
| ,, ,, | 60 to 80 | ,, | ,, | | 4 to 5 |

He concluded with a forthright exposition of the need for self-restraint, whereby the periodical bonus additions would be regulated and confined:

From the conduct and circumstances of this Society, it will be readily perceived, that it is much easier to establish, than to provide for the future management of such an institution. The mere computations of the premiums of assurance is a very subordinate work; and, by the aid of those rules which have been published by different mathematicians, may be performed mechanically, without the least knowledge of the principles on which they are founded. But what signify those premiums, however correctly computed, if no means are provided for ascertaining, at proper intervals, the real state of the institution, and for disposing of its profits without endangering its security, either by a direct or an indirect invasion of its capital? Had this Society been so constituted, or, in other words, had its whole plan been formed by persons properly acquainted with the subject, we should not have been reduced to the necessity of repeatedly breaking through one of its fundamental laws, in order to preserve it from destruction. Can anything be more absurd, or betray greater ignorance, than to propose an annual profit and loss account in a concern of this kind; or to regulate the dividend or the call by the success or failure of each year? From the very nature of such an institution, this is impracticable; but particularly in the earlier period of its existence, when the small number and short continuance of the assurances render it utterly impossible to form any accurate judgement of its profits or deficiencies: and even when many years have elapsed after its establishment, the real state of its finances can only be investigated at distant periods; for, exclusive of the immense labour of such an investigation, the events of one year vary so much from those of another, that no general conclusions respecting the affairs of the Society can be safely deduced from the experience of so short a term. In this Society, indeed, the number of lives is now so great as to render the decrements in every year very nearly the same. But even here, from the great difference in the sums assured on each life, the amount of the claims is so uncertain, that it shall often happen that events prove peculiarly unfavourable to the Society in a year which has been attended with no uncommon degree of mortality. This was particularly the case in the years 1796 and 1797, when the claims, though nearly equal in number, having fallen chiefly on the large assurances, increased to double their amount in the two preceding years. On every consideration, therefore, the idea of an annual dividend, arising from the balance of the Society's accounts in each year, should be for ever abandoned: And since the distribution of no part of the profits, or rather of the capital of the Society, ought to be hazarded without a minute investigation of the real state of its affairs, it is evident, from the length of time which the present computations have required, that such a distribution, so far from being annual, can only be repeated after long intervals of experience and success.

William Morgan had the solid backing of the Court of Directors and a good President. The General Court agreed (G, April 24, 1800) to the additions at the rate of 2 per cent for each year's payment before May 1, 1800 and resolved to make three bye-laws (which could only be varied or repealed by the votes of three successive General Courts): '(1) that a careful investigation of the value of each policy of assurance, similar to the investigation which has now taken place, be repeated once in ten years; (2) that in future no addition be made to the claims, nor any other mode of distribution of the profits of the Society be adopted, without such investigation previously had; and (3) that the addition made to the claims, do not in any instance exceed in present value two-thirds of the clear surplus stock of the Society'. Morgan must have been well content that day.

The members, meeting in the General Court, tended to play a much larger part in the affairs of the Society than would be customary nowadays. A striking instance of this is found in the practice of submitting petitions to the General Court so that matters of doubt could be resolved by the fellow members of the one who felt aggrieved. The practice started in 1786 and can be attributed to the wise guidance of Gould as President. It assured each member of equitable treatment, so far as possible, and gave a desirable firmness to decisions on questions of some difficulty.

By the terms of the policies, premiums had to be paid not later than thirty days after the due date; if the life assured had died within the thirty days, the premium still had to be paid within the stated time or the claim would not be admitted—the sum assured, of course, was not payable until six months later. Several of the petitions concerned unpaid premiums.

The premiums on Joseph Holl's assurance were due on May 12th in each year and had been regularly paid on that day. On May 11, 1786, he was suddenly taken ill, lingered until the next day and died. His brother and administrator, Benjamin Holl of the Navy Office, procured the required evidence and was told that the claim would be allowed but that the premium was due and must be paid. Benjamin Holl did not have sufficient money with him at the time and, going into the country, his return was delayed by public business longer than he expected. He pleaded 'an entire ignorance' of the regulations. The Court resolved that he had no right to relief but the money would be paid as a gratuity (G, December 7, 1786). His letter of thanks (dated from the Navy Office February 28, 1787) is worth quoting:

> I beg to return you my most grateful acknowledgment for the indulgence you were pleased to shew me, at your last General Court, in allowing my claim upon my late brother's policy, altho' the premium was not paid in due time . . . but I have not yet been able to benefit by that kind indulgence for want of the policy, which is either lost or mislaid and cannot be produced. I am therefore humbly to request your further indulgence, in dispensing with the want of such policy, upon my giving the Society such indemnity for any claim that may in future be made on the same, as you may be pleased to approve.

This prayer was also granted.

A member named Joynes had assured the life of Isaac Cook and had paid the premiums regularly for 15 or 16 years but forgot to pay it, as it happened, in the year that Isaac Cook died. He prayed that 'it was peculiarly unfortunate for him that the man should die in the very year it was omitted . . .'. His petition was rejected (G, September 1, 1791).

Mercy was, however, shown to a maidservant named Mary Price who had assured £300 on the life of Edmund Phelips and who, being out of town, could not pay the premiums personally; she relied upon a friend to make the payment for her. One year, the friend inadvertently omitted to do so and Phelips died three days after the expiry of the days of grace. She asked for 'some relief as the loss to a person in her situation of life and at the age of 66 years will be very sensibly felt'. She was granted an allowance, as a free donation, of £20 per annum payable half-yearly during her life (G, December 6, 1792).

Another class of case concerned the clause which excluded claims on deaths at sea, known as 'sea risque'. Edward Rogers of Liverpool had assured the life of Lieut. William Richard Rumbold on whose life he had purchased an annuity. On the advice of his doctors, Rumbold went to Lisbon for the benefit of his health but was returning 'to his native air as the only means left of prolonging his life' when he died at sea. Edward Rogers tried two lines of attack. He pleaded, first, that Rumbold was within the limits of Europe as required by the policy and, secondly, that 'a natural death occurred, not being induced or accelerated by his being on the sea'. Rogers contended that the clause meant to exclude only those dangers which were peculiar to the sea. After 'due deliberation' it was decided that the prayer could not be complied with (G, June 7, 1787).

As a result of this case, the Court of Directors gave further thought to the wording of this clause but decided not to make any alteration. The question is one of a type that still gives difficulty though 'sea risque' is no longer a source of trouble. In general, it is difficult to distinguish between causes of death and, if an exclusion is necessary, it is better to avoid an exclusion based upon the cause of death.

In 1788, Sarah Stearndale assured the life of George William August Courtenay, Captain in the Royal Navy. When he was ordered on duty in 1790, she paid, as she thought, the extra premium required for sea risque. Courtenay was killed in action on board the *Ship of Boston* in America on August 1, 1793. The claim was refused because the extra premium for sea risque extended only to the Mediterranean and more should have been paid for wider cover. Sarah Stearndale pleaded ignorance; the Court resolved that she had no legal claim but that payment should be made as a matter of grace (G, September 1, 1796).

These examples are sufficient to show how a real attempt was made through these petitions to deal equitably with cases of hardship, rather than to decide simply on the letter of the law.

The finances of the Society during the last decades of the eighteenth century need to be seen against the larger background of the national finances. The prudent management which was so successful in the Society's affairs should, Price and Morgan thought, be applied also to the national finances. They were consistent advocates of economy in expenditure, combined with sufficient taxation to make some provision, also, for the redemption of debt.

Citizens of the twentieth century are so accustomed to the notion of a vast Government debt which will never be repaid, that the gloomy views held in the eighteenth century seem otherworldly. But, then, the national debt was a comparatively new problem; the practice of raising money for supplies by borrowing against future taxes had begun with the 'otherwise glorious Revolution', as Price called it (i.e. the Revolution of 1688); and the belief was widespread that the debt could and should be repaid.

The fears were real. The power of the national purse is a political power, which in the limited franchise of the time, increased dependence on the crown 'by jobs and places without number'. The exorbitant public debt occasioned the 'execrable practices of the Alley' (i.e. stockbroking), rendered us 'tributary to foreigners' (i.e. on the debt held abroad), and raised 'the price of provisions and labour . . . checking population and loading our trade and manufactures'. What mattered most to Price was that the spirit of liberty might be checked: 'The tendency of every Government is to despotism . . . Opposition . . . and resistance are often necessary'. Those who were concerned with the stability of the funds would be restrained from criticism and inclined 'always to acquiescence and servility'.

These views were not exceptional; they were shared by many others. In some essays published in 1752, David Hume, the philosopher, had said: 'Either the nation . . . must destroy public credit (i.e. the debt) or public credit will destroy the nation'. Price, quoting him, added 'a dreadful alternative surely'. A quarter of a century later, in his *History of England*, written in 1776, Hume commented: 'the endless increase of national debt is the direct road to national ruin'.

The widespread interest shown in the problem of the public debt can be illustrated by a curious circumstance. Augustus Toplady used the theme in *The Gospel Magazine*, which he edited. In the year 1776, he included 'a remarkable calculation', which consisted of questions and answers relative to the national debt, by someone who wrote under the initials J. F. The questions led up to:

Q. When will the government be able to pay the principal?
A. When there is more money in England's treasury alone, than there is at present in all Europe.
Q. And when will *that* be?    A. Never.

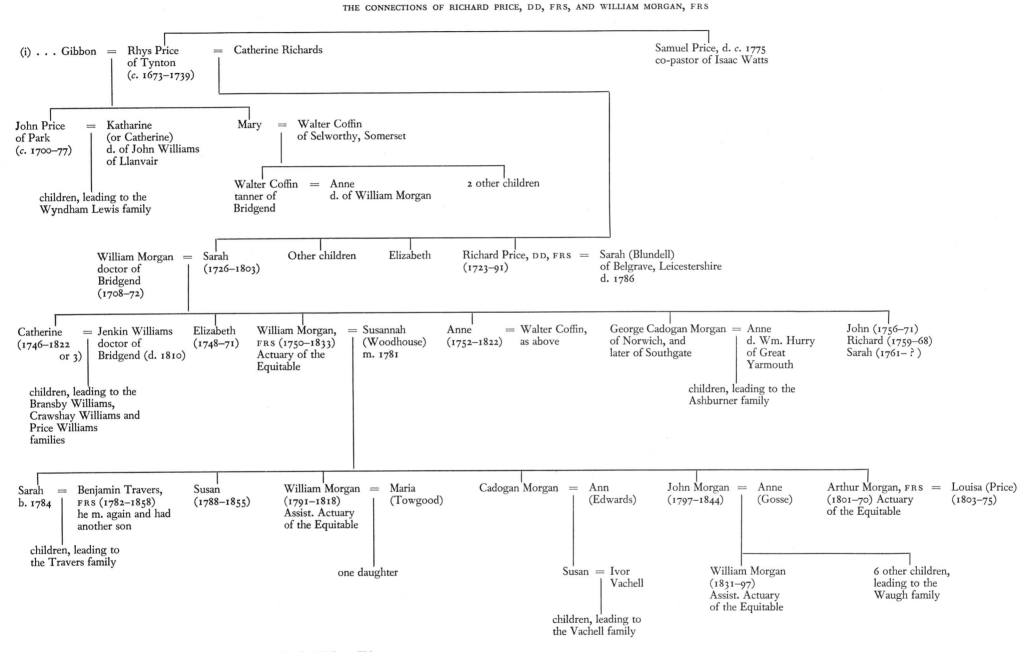

The connections of the family are described by Sir William Elderton, in *The Genealogist's Magazine*, Vol. 12, No. 10, p. 329 (June 1957).

Augustus Toplady used this theme for 'spiritual improvement' and, at the end of his article, he printed his well-known hymn, *Rock of Ages*. The thought of the magnitude of our own indebtedness echoes in it, especially in the lines:

> 'Not the labour of my hands
> Can fulfil Thy law's demands'.

In the years 1773 to 1776, Adam Smith was living in London while he was writing *The Wealth of Nations*. Richard Price and Benjamin Franklin were members of the circle of friends in which Adam Smith moved and he was in the habit of discussing with them the sheets of his book as it was written. Price would have been well acquainted with his views and Adam Smith thought that bankruptcy would follow any great increase of public debt.

Richard Price advocated two remedies, neither, of course, original:

> No money should be borrowed except on annuities which are to terminate within a given period . . . and time would do that necessarily for the public, which, if trusted to the economy of the conductors of its affairs, might possibly never be done . . . And, by providing an annual saving to be applied invariably, together with the interest of all the sums redeemed by it, to the purpose of discharging the public debts: or, in other words, by the establishment of a permanent sinking fund. . . . It would give a vigour to public credit, which would enable a state always to borrow money easily, and on the best terms.

The general principles which Price enunciated in his earlier writings are easier to accept than some of his arithmetical applications of them and the developments of his arguments to which he was led in the course of the later controversies.

Price has been criticized because he emphasized the power of the sinking fund to redeem debt, whereas it is argued that national debt can be redeemed only by an excess of revenue over expenditure. Yet this was explicit in his early writings. He called the sinking fund an 'annual saving'. He said that 'it would have been easy to have annexed to each loan a fund producing a surplus of 1 per cent after paying the interest'. Later, in discussing the current situation, he assumed a sufficient surplus to cover the existing loans and also the burdens of future expenditure for twenty years. 'If this is not true,' he said, 'we have, I think, nothing to do but wait the issue, and tremble.'

These quotations show that it is untrue to charge Price with a lack of understanding of the economic truth about public debt. But in his anxiety to compel governments to financial virtue by the rigid operation of a sinking fund, he gave insufficient weight to the consequences if virtue were not in them. This is strange because he would have maintained that individual men and women cannot be compelled to be virtuous by law. Why should it be possible to compel governments to produce a real financial surplus when the will was lacking?

There is no space to describe how the sinking fund was established by Pitt in 1786, with the help and advice of Dr Price, and put in charge of the Commissioners for the Reduction of the National Debt (now known as the National Debt Office). The financial dam of the sinking fund was swamped by the flood-tide of revolution in France and the French wars. Richard Price died in 1791 and his financial mantle fell on his nephew, William Morgan, who became a sharp critic of Pitt's administration.

The blame for the failure of the sinking fund arrangements has been put wholly on Price but this is scarcely fair. The root of the trouble was that the scheme was visionary. It was altogether too ambitious to be viable in the world of practical politics. And it was completely out of touch with reality in a world at war. The sinking fund was mismanaged in peace-time. The impact of war expenditure on the finances left Morgan despairing:

> I do not know even whether . . . it would not have been better that the sinking fund had never been established . . . the nation might perhaps have been awakened into a sense of its danger. . . . But instead of this it has been led to place its whole reliance on an impotent plan.

The implication is that Morgan would have stopped the plan there and then. The drain of bullion caused a general alarm about the currency. Panic caused a run on the country bankers. The Bank of England became alarmed and on Sunday, February 26, 1797, the Privy Council ordered the Bank to stop payment (i.e. in gold) on the following day. Thus the paper currency became inconvertible. Morgan was unsparing in his criticism of Pitt:

> The diminution of specie in the Bank appears to be the effect neither of this alarm, nor of that instance of prodigality. The evil has been gradually increasing for more than two years; nor can the minister deny that, during the greater part of that time, he has been repeatedly warned of its progress.

The circumstances of the French wars must be borne in mind when reading these criticisms. Morgan was opposed to the whole policy of war as well as to the financial administration.

Such methods of finance must end in inflation. Some idea of the damage to the currency can be gained from Silberling's cost-of-living index:[1]

| Year | Index |
|------|-------|
| 1790 | 100 |
| 1798 | 121 |
| 1799 | 143 |
| 1800 | 170 |
| 1801 | 174 |
| 1802 | 138 |

The note circulation averaged £6,800,000 in the years 1780–86 and £11,000,000 in 1791–97, with a peak of £14,000,000 in February 1795, a sure sign of inflation.

In 1803, Morgan reviewed the whole course of Pitt's financial administration in nineteen years of office. His criticism rises to a strident note. More had been added to the national debt during nine years of war than during the whole of the preceding century. The stoppage of gold payments had been calamitous:

This fatal blow to public credit has been succeeded by an inundation of paper money, which . . . has . . . reduced the greater part of the nation to distress and misery. And yet in the midst of all these calamities . . . the Minister can resign his employment in triumph, and congratulate the country on an envied state of prosperity to which it has been raised during his administration.

The exigencies of war had brought forth new modes of taxation— and drawn Morgan's sarcastic fire:

Happily, by the assistance of his sapient counsellors at the Mansion House, the Minister discovered a new and solid system of finance . . . founded on the humane and equitable principles of the income-tax, so congenial with the dignified feelings of liberty and independence.

By the time a second edition of Morgan's pamphlet was produced later in the year 1803, war had broken out again and Morgan's pessimism and his patriotism were in conflict:

Being now unfortunately engaged in another war, which will probably demand the utmost energies of the nation, it is farthest from my wishes to damp those energies, or in the slightest degree to discourage that proud spirit which should animate us to defend our rights, and to maintain our dignity as a free people.

He must, however, have regarded the increasing cost of war with

[1] *Review of Economic Statistics*, 1923, p. 235 (quoted by Ashton).

horror and his sense of pessimism for the future must have been deepened.

In the years 1795 to 1799, a skirmish was first won, then lost, which has had a considerable effect on the business of life assurance in this country. A new and prosperous industry, such as was life assurance at that time, rather naturally seemed a promising field for new revenue. Pitt, speaking as Chancellor, announced in the House of Commons on February 23, 1795 that the next tax would fall upon 'insurances on ships, cargoes, and lives, from which would result a sum of £160,000'.

Sir Charles Morgan, the President of the Society, happened to be also the Chairman of a Committee of the House of Commons, which reported on February 23, 1795, on the projected duty of 10 per cent on life assurance premiums. Such a duty would have been a severe discouragement to a valuable form of thrift. The Court of Directors met specially at 10 o'clock on the morning of March 5, 1795; their feelings can be imagined but they mildly recorded 'several objections presenting themselves against that mode of ascertaining the tax (if any tax shall ultimately be deemed requisite)'. A few days later, Sir Charles Morgan had an interview with the Chancellor and hoped to secure some modification of the tax. On March 25, 1795, Sir Charles took the chair at first but then left the meeting and went off with Richard Frewin for a second interview with the Chancellor. They returned in time for Sir Charles to resume his place in the chair and to report on what had taken place. The Chancellor had determined to recommend a modified tax which would apply to new assurances only and which would be calculated upon the sum assured—at the rate of £1 per £100 in the first year and 10s per £100 in each subsequent year. This would raise much more tax from temporary assurances, which escaped comparatively lightly under the original proposals, and so it might be hoped that whole life assurances, the more provident type of life assurance, would be encouraged instead of being discouraged.

The representations, however, were even more successful because the Chancellor found that the duty on Scots spirits would produce considerably more than he had estimated and he was able to heed the 'forcible objections' that had been made against the expediency of the tax upon life assurances. 'The idea of imposing any tax upon life assurances has been altogether relinquished' (W, April 1, 1795).

The Society subscribed £50,000 to a public loan in 1796. When, however, invasion was threatened and a public subscription was raised as a kind of voluntary tax 'for the defence of the country at this important crisis', there were doubts about the propriety of voting money to the subscription. Counsel advised that the General Court had no authority to subscribe 'without the consent of each individual member' (G, March 27, 1798).

The most serious challenge was to come. Later in the year 1798, a Bill was introduced into Parliament which sought to impose a tax upon income. A first perusal of the Bill left the directors with the impression that its provisions did not 'attack upon the revenues of the Society'. At an early stage of the Bill, a provision had been inserted which directed the two chartered corporations and the Equitable to nominate commissioners for the general purposes of the Act but, on consideration of the different constitution of the Equitable, it had been relieved of this requirement. Friendly societies were exempt and, by analogy, the Equitable should also escape taxation. The directors, however, deceived themselves; it is interesting to speculate what might have been, had the Court made strong representations in time.

The Commissioners appointed by the Act at once sent demands to the trustees of the Society. In reply, the Court of Directors prepared a memorial claiming that the Society was exempt, as were friendly societies; the Commissioners acted with remarkable speed for within a week they had written rebutting the memorial. William Bray was instructed to take Counsel's opinion but, unfortunately, Counsel agreed with the Commissioners. Further resistance seemed 'inexpedient and fruitless'. The Court of Directors, therefore, decided to make a compromise offer of £3,600 for one year's tax on the average amount, over the previous three years, of the interest on the mortgages and the dividends on the stock of the Society less the expenses of management (W, May 29, 1799). Presumably, the premiums were regarded as being the Society's 'capital', a word then used in that context, and the interest and dividends the Society's 'income' earned on the 'capital', which income, after allowing for expenses, would be chargeable to income tax. The actual amount paid was £3,522 16s 6d, some discount being allowed.

In the closing words of Morgan's speech in 1800 he referred to the 'pre-eminence' of the Society, which does suggest that by that time there were competitors in the field of life assurance. The Society was left to develop life assurance on its own for about twenty years but the beginnings of competition are seen in the closing years of the century.

The first office to compete directly with the Equitable was the Royal Exchange Assurance, one of the two corporations founded by Royal Charter in 1720. Life assurance by yearly contracts, similar to those for other insurance risks, had no great success; its appeal was too limited in character. The total life premiums collected by the Royal Exchange Assurance in the whole period of sixty-two years 1721–83, amounted to £33,840. The claims amounted to £18,263, i.e. seven-thirteenths of the premiums. Considering that the usual rate of premium was 5 per cent for a year's assurance, the rate of mortality was comparatively high though a knowledge of the ages would be required for a sound judgment of the experience. In the year 1783, the Royal Exchange Assurance commenced a new life assurance fund for the transaction of temporary and whole-life assurances with premiums suitably graduated for age and the number of years the assurance was to run. It thus put its life assurance business on a scientific basis comparable to the Equitable. It would be interesting to know what table of mortality was used and who made the actuarial calculations, but there is no surviving record of either the person or the table. The scale of premiums for assurances for the whole of life was at about the same level as was charged by the Equitable between 1777 and 1782, i.e. before the Northampton table was introduced. The premiums were less at the ages of 30 and 40 but were more at the youngest and oldest ages than would have been charged by the Equitable.

Some six years later the first moves were made towards the establishment of another life assurance society which would be modelled more on the lines of the Equitable, except that a capital was to be raised so that the office would be a proprietary one. The promoters hoped to obtain incorporation by Act of Parliament but the Amicable opposed the petition and it was unsuccessful. The office was finally established three years later, in 1792, as the West-minster Society for Insurance of Lives and Survivorships, under a deed of settlement which provided for a capital of £150,000, of which £50,000 was paid up. It was the first proprietary life office. In the early years of the nineteenth century, it had a common management and directorate with the British Fire Office.

Little is known about this Society. Charles Hutton refers to the equitable terms on which the Westminster Society proposed to deal and the known ability and accuracy of the mathematicians and calculators employed in conducting it. The scale of premiums for assurances for the whole of life was a little less than the one used by the Equitable between 1782 and 1786 (before the 15 per cent addition was removed). The Society had a life of seventy-one years and was amalgamated with the Guardian Assurance Company in 1863. It should not be confused with the composite office of a similar name which was founded many years later and was also amalgamated with the Guardian.

The only other competitor before the end of the century was a life office which was started in conjunction with a fire office. The Phoenix Assurance Company (established as the 'New Fire Office' in 1782) formed a separate life office under the name of the Pelican Life Insurance Office in 1797. The name 'Phoenix' seems a fairly obvious choice for a fire office but the name 'Pelican' seems less obvious for a life office and it would be interesting to know whether the choice was influenced by the fact that the seal used by the trustees of the Equitable from the early days had a design based upon a pelican feeding its young. The Phoenix and the Pelican were amalgamated in 1907.

In the *Courier and Evening Gazette* for Tuesday, November 28, 1797, the Pelican referred to the 'increasing demand for life insurance in its various branches' and held forth 'an ample capital in Government securities' as being a 'proper basis for public confidence'. Policyholders were 'not liable to any calls'—a dig at the Equitable. The scale of premiums was set at a little lower level than the Equitable's.

As it happens, a copy of Morgan's book of 1779 has been preserved which originally belonged to George S. Griffin Stonestreet and which contains marginal comments (presumably written by him) on Dr Price's preface. His signature is dated 1800 and the comments would have been added at about that time; they are vitriolic. George Griffin Stonestreet was one of the original directors of the Pelican; the writer of the marginal comments would have been related to him and possibly got some of his opinions from him. The comments show the kind of criticism that could be levelled against the Society by a competitor.

*Dr Price:* 'They (the Directors) might have reduced them (the premiums) much more . . .'—an allusion to the 15 per cent addition made when the Northampton table was first introduced.

*Comment:* 'but it (the Society) had assumed the stile [*sic*] of Equitable during many years in which its rates were exorbitant by the Learned Doctor's admission'.

*Dr Price:* 'When I speak of full security, I must be understood to mean all the security that property in the public funds can give. It is earnestly to be wished this was greater than it is. . . .'

*Comment:* 'A Morganic sneer!'—actually, of course, it was Dr Price's remark.

*Dr Price:* 'It (the return of the whole "overplus" paid in premiums) is in itself a measure of the most pernicious tendency. . . .'

*Comment:* 'Ergo—A Society or company not encumbered by such engagements may safely make that reduction and charge only as much premium as the value of the life requires.'

Dr Price had recommended Dr Haygarth's *Register of Mortality* at Chester as 'fitted for shewing the true law (of mortality)'.

*Comment:* 'Who (i.e. Dr Haygarth) has himself declared their imperfections.'

*Dr Price:* '. . . it is of particular consequence that the Society . . . should distinguish between those cases in which its interest requires it to compute from observations that give the chances of life too high, rather than from those which give them too low'.

*Comment:* 'i.e. that they should abide by their Table or depart from it, as suits their inclination'.

*Morgan:* 'It is obvious that so far as it (a life office) does not regulate itself according to these principles, it must proceed in the dark, and be either requiring exorbitant contributions on the one hand. . . . *Comment:*—like the Equitable—or laying the foundation for future disappointment on the other.'

*Morgan:* 'The probabilities of life in a society should always be a little higher than those in the tables, in order to balance the necessary expenses of management, and to enable it to lay up against any particular season of mortality.'

*Comment:* 'Vide Northampton Table for that.'

After a comparison of the mortality experience with various tables . . . the comment is:

'Ergo—Dr Halley's and De Moivre's Tables are nearer the truth than your Northampton.'

As the eighteenth century drew to its close, the standing of the Equitable Society can be seen from an article 'Assurances' in *A Mathematical and Philosophical Dictionary* by Charles Hutton, LL D (1796). Set somewhat incongruously in the midst of articles on various subjects in pure and applied mathematics, this article discussed the various kinds of life assurance then available—possibly because the transaction of life assurance requires an understanding of the mathematics on which it is based. The article mentioned five 'principal offices' for making life assurances—the two chartered corporations, the Amicable, the Equitable and the Westminster. The Pelican was ignored. The Equitable received its full title, 'The Society for equitable Assurances on Lives and Survivorships'; 'equitable' is spelled with a small 'e' and was clearly thought of as an adjective, rather than a name. In short, the article says there are 'no kinds of assurances on lives and survivorships which this Society does not make. . . . In doing this, the Society follows the rules which have been given by the best mathematical writers on the doctrine of life annuities and reversions'.

The business of the Society required skilful mathematicians to conduct it; if it came into the hands of persons not possessed of sufficient ability, such mistakes might be committed as would prove 'detrimental and dangerous' but, the article continues:

There is reason to believe that at present the Society is in no danger of this kind; one of the great public advantages attending it, is that it has established an office where not only the business (of life assurance) is transacted with faithfulness and skill, but where all persons who want solutions of any questions relating to life annuities and reversions may apply and be sure of receiving just answers.

The amount of space given to the Equitable and the approval with which Hutton wrote of its affairs clearly show that he placed that Society far ahead of its rivals and that the talents of William Morgan were no small influence in the formation of this favourable opinion.

# CHAPTER X

# THE TREDEGAR FAMILY

THE Tredegar family[1] gave three Presidents to the Society. As has been seen, Charles Gould took the over-all direction of the Society at a time when it was weak and divided. His strength of character brought it through this difficult period. He was fortunate in his advisers, and especially in Dr Price and William Morgan, but they were fortunate in his steady support.

Gould was a man of good family who rose by his own abilities and exertions to high office and who, by a fortunate marriage, was led into a position of great power and influence. He was the elder son of King Gould of Westminster, the Deputy Judge-Advocate—presumably a lawyer though he was not a member of any of the four Inns of Court. Charles was educated at Westminster, and proceeded to Christ Church, Oxford, in 1743. His chosen profession was the law and on January 11, 1742 (1743 N.S.) he was admitted to Lincoln's Inn.[2] In the following June he matriculated at Oxford; he would have been in residence at Christ Church from 1743 to 1747, when he graduated BA, and from 1747 to 1750 in Lincoln's Inn. He was called to the Bar on November 20, 1750 and in the same year received his MA.

In Charles's early years as a barrister, he helped his father with the work of the office of Deputy Judge-Advocate. King Gould was friendly with John Bradstreet, who at that time was Deputy Governor of St John's, Newfoundland; Charles's correspondence with Bradstreet provides a lively commentary both on the military situation in America and the political situation at home. Thus, on April 18, 1755, Charles Gould wrote: 'Our world here is lottery mad: a subscription having been opened for a million, in five days it became

---

[1] The Tredegar papers are at the National Library of Wales, Aberystwyth.
[2] Not Middle Temple as stated in various works of reference.

near four times full, £3,880,000 being subscribed for.' On August 2, 1756, Charles Gould told Bradstreet of his 'distress for the loss of the best of fathers', whose 'old complaint' had ended in a mortification of the foot.

The Gould home was at Ealing and another letter of January 3, 1756 gives a glimpse of happiness in the time spent 'round our Christmas fire'. Charles Gould's housekeeping accounts at Ealing start with 1756, the year of his father's death. He was friendly with the Morgans of Tredegar, a family of ancient Welsh descent, with vast estates in South Wales and Monmouthshire. At a guess, the friendship started with William Morgan, who entered Christ Church at the same time as Charles Gould and who was then described as being the son of William Morgan of Westminster, though he was in fact the heir to the Tredegar estates.

William Morgan's cousins lived at Ruperra Castle, another seat of the Tredegar family, just over the county border in Glamorgan. There were five children in this family, Thomas, Jane, Katharine, Charles and John, and Charles Gould became friendly with Charles Morgan. Possibly, Charles Gould had been invited to the Tredegar home; he was taken into the family circle and, in February 1758, married Jane Morgan, his friend's sister. At the time of the marriage, he could have little thought that it would lead him into a vast inheritance, for his father-in-law had not then succeeded to the baronetcy; the Tredegar estates were in the possession of the elder branch of the family and, even if his wife's family should succeed to the estates, she had three brothers who would rank ahead of her. As it happened, William Morgan died unmarried in 1763 and Thomas Morgan of Ruperra succeeded to the baronetcy and the Tredegar estates.

Charles Gould's outstanding abilities were recognized by his appointment as Judge Advocate-General in 1771. In the following year he was appointed Chancellor of the diocese of Salisbury and Chamberlain of Brecknock, Radnor and Glamorgan. In his appointment as Recorder of Newport in 1775, family connection played some part because Charles and John Morgan, and also Charles Van who had married Katharine Morgan, were among those who officially attested the appointment, but he had the requisite abilities, too. None of these appointments required his absence from London for long at a time and most of his correspondence was conducted from his chambers at the Horseguards, Whitehall. Thus, on September 16, 1789:

> I am at present only in town for an hour or two in a day, as business requires, my apartments being under a general repair and not a bed standing. I believe I shall set out for Breconshire on Tuesday next and cannot speak with certainty of my return into Middlesex till the beginning of November.

Gould kept an open house in the social life of his days as, for example, when he was at Bath in 1776. Boswell, on Sunday, April 28, 1776, 'went to Gould's and played a rubber'. Two days later, he noted: 'Pump room gay. Breakfasted at Gould's . . . called on the Heron's at Mrs Cochrane's and sat with Gould a little.'

With the help of the Morgan family, Gould was duly elected M.P. for the borough of Brecon in 1778, and for the county of Brecon—conferring a higher social status—in 1787. As Judge Advocate-General, he held office under the Crown and was one of those useful members who could usually be relied upon to support the King's government, whichever faction happened to be in power. He was knighted in 1779.

Gould subscribed in 1769 to Syprut's Society for Annuities Encreasing to the Survivors. He was not one of the original trustees but he became one in or before 1788, since there was no meeting for the election of a trustee between 1788 and 1802, and he took the chair as one of the trustees at the general meeting on February 18, 1802 at the Jerusalem Coffee-house in Cowper's Court, Cornhill. The other trustees were Henry Thornton, the well-known banker and economist, Thomas Henry Hume and William Masterman.

His wife's three brothers, Thomas, Charles and John Morgan, successively held the Tredegar baronetcy and when John died the male line became extinct. John Morgan left the Tredegar estates to Charles Gould as being the husband of the elder sister, the condition being that he should assume the name and bear the arms of the Morgan family, which he duly petitioned the Crown to do. He was created a baronet on November 15, 1792, and assumed the family name of Morgan on the following day. The arms granted to him incorporated the chevron with thistles and roses which had been his as Gould.

As Sir Charles Morgan, Bart., he became one of the great magnates and he played this part worthily, with care for family interests and (for example) gifts of clothing to the poor at Christmas—listed in 1794 but probably a regular practice—and subscriptions to the charity school at Ealing and to the Ealing Sunday School. In due season, on September 22, 1802, he took the oath as Privy Councillor. One ambition eluded him; he thought himself worthy of a peerage, especially by reason of his long service as Judge Advocate-General, and he had the means to support the dignity. In the years 1802 and 1803 he tackled Lord Sidmouth on the question but the honour was denied him.

In 1806, at the age of 80 years, he felt he had to retire both from his seat for Monmouthshire and from his office as Judge Advocate-General. The formal address by the Grand Jury of Brecon on this occasion showed the esteem in which he was held, referring to 'a length of judicial services far exceeding any on record'. He continued to serve the Equitable, though he could not be present as frequently as formerly. After the annual meeting in May 1806, when he was re-elected President, he wrote from Downing Street:

My son informs me that the Directors have done me the honour of appointing me President . . . nominate Mr Chamberlain Clark and Mr Silvester, the Recorder, to be my Vice-Presidents.

Before the end of the year he was dead. The cause of his death, on December 6, 1806, was recorded as 'decay of nature'—the natural ending of a long and healthy life. It is interesting that his assurances, originally for £5,000, produced with bonuses a claim for £9,965, virtually double the amount assured.

When the shadow of death falls across such a man, the tributes paid to his memory tend to be mere eulogies. But making allowance for this, it is clear that Gould was a man of exceptional ability and firm character, well worthy of the greatness that came upon him. How fortunate was the Equitable in having such a leader.

A talented and successful father may be a handicap to the son who has to follow him. Charles Gould's eldest son was born when Gould was a young man, just making his way in his chosen profession. By the time Gould had inherited the Tredegar estates and become Sir Charles Morgan, Bart., the son himself was already in his thirties. He was one of a family of four children—Jane, Charles, Elizabeth and John.

The father and his two sons all went to Westminster School but the sons did not follow their father to Oxford. The American War of

Independence had broken out and in 1777, at the age of 17, Charles became an ensign in the Coldstream Guards. He served in America and gained his Lieutenancy (with rank of Captain) in the spring of 1781. He was captured at Yorktown in the autumn of that year. In the spring of 1782, his younger brother John was killed in the naval battle off Dominica, when Rodney won back for England the control of the Atlantic. The war ended with the acknowledgment of American independence on November 30, 1782.

The younger Charles Gould had sufficient ability to follow his father as M.P. for the borough of Brecon, which seat he held from 1787 to 1796, and for Monmouthshire from 1796 to 1831. But whereas his father's interests had been centred in London, his own seem to have been more in his country estates, though he was regular in attendance at the Society's meetings when he was in London. Parliamentary business would have required his presence there and in 1810 he bought the lease of 70 Pall Mall. In 1847, soon after his death, his son sold the remainder of the lease to the Guards' Club.

With the change in family fortunes in 1792, Charles Gould, jnr., took the surname Morgan and, as heir to the inheritance, he made his home in Ruperra Castle at Machen, where he was within a few miles of Tredegar Park. He had a large family—four sons and four daughters—and, when he succeeded to the Tredegar estates, he established himself as a friendly and hospitable country gentleman. Christmas parties became a tradition at Tredegar House, large numbers of guests being invited to stay for the festivities. A 'delightful Christmas' in 1809 was paid an enthusiastic tribute in verse. Sir Charles kept up the homely tradition for forty years. When he went on a tour of Scotland in 1813, he described it all in rhymed couplets—but they are (regrettably) too pedestrian to be quotable.

He was generous in mind and in act. As a thank-offering when his son and heir came of age in 1813, he made a gift to the building fund of the Calvinistic Society of Newport—and received an address of thanks from the minister, the Rev. John Rees. At Christmas in 1814, he arranged for his agent, Thomas Bold, to distribute £100 among the poor of Brecon; this kind of action was a regular feature of his life.

Sir Charles Morgan was a munificent supporter of the agricultural interest. He is said to have spent £5,000 a year in prizes for the cattle shows at Tredegar. He erected the market place in Newport at his own expense. By way of testimony for his services to the county, the people of Monmouthshire presented him with plate worth £3,000.

Like his father, he was ambitious for the dignity of a peerage and, in 1814, he made a determined attempt to secure it. His first approach to Lord Sidmouth was rejected out of hand. Undaunted, he tried the Duke of York and received a friendly answer, but nothing came of it. The peerage had to wait for the third generation of the family.

One fact is clear from his correspondence. A warm friendship sprang up between Sir Charles Morgan and William Morgan. Sir Charles was ten years younger than the Actuary and lived in a different social milieu. But he had a warm admiration for William Morgan's abilities and gave him his firm support throughout the difficult years.

Though Sir Charles lived to the advanced age of 86 years, he retained his faculties to the end and was in church at Bassaleg Cheval as usual about a month before he died. His death on December 5, 1846 was ascribed to a 'continued fever' but it cannot have lasted long and would have been some kind of acute infection. It was characteristic of him that 'a genuine and warm philanthropy . . . marked almost every day of his long and valuable life'. He was held in such esteem that a public subscription was raised for the erection of a mound on the top of Coed y Defaid as a testimonial to him; the mound cannot be traced and may not have been, in fact, erected.

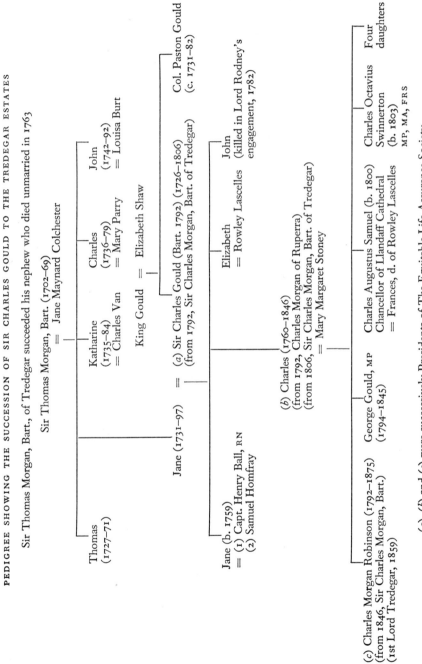

PEDIGREE SHOWING THE SUCCESSION OF SIR CHARLES GOULD TO THE TREDEGAR ESTATES

Sir Thomas Morgan, Bart., of Tredegar succeeded his nephew who died unmarried in 1763

Sir Thomas Morgan, Bart. (1702–69)
= Jane Maynard Colchester

Thomas
(1727–71)

Katharine
(1735–84)
= Charles Van

Charles
(1736–79)
= Mary Parry

John
(1742–92)
= Louisa Burt

Col. Paston Gould
(c. 1731–82)

King Gould = Elizabeth Shaw

Jane (1731–97) = (a) Sir Charles Gould (Bart. 1792) (1726–1806)
(from 1792, Sir Charles Morgan, Bart. of Tredegar)

Elizabeth
= Rowley Lascelles

John
(killed in Lord Rodney's
engagement, 1782)

Jane (b. 1759)
= (1) Capt. Henry Ball, RN
(2) Samuel Homfray

(b) Charles (1760–1846)
(from 1792, Charles Morgan of Ruperra)
(from 1806, Sir Charles Morgan, Bart. of Tredegar)
= Mary Margaret Stoney

(c) Charles Morgan Robinson (1792–1875)
(from 1846, Sir Charles Morgan, Bart.)
(1st Lord Tredegar, 1859)

George Gould, MP
(1794–1845)

Charles Augustus Samuel (b. 1800)
Chancellor of Llandaff Cathedral
= Frances, d. of Rowley Lascelles

Charles Octavius
Swinnerton
(b. 1803)
MP, MA, FRS

Four
daughters

(a), (b) and (c) were successively Presidents of The Equitable Life Assurance Society

144

The Armorial Bearings of the Society

# CHAPTER XI

# FLOOD-TIDE (1801–1819)

WITH the opening of the new century, the tide was flowing strongly and the life assurance business was rapidly increasing. The growth in business brought its own problems and why this was can be seen by considering the rather primitive structure of the companies at that time.

In 1720, at the time of the 'South Sea Bubble', a statute was passed with the object of restraining the promotion of wild schemes:

Whereas it is notorious that several undertakings or projects . . . have, at times since June 1718, been publicly contrived and practiced within London . . . and the persons who contrive or attempt such dangerous and mischievous undertakings or projects, under false pretences of public good, do presume . . . to open books for public subscriptions, and draw in many unwary persons, to subscribe therein, . . . ; and whereas in many cases the said undertakers or subscribers have presumed to act as if they were corporate bodies, and have pretended to make their shares in stocks transferable or assignable without any legal authority. . . .

Section 19 enacted that all such unlawful undertakings and attempts should be deemed public nuisances.

The thought behind the Act was that every promoter of a project must be liable to answer for its debts with all his fortune; he was to be denied both the limitation of liability which could be gained by incorporation and the possibility of shuffling his liability on to an unwary third party by transfer of shares. The Act served its purpose because little use had to be made of its provisions and it remained dormant for the best part of a century, when it was suddenly revived in quite altered circumstances.

The growth of business activity had led to the establishment of business concerns which appeared to have the form of companies, though they were, in law, partnerships. A promoter named Dodd, in 1807, made the mistake of thinking that the subscribers' liability could be limited to the amount of the subscription. When his schemes were published, the Act of 1720 was invoked to prevent his carrying them into execution. *The King v. Dodd* (9th East 516) was the first of a number of such cases.

The system of mutual guarantee, whereby each member was, at law, liable for the whole debts of the concern, was quite unsuitable for the large businesses that were developing. It placed an unwarranted liability on the individual member, who might have taken little part in the promotion of the project. It virtually required each member to have a say in the running of the business. And the concern could only sue and be sued at law in the names of all members of the partnership, unless the funds were held by the trustees.

The fear of an unlimited liability could be a severe handicap to the growth of the business of a mutual assurance society, because the contingent liabilities could be so large. It was only natural that extreme caution should be shown in the distribution of surplus. The prime consideration was to establish the credit of the business on an unassailable foundation. However, caution also had its dangers. If too much surplus were held back, those members whose contributions had built up the fund would have passed on before the surplus was distributed. Hence, the next generation would reap where the first generation had sown. The system worked well so long as each generation was content to pass on the heritage it had received from the previous generation of members. But suppose that new members, attracted by the large reserved surplus, came flooding in with more thought of benefit to themselves than of provision for their families? In a society always open to new members, the danger was a real one.

Had the business had the benefit of incorporation, its permanent existence would have been protected. But the loose form of organization of a mutual society, with the character of a partnership, could be too easily dissolved or disrupted. There was an especial danger of such a happening when the existing members felt that too much surplus was being held back and too little distributed for their benefit. Since it was only human for the members to want as large a distribution of surplus as possible, the Court of Directors, under the advice and guidance of the Actuary, had to act as guardians of the interests of future generations as well as their own. The problem was one of equity between different generations and yet not merely one of equity. There could well be a conflict between the professed equity of the mutual system and the practical needs of the business for building up the surplus to give permanent security.

Members of the Equitable had ample opportunity in the quarterly meetings to bring forward their own pet ideas regarding the way the business should be run. For example, an attempt was made to secure the future (and tie the hands of the directors) by the provision of a capital of £2,000,000, invested in the 4 per cent and 3 per cent stocks, and held as a reserve in perpetuity under a Charter; the motion was negatived (G, June 2, 1803) and a bye-law was adopted which required notice of any motion affecting the Society's cash—an additional safeguard to the rule that resolutions should not take effect until they had been confirmed by two General Courts.

Five directors were elected each year and the Court of Directors had been accustomed to recommending the names of suitable candidates. One member, who wished to curb the powers of the Court, proposed that the practice be discontinued and another, that directors who had served three years should be ineligible for re-election for two years; the latter proposal was referred to Counsel (Sp. Perceval, Thomas Manners Sutton, Wm. Garrow) who did not think that it was 'competent to the General Court to make a bye-law so contrary to the terms of the original Institution as that proposed would be . . .' (G, December 1, 1803).

In the same year, notice was given of a motion that the 'expediency of petitioning the Crown for a charter' should be considered. Nothing more was heard of this, though it would have been the best solution of the problems, assuming that, by this time, the petition had a reasonable chance of success. Were soundings made? It seems unlikely that they would have gone unrecorded.

Within five years of the last distribution of surplus, some members were thirsting for another one. They went to the length of requisitioning the Actuary to convene a special meeting of the General Court, but the Court of Directors reacted vigorously (G, February 28, 1805):

. . . it would argue an improvident avidity and excite an opinion by no means conducive to the credit and stability of the Society to be so soon looking out for a further increase of the claims . . . a period of ten years affords not more than a reasonable pause for an accumulation of profits.

Though the Court of Directors was firm in opposition to such requests, it was generous—as far as it could be—in the settlement of claims; this is clearly shown by the attitude of the Court to a well-known case. William Pitt's coachmakers had insured his life with the Pelican Life Assurance Company for the sum of £500 for seven years at an annual premium of £15 15s. Pitt died on February 23, 1806, when three years' premiums had been paid. Throughout the period of the insurance, Pitt had been indebted to his coachmakers for more than £500 and he died insolvent. However, Pitt had served his country well and money granted by Parliament enabled his executors to pay the debt (£1,109 11s 6d) in full. The Pelican resisted the claim on the ground (amongst others) that the interest which had been insured was a debt, and the debt had been paid. Counsel for the coachmakers pleaded in vain 'it is not the debt *qua* debt that is insured, but the life of the debtor . . .'. Lord Ellenborough, CJ—in a judgment which stood for many years, though it was the source of many misgivings in the insurance world—laid down 'This assurance . . . is in its nature a contract of indemnity, as distinguished from a contract of gaming or wagering', and he upheld the Pelican's objections to the claim.

Doubts about this judgment were in the minds of members of the Equitable Society and the directors were asked to consider what their own course of action would be in such a case. Behind the carefully phrased wording of the report, it is apparent that the Court of Directors felt that the Equitable should settle its claims in a more generous spirit:

> This Society has hitherto been distinguished by the liberability of its conduct, they mean as far as is consistent with its permanent interests to persevere in the same course.

In the summer of 1808, there was a renewed attack on the surplus. At the usual quarterly meeting (G, June 2, 1808) a member proposed what seems on the surface an innocent resolution and, when he was unsuccessful, the members behind it requisitioned a special meeting, which took place on the last day of the month, when 238 members were present. The requisitionists were among the older members because they were concerned to ensure that no one would lose a share in the next distribution by dying too soon. Their proposal was that all claimants in respect of deaths after Lady Day 1808 should receive the increase to be allotted in 1810, but they failed to give due notice of their motion and it was declared out of order. The attempt had been foiled.

The end of the ten-year period which had been set was now near; the work of calculating the values of all the policies was put in hand in good time so that the results were available before the end of 1809. There were 7,320 policies in force for total assurances of £8,023,928 and annuities of £11,350. The investigation disclosed a surplus of £1,615,940, a magnificent result; it was well over three times the amount ten years earlier and amounted to about 53 per cent of the assets. Morgan (G, December 7, 1809) sought to satisfy the legitimate desires of members, while preserving the same kind of restraint as formerly:

There are two classes of persons (of very different descriptions indeed) who seem to wish that the investigations were made at shorter intervals. I mean the very old and the new members: the former from the fear of not surviving a period of ten years, the latter from an eagerness to partake of profits from which they have never yet derived any benefit, and towards which they can have contributed but in a very small degree. Happily the liberality and good sense of the great majority have hitherto succeeded in quieting the fears of the one, and checking the impatience of the other, and thus in promoting ultimately the real interests of both. . . . It should be remembered that the original, and indeed the only intention of this Society was to secure the payment of a certain sum on the death of the assured, and that the premiums were computed solely with that view, and not with the remotest idea of any further advantage. I am sorry, however, to observe that other views have lately been cherished, and that many have been induced by the great wealth and prosperity of the Society to assure their lives with most extravagant hopes of benefit to themselves and their families. It will, I am afraid, be very difficult to satisfy the expectations of such persons, and I shall despair of leading them to entertain more just and sober opinions, if what I have already said on the subject shall fail to produce this effect. It is very probable that the term at present appointed for the investigation of the affairs of the Society may appear rather long and perhaps discouraging to some of the older members; but they should recollect that every addition to their claims is much more valuable than it can be in the case of the younger members, and therefore, if the probability of their participating in any future addition is less, the amount of it, should they survive the period, is so much greater as to make their expectations as nearly of the same value with those of the younger members as circumstances will admit. It is, I believe, impossible to devise any method of giving each member his exact share of the profits of a Society which is always open for the admission of an unlimited number of persons to partake of them.

The increase in the claims was £2 10s per £100 assured for each year's premium prior to January 1, 1810. By way of meeting the criticisms of the older members, who feared that they would not survive the full ten-year period to the next investigation, Morgan also recommended, for all assurances existing on December 31, 1809, a further addition of £2 per £100 assured for every payment made after that day so that, in effect, claims would receive some increase for every payment made. This second addition, which would now be called an 'interim bonus', was to cease on January 1, 1820 when it would be replaced by other additions on the customary plan, if all went well.

The magnitude of the bonus declared in 1809 can be seen by considering an assurance effected in the year 1770. On such an assurance, the premium paid in 1809 would be the fortieth year's premium and so the addition to the sum assured at that time was forty times £2 10s, i.e. £100 for each £100 assured. The previous additions amounted to £190 (or slightly less for assurances effected on or after May 1st) and so each £100 originally assured in 1770 had become £390 and was to be increased by £2 for each further premium.

The members accepted the recommendations, with the minor amendment that the £2 10s addition should be given to all assurances existing on December 7th, when the results were announced, and showed their appreciation of Morgan's qualities by recording their thanks:

> For very able and perspicuous report . . . and in particular for the forcible manner in which he has recommended a steady perseverance in the wise, temperate and prudent line of conduct to which the present flourishing state of the Society has been principally owing and which is now more than ever necessary from the increased magnitude of its concerns. . . .

The wording reflects the steady support of Sir Charles Morgan, who had succeeded his father as President on December 17, 1806.

The remarkable results of the 1809 investigation were followed by a flood of new assurances in the first quarter of 1810, when new assurances came in at about double the usual rate at that time, encouraged perhaps by the proposal to grant interim bonuses to new assurances from the day the first premium was paid.

When Morgan made his report on December 7, 1809, he proposed that new assurances effected after December 31, 1809, should also receive the interim bonus but this recommendation was not accepted by the meeting on December 19th and evidently further thought was to be given to the question. A few weeks later, on January 23, 1810, notice was given of a motion by which the additions to claims would not take effect until the sixth year's premium had become due and been paid. This motion was taken in leisurely fashion at the quarterly Courts on March 1, June 7 and September 6, 1810, when the rule was finally confirmed. The mere announcement of the rule may have been enough to check too extravagant expectations, but it seems more likely that the flood of business was just the effect of the announcement of the bonus and did not last more than a few weeks.

In the first decade of the nineteenth century, some five or six more life offices opened for business. The relative position of the Equitable can best be seen through the eyes of Francis Baily F R S, a member of the Stock Exchange, in his pamphlet: *An account of the several Life-assurance Companies, established in London, containing a View of their respective Merits and Advantages*. The preface is dated from his office, No. 13 Angel Court, Throgmorton Street, January 1, 1810. The pamphlet was actually a chapter from his standard work, *The Doctrine of Life-annuities and Assurances* (1813), but was produced separately in advance of the main work, because of its topical interest.

He asserted (what was substantially true) that all life offices at that time charged the same scale of premiums:

> So that, whether a person makes an assurance at the Equitable Society where the sum assured is continually increasing in value, or whether he effects it at any other office where no additional advantage is derived, *he pays precisely the same premium*. Surely this important fact cannot be known by the public, else it is difficult to conceive how any of the newly established offices should ever have been able to extend their business beyond the limits of their own proprietary.

In this, Baily was unfair to those offices that were mutual in character because they would presumably be able to add bonuses to their policies later on, when the surplus had been built up. The superior security of the Equitable:

> Originated from, and is principally maintained by, the power which each member possesses (in his own right) of giving his vote and opinion on all the proceedings of the Society: so that no unfair advantage can be taken by any particular class of the assured.

While, as Baily suggested, the vote can be an important safeguard, what every life office needs is strong leadership by a Board of Directors who act in the manner of trustees for the various, and possibly conflicting, interests:

> A more just and equitable scale (of premiums) ought to be adopted by those societies who do not make any return to the assured of the vast profits that arise from this species of daily traffic; and would tend more to the increase of their business in this way, and would likewise be more honourable to themselves, than the disgraceful practice of *bribing* solicitors, agents and others to effect assurances at their offices: thereby notoriously inducing those parties to *sacrifice* the interest of their employers and their friends. For the money . . . would be more properly and more equitably employed in being appropriated towards a reduction of the rate of the assurance (i.e. the premium): since, if the Company can afford to allow it to the agent, it can surely afford to allow it to the principal and it evidently belongs more justly to the latter than to the former.

By way of explanation, Baily added in a footnote:

> Many of the public companies, who do not make any return of the profits to the assured, allow a liberal premium (generally 5 per cent on the payment made) to any person who will procure an insurance to be effected at their office: and this commission is also allowed to any person who makes the annual payment provided it be not the party himself! ! ! An artifice which is easily seen through: but which opens a door to fraud and imposition, that it cannot be too severely reprobated. . . . I omit to give the names of those companies who have adopted this nefarious practice, under the hope that this mean and improper artifice will not be encouraged in future.

Baily's hope was unrealized; yet there must have been some laxness in the commission arrangements, if his assertions were well founded.

At this stage in the development of life assurance, it is clear that the Equitable had a lead which placed it far ahead of its rivals, notwithstanding that the oldest of them had been operating in competition for some thirty years. The 'reserved third' of surplus had created a wealthy society with a strong appeal to those seeking life assurance, with the additional attraction of a good investment.

The Court of Directors, acting on the advice of the Actuary, was the guardian of the surplus against all manner of encroachments, whether from those who wanted the Society to pay claims in unjustifiable circumstances or from those who simply wanted a larger share of the surplus. The very size of the business, too, made it essential to keep a tight rein on the finances, if losses by default or worse were to be avoided.

John Williams of Fetter Lane had died by his own hand, a contingency which was excluded by the terms of the policy, and the

Court of Directors took its stand on the principle that such claims should not be paid (S, October 10, 1810). However, when the members next met, one of them gave notice of a motion to pay the claim. The Court of Directors re-affirmed the decision not to pay, but the members carried the motion to pay the claim, against their advice (G, March 7, 1811). Three months later the motion was quashed, so that in the end the advice of the Court of Directors was accepted.

Early in the following year, the Society ran into a danger of another kind. On January 2, 1812, the Actuary received a simple but devastating letter from the Society's bankers:

Messrs Boldero's & Co. with the deepest concern inform Mr Morgan that they are under the unavoidable necessity of suspending their payments tomorrow.

By a stroke of ill-fortune, the balance had been temporarily swollen by a sum of £14,000 which had been reserved for a mortgage; the borrower had said he was ready to complete and then put off completion unexpectedly. Including this £14,000, the total balance at stake was £25,781 9s 6d. But one fortunate outcome of this unfortunate affair was that the Court of Directors immediately opened a new account with the Bank of England (S, January 4, 1812) and so began a happy connection which has continued ever since.

Counsel advised that the loss must clearly fall on the Equitable. In the end, something was saved out of the wreck, though it took a very long while. In the years 1818 to 1837, a total of £11,064 was recovered and further dividends from Boldero's estate brought the total to £11,562 by 1864. Thus a total of £14,219 was lost and interest on the money for a quarter of a century. The crash brought down some country banks but caused scarcely a ripple on the surface of the Equitable.

Another danger came from within. One of the clerks, James Jones, who had been appointed to the staff on April 1, 1812, was generally entrusted with the responsibility of taking the cash of the Society into the Bank of England. Just what happened is unrecorded, but he committed some fraud which was possibly discovered by the Bank, who told the trustees, for the fraud came to the ears of the trustees before the Court of Directors knew about 'the serious deficiency in the accounts of the Society' (S, September 27, 1815). It was not until November 1815 that James Jones was reported to have been dismissed, so that the fraud probably took time to be investigated. The next quarterly accounts contained the bleak statement: 'By cash embezzled by James Jones, one of the clerks, £2,979 2s.'

These events need to be seen against the background of the political situation, both internal and external, for they coincided with a dark period in Great Britain's history. At the beginning of 1812, Napoleon seemed to be all-victorious, though the year is remembered, now, for the destruction of the French army in Russia. High prices, with the disruption of economic life by war, and the first effects of the introduction of machinery, the throwing of men out of work, led to the Luddite riots of 1811–12. Industrial unrest was met by repression. Even the peace which followed Waterloo was itself not an unmixed blessing, for the transition from a war to a peace economy led to an acute trade depression in 1816.

As Morgan looked out on the Society's affairs and tried to plan for the future, there is little wonder that his thoughts took a pessimistic turn. He must have felt that the Society was getting out of hand, that he was ageing—his 65th birthday fell in 1815—and that some drastic action was needed to secure the future. He put his thoughts down in some 'observations on the present state of the Society' (S, December 22, 1815). No copy survives; how we would like to know what was in his mind at this time! The observations were considered at three summoned meetings, without any decision being reached; possibly the subject was resumed on May 1, 1816, when the Court gave 'prospective thinking' to the problems of 1820, the next investigation.

The busy minds of certain members of the Society were still at work, devising means for their own enrichment. Was it touched off by the 'prospective thinking' of the directors, or was it merely the sporadic outbreak of an endemic disease? A member gave notice of a motion that would give to members of fifteen years' standing the 'option of accepting stock transferable in lieu of the benefit accruing from their policies'; the idea was to convert the wealth of the Society into usable assets for the then existing members. The motion asked for an application to Parliament and the appointment of a committee which should 'be empowered to examine the Actuary, and his Assistants, and be at liberty to inspect the books of the Society' (G, June 6, 1816). Fortunately the General Court refused to have anything to do with such a suggestion and the motion was still-born. However, it served to determine the directors to take some action to curb members' desires. Two weeks later, Morgan was requested 'to lay before the directors any plan which may occur to him as most likely to prevent an improper increase of new members'.

Within a month, Morgan was ready with some observations on the state of the Society. Whether these were the same as had been circulated in the previous December is unknown, for neither report has survived; it would have been interesting to see how Morgan's ideas had developed in those seven months. Another four months were needed for reflection on his ideas and then, on November 25, 1816, Morgan submitted to the Court of Directors a plan for the future regulation of the Society which was approved nine days later.

The general idea was an extension of the rules adopted in 1810, whereby bonuses did not vest, and the member had no right to vote, until the assurance had been in force five years and the sixth year's premium had been paid. The new member lost little by this rule; if the assured life died within the five-year period, no bonus would be payable, but this was little hardship; if the assured life survived the five-year period, bonuses would thereafter be payable with the claim in the same way as if the assurance had ranked for bonuses from the outset. Morgan had the idea that the waiting period could be extended with advantage and without much harm to the interests of new members. He proposed that no member should have the right to vote and no bonus should be payable with any claim until the assurance had become one of the 5,000 oldest policies in the Society. In effect, this would lead to a flexible waiting period which would lengthen as the number of new assurances grew, or shorten if they lessened.

At the time, the number of assurances in force was about 9,500 but the numbers would be reduced by discontinuances as well as deaths. Many assurances were surrendered or given up for one reason or another and Morgan thought that the number then in force would soon be reduced to 5,000—probably within a period little longer than the existing five-year waiting period.

A waiting period for full membership was not an unreasonable requirement. The varying waiting period was ingenious because however many new members were admitted the balance of voting power would not be upset; effective power would remain with a manageable number of not more than 5,000 members. This corps of older members would not be a static one but would be continually replenished by those recruits who had completed the waiting period. The interests of the older members would tend to be improved by the admission of new members because the early claims amongst the new members would get no bonus. Yet the new members would suffer little loss, because those that survived the waiting period would thereafter be entitled to the full bonus both declared and to be declared in respect of past as well as future premiums. The only ones to suffer would be the early claims amongst the new members, and the early claims are those that by the nature of things do well out of a life assurance fund.

When Morgan put the plan to the members (G, December 5, 1816), he argued that the restrictions already imposed on new assurances proved that the General Court had the legal right to impose such restrictions; also that the flourishing state of the Society proved the wisdom of those measures. He continued:

> The evil, however, though lessened by these laws, has not been entirely removed: the increase of the Society, though rendered more gradual, still remains *unlimited;* and the management of its concerns must in consequence be ultimately exposed to all the difficulties and dangers arising from the overgrowing number of its Members.

> Various plans have been proposed at different times to guard against this evil; but they have generally tended to an alteration of the whole constitution of the Society, and required an application to Parliament to carry them into effect. This of itself has been considered a sufficient objection to them, and all of them have consequently been laid aside. It is indeed highly desirable, whatever laws or regulations are in future adopted, that they should deviate as little as possible from the original plan and design of the Institution. That the Society has the power of restraining the future Members from the participation of the benefits enjoyed by the existing Members during a limited time, has been established by the adoption of the Bye-Laws in 1810. That it has, therefore, the power of *postponing* that participation to a more distant period can admit of no doubt; nor can it make any difference whether the term is limited to a certain number of years, or is made to depend on contingencies which may either shorten or prolong the duration of it. But if it should appear that this alteration, while it improved the interest of the present Members, will render the Society more secure without lessening its usefulness to the public, it becomes not only justifiable but necessary. . . .

> From a comparison of the number of assurances for the whole continuance of life which have been made in the last ten years, with the numbers which have been cancelled during the same time, it appears that the Society has increased upon an average at the rate of more than three hundred in each year. Hence may be inferred

the probable increase during the next ten years; and consequently the inconvenience and danger to which the Society will be exposed, from the great number of those who will have a right to share in the management of its affairs, and an interest to support the premature division of its surplus.

Were the admission of future Members to depend solely on the *deaths* of those already assured, the period would perhaps be postponed too long; for according to the probabilities of life in the Society during the last forty-five years, not one in sixty will die in each year. But the reduction in the number of assurances by forfeiture and surrenders will, agreeably to the experience of many years, be so much accelerated, that the term, were they limited to half their present number, will not be very considerably prolonged beyond the period allotted by the present Bye-Laws of the Society. These regulations, therefore, will probably have little or no effect in preventing the Society from going on to increase as it has done of late years. The prospect, however remote, of participating in the profits of an Institution possessed of such an immense capital, will always secure a preference; and the care thus taken to guard against the improvident distribution of that capital, instead of retarding, must rather accelerate the increase, and add to the credit of the Society. . . .

Possessed of such a capital, it is no wonder that extravagant opinions should be entertained of the Society's opulence, and that many persons should be induced to assure their lives from the hope of soon sharing in the distribution of it. The Society, constituted as it is at present, is open to the public at large; and thus the number of those is continually increasing whose expectations are in danger of being too sanguine . . . the liberality of the Society should not be exercised at the risque of its welfare and security. . . . Were every person in future assuring in this Society to have an addition of £2 *per cent per annum* made to his assurance, and repeated every ten years in the manner hitherto pursued, not one in seven of those assured under the age of thirty will live long enough to pay the accumulated sum which will become due at his decease, nor one in ten under the age of twenty: and yet I very much doubt whether the expectations of those persons would not lead them to anticipate larger and more frequent additions.

A variety of computations (were it proper to introduce them here) might be added to show the utter impossibility of persevering in the present indiscriminate admission of the public to a proportionate share of the Society's surplus, without either lessening the future additions on the one hand, or increasing the annual premiums on the other. . . . The Resolutions now proposed . . . have not arisen from any alarm as to the immediate safety of the Society. On the contrary, . . . its success and prosperity continue uninterrupted—the probabilities of life in the Society bear the same ratio to those in the Table of Observations from which its premiums are computed that they have done for the last forty years, and . . . no circumstance has hitherto occurred to disappoint the reasonable expectations of its Members. . . .

The method of adding to the claims rather than immediately dividing the surplus among the Members, and of restraining the additions to a period of ten years rather than repeating them at shorter intervals, has had the best effect in establishing the credit and promoting the interests of the Society. But while the

Members are daily increasing, and no limits are set to the number of those who are to have a control over the affairs and to partake of the surplus stock of the Society, it is impossible to say that the one shall not at last become too complicated, or that the other, from being divided among so many, may not ultimately be diminished so much as to produce all the evil consequences of disappointed hopes and expectations. . . .

I hope that no person will so far misunderstand me, as to suppose that I wish to infuse any alarms into the minds of the Members respecting the *present* state of the Society. On the contrary, there is every reason . . . for congratulating the General Court on the uniform progress of its success and prosperity. My apprehensions arise not from a *retrospect* of the measures which have been pursued, for no evil has yet been incurred by them, but they arise from looking *forwards* to the measures which may hereafter be adopted, when a new interest may prevail over the prudence and discretion which have always distinguished the Resolutions of the Society. From a small body, possessed of a few thousands (when I first officiated as Actuary), it has, during the course of more than forty years, grown to an institution of great public importance, and become possessed of several millions. It is obvious, therefore, that the Rules and Regulations which were well adapted to its circumstances in an infant state, may now have become altogether impracticable. On this ground the present Resolutions are proposed, as the best means of securing and improving the interests of the present Members, and *in due time* the interests also of those that shall succeed them.

Morgan (in 1829) said that, by the desire of the Court of Directors, he had laid before them two plans. 'The first, being deemed impracticable without an act of parliament, was declined.' For a complete judgment on Morgan's proposal of 1816, it would be necessary to know what was in the alternative plan that had been rejected; on this, the records are silent. Is there some significance in Morgan's reference to the rejected plan as being the 'first'? Can it be inferred that the rejected plan was the one that Morgan would have preferred, had it been practicable? He was, of course, merely explaining what had happened, but he may well have unconsciously shown us which of the plans he favoured; otherwise, why mention that there was another plan?

The fact that the rejected plan would have required an Act of Parliament suggests that it contemplated an alteration of the constitution of the Society. What this new structure was can only be guessed. Greater authority was needed at the centre of the organization, freed from the hazards of government by meetings of the General Court. The Society, too, needed the permanent structure of a corporation rather than the loose form of a partnership, which was unsuited to the affairs of so large a body of members. The 'reserved third' of surplus, which was the foundation of the Society's prosperity, was at the mercy of greedy hands unless the majority of members could be convinced of the wisdom of restraint; some arrangement was needed to establish the reserve more securely. These are mere guesses; the plan is unknown.

When the proposed regulations came up for approval, it was easy to dispose of an amendment which would have confined voting power to the first 4,000, instead of the first 5,000, assurances. Then came an amendment which, while seemingly innocent, in fact substantially altered the character of the scheme and had a profound influence on the future course of events. The amendment was that when an assurance began to participate in bonuses, because the earlier assurances had been reduced below the specified 5,000 in number, the assurance should be entitled to bonuses thereafter *in respect of all the payments made subsequent to such ascertained reduction*, i.e. the premiums paid during the waiting period would not rank for bonus, and the assurance would receive bonuses as if it had been effected when the waiting period was completed.

Consider, for example, assurances effected in the year 1817. The waiting period for these assurances turned out to be at least fourteen years, when they began to come within the first 5,000 assurances. If this was in the year 1831, the assurance thereafter received bonuses as if it had been effected in 1831, and not in 1817. The penalty was a continuing one because bonus was allotted in respect of the whole period of the assurance and fourteen fewer years would rank for bonus on each occasion; the regulation thus affected all claims, not merely those during the waiting period, and the penalty was cumulative.

When the amended resolution came up for confirmation, it was moved and seconded that the original resolution should be adopted in its stead but the motion did not succeed and the amended resolution was confirmed. William Morgan has left no written record of what he thought of this amendment to his scheme, but a glimpse into his mind is granted to us in a letter written many years later (May 29, 1839) by his son, Arthur Morgan, to Thomas Windus, a complaining policy-holder who had inadvertently let his assurance lapse and had it replaced by a new one at the same premium but dated 1817 instead of 1812:

I enclose for your perusal a copy of the bye-laws recommended by my father to the General Court in December 1816, and you will see by attentively reading the fourth clause that he was fully justified in stating to you that it would make comparatively little difference in your position whether your policy were dated in 1812, or 1816,[1] the same being re-issued at the premium chargeable on your life in the former year, as, under the clause as he had penned it, you would now have taken the benefit of the appropriation made in 1820, in 1829, and to be made in 1839, for every payment made upon the policy. Unfortunately for you, the General Court of that day thought fit to make a material alteration in the proposed bye-law, which my father always regretted, and which I have no hesitation in declaring to have been in my own opinion an inequitable extension of the restriction contemplated in the original propositions. Please to return the address and bye-laws when you have copied such parts of the letter as you may wish to extract, as I prize this copy, the only one I have ever seen preserved of the address and bye-laws embodied as they were circulated among the members of the Society.

If William Morgan 'always regretted' the amendment, why did he not try to get it altered subsequently? The answer must surely be that he was loyal to the decision of the General Court, even though he thought it an unwise decision, and would not thereafter challenge it.

What the members thought of William Morgan is shown by a little ceremony (G, June 5, 1817) when Sir John Silvester, Vice-President of the Society, presented to him a silver vase with the inscription:

As a gratefull testimony of the Eminent Services rendered to the Society for Equitable Assurances by William Morgan, Esquire, their Actuary, to the wisdom of whose counsels and to whose indefatigable exertions during more than forty years the unparalleled prosperity of the Institution is in a great degree to be attributed, and to record to his posterity the sense which the Society entertains of those services,

THIS VASE,

was unanimously voted at a General Court of Proprietors on March 6, 1817.

The accounts for 1817 show a gratuity of £1,000 to William Morgan and a payment of £210 to Rundle & Co. for the silver vase. At the same time, William Morgan's portrait was painted by Sir Thomas Lawrence for the benefit of the Society. The portrait now hangs in the Board room; a copy, originally made for a member of the family about 1900, adorns the hall of the Institute of Actuaries in Staple Inn.

[1] The assurance was not, in fact, replaced until 1817.

William Morgan, FRS, by Thomas Lawrence

In spite of the increased business, at this time there were only seven members of the staff (G, March 7, 1816).

| Name | Appointed | Salary in 1816 |
|---|---|---|
| William Morgan, *Actuary* | February 1775 | £800 plus £700 gratuity |
| Thomas Cooper, *Assistant Actuary* | March 1775 | £500 plus £250 gratuity |
| Thomas Hampshire, *Prime Clerk* | March 1797 | £300 plus £200 gratuity |
| William Morgan, jnr. | April 1809 | £300 |
| John Stephenson | June 1809 | £250 plus £50 gratuity |
| Edward Lovelock | November 1815 | £250 |
| John Scott Martineau | January 1816 | £200 |

Clerks: William Morgan, jnr.; John Stephenson; Edward Lovelock; John Scott Martineau

Not much is known about the qualifications of the staff but the two Morgans, Cooper, Stephenson and Martineau were all mathematicians.

The post of Principal Clerk had been created in 1783, when the number of clerks was increased to three. Edward Fastnedge, the first Principal Clerk, became blind with cataract but was cured by the old operation called 'couching'; he was given a gratuity towards the cost of hospital treatment (S, February 8, 1786). When he died of consumption, at the age of 54 in 1812, he left a family of two unmarried daughters and three young sons, who were all granted annuities. His place was taken by Thomas Hampshire.

By 1817, Thomas Cooper had completed forty-two years' service as Assistant Actuary and, being in the sixty-fifth year of age, felt the time had come for him to retire. The Court of Directors recommended a pension of three-quarters of his salary 'the same being the proportion allowed by Act of Parliament to such persons as have faithfully served in any office under Government during a term of not less than forty years'. The General Court generously amended this to a pension of the full salary of £750.

Thomas Hampshire died early in 1819 of jaundice, at the age of 57. He left a widow aged about 48 and a daughter aged 18. The only provision he had been able to make for them was said to be a sum of about £800 from assurances on his life. (Actually, he had effected assurances for £1,000 which were worth £1,306 10s at his death.) The Court of Directors recommended the grant of an annuity of £150 to the widow but the General Court amended this to a lump sum payment of £1,000.

William Morgan's eldest son, William Morgan, junior, had been a member of the staff since 1809 and the retirement of Thomas Cooper made the opening for him to be appointed Assistant Actuary in Cooper's place. It is clear that the father had already made his son his special confidant, looking to him to carry the burden of affairs in due course. It was not to be. He died of 'inflammation of the chest'— presumably tubercular in origin—at the early age of 28, on October 5, 1819. He had much ability and was universally beloved. He had taken a substantial part in the calculations for the decennial investigation; the General Court increased his gratuity of £500 to £1,000 for his dependants. The 'melancholy event' of his death left a gap in the staff arrangements which it was difficult to fill.

The immediate gaps left by the two deaths were filled by the promotion of Stephenson, to be Assistant Actuary, and Lovelock, to be Principal Clerk, but the circumstances of the time made it just as necessary to provide some confidential assistance to William Morgan and his youngest son, Arthur Morgan, was appointed to that office, 'in like manner and with the same salary as his late brother had had at the time of his appointment'. This was the strengthening of the team, desired by his father.

One aspect of the growth of the business that is somewhat puzzling is the accommodation of the Society's premises. In the first quarter of the nineteenth century, it was usual for over 200 members to attend the quarterly meetings and sometimes over 400 were present; they would need a room of considerable size. In 1809, 'the present house having been found too small for the business of the office and for the accommodation of members attending the General Courts', the decision was taken to buy the lease of the house next door for £4,500. Fixtures and fittings brought the total cost to £4,619 12s (G, June 1, 1809). There is no plan of the combined office but perhaps certain rooms were knocked into one, so as to provide a sufficiently large Court room.

The results of the mass of calculations required for the decennial investigation were ready for the Court of Directors on November 23, 1819, just seven weeks after the son's death. There were 9,806 policies in force for total assurances of £12,626,818 and annuities of £8,773. The investigation disclosed a surplus of £3,210,855, which was double the amount ten years earlier and amounted to about 50 per cent of the assets. When Morgan reported the results (G, December 2, 1819), what a contrast there must have been between the splendid figures he had to announce and the ache in his own heart for the son, who had died so untimely:

I know not to what extent the expectations of those persons may have been lately raised who, viewing the amount of the capital (i.e. the funds) without having any regard to the immense claims with which it is charged, consider every addition to that capital as so much addition to the surplus stock of the Society. I must, however, observe to them, that there cannot be a delusion more to be deprecated, nor which in the present circumstances of the Society would lead to more ruinous consequences. Although the capital has increased within the last ten years above three millions, this of itself affords no decisive proof of prosperity. It should be remembered on the other hand, that the sums assured have increased more than double that amount—that half the number of the present assurances have been made since the year 1809—that the other half is composed of assurances on lives ten years older than they were at that period, and consequently so much more valuable—that while the number of assurances is annually increasing, or even while it continues the same without any variation, the stock must necessarily go on to accumulate for many years to come, and that if any measures were adopted to prevent that accumulation, the Society would soon find itself in a state of insolvency. . . .

In the year 1817 the Society commenced a new era, and the experience of every day has served to prove the wisdom of that measure. Though in the short term of three years it could not be expected to have done much in improving the present interests of the Members; yet even in this early stage its operations have not been altogether without effect; for had no such measure been adopted, the assurances entitled to the additions would in that case have exceeded their present number by more than 1200. But its benefits hereafter are likely to be much more considerable. Not only will the Society be rendered more secure, but by confining the future additions to a limited number of claims, these additions must necessarily be increased, and may possibly admit of having a larger proportion of the surplus appropriated to them. Nor are the present Members the only persons likely to profit by the late regulations. Although the expectations of future Members are postponed, they are not taken away. What they lose by having the accomplishment of their wishes deferred to a later period, will be more than compensated to them when they are fulfilled; and if regarded in a proper light, these regulations should be considered as so many precautionary measures, more effectually to guard their interests against the danger arising from the participators in the Society's surplus, at one and the same time becoming too numerous to have their over sanguine expectations gratified to their full extent, without sacrificing the interests of those who are to succeed them. It is a matter of little consequence to the Society whether its Members do, or do not increase; nor is it necessary to point out the great benefit which it has produced, and still continues to produce to the public. The immense capital which it possesses, and the prospect which it holds forth not only to its present, but to its future Members, raises it above all competition, and must ever render it an institution of the highest importance. From the experience of the last three years, the regulations of 1817 appear to have had no other effect than that of rather lessening the number of new assurances, which however, considerably exceed the number of old assurances cancelled, so that the Society still continues to increase, though more slowly. This is the necessary consequence of such a measure, and was to be expected. But it should be observed on the other hand, that the Society may now regard its increase without apprehension . . . it is in no danger of ever becoming too numerous, or of being composed of a multitude of new Members, who, assuring their lives more with the view of present advantage to themselves than of providing for their families, would always be urging an improvident distribution of the Society's stock. . . .

Being arrived at a period in which it is altogether improbable that I should ever be able to engage in another work of the same kind, however ardent my wishes might be to serve the Society, I cannot help being solicitous for the permanent welfare of an Institution so beneficial to mankind, and so much the object of my care and attention during the greater part of my life. The lapse of forty-six years must necessarily be expected to impair the human constitution—nor has mine survived them without injury. The ravages of time, however, had in a great measure been repaired to me by the accession of a near and dear relation to participate in my labours; and who, I had fondly hoped, would have lived to deserve the approbation and confidence of this Society. But all my hopes with regard to him are for ever gone. His assistance, without which I never could have accomplished this work, closed with those laborious computations which are now laid before the General Court, and the fond expectations I had once cherished must now be exchanged for a wish that the Society may ever be served by a person of equal worth and integrity.

For all assurances made before January 1, 1815, and existing on January 1, 1820, the claims were to be increased by £2 10s per £100 assured, for every year's premium due and paid before January 1, 1820. Assurances made between January 1, 1815, and January 1, 1817, were to share similarly in the increase when the required six years' premiums had been paid. Assurances made in and after 1817 came within the regulations of 1816 and did not participate in respect of premiums so far paid.

As on the last occasion, claims before January 1, 1830, were also to receive an increase in respect of each year's premium paid after January 1, 1820 (subject to the same restrictions for assurances made after January 1, 1815), but the amount was raised to the full £2 10s for each £100 assured in respect of each such year's premium.

The magnitude of the bonus declared in 1819 and the comparison with 1809 can be seen by considering an assurance effected in the year 1780, on which forty years' premiums had been paid. The new addition to the sum assured would once again be forty times £2 10s, i.e. £100 for each £100 assured, but the previous additions on this occasion amounted to £180 (or slightly less for assurances effected on or after May 1st). Each £100 originally assured in 1780 had become £380 and was to be increased by £2 10s for each further premium; the comparative figure for an assurance in its fortieth year in 1809 was £390, increased by £2 for each further premium.

# CHAPTER XII

# THE DEFENCES HOLD (1820–1828)

F AR from being satisfied by the wonderful results of the decennial investigation, some members used the occasion for a renewed attempt to secure a larger share of surplus in one way or another, but this time the directors had an effective weapon to counter the attack—-the regulations of 1816.

One of the members wrote to the President, proposing the distribution, also, of the part of the surplus that remained unappropriated but the proposition was rejected out of hand; the older members could not be so benefited without the individual consent of each person assured since 1816. About a year later (was it the same member?), a proposition was made which was more dangerous because it was both more moderate and more specific—either the allocation of a larger share than two-thirds of surplus or a reduction in premiums for policies which had been ten years in force. The directors prepared a considered reply:

> The adoption of such measures would be highly injurious to the credit and security of the Society and is not justified by any extraordinary decrease in the mortality of its members, or by any other circumstance peculiarly favorable [sic] to its finances, except it be the late temporary rise in the public funds, which may (as hath often happen'd) be succeeded by as great a fall, and thus afford as good a reason for increasing the premiums, as it does in the former case for reducing them. Admitting the affairs since the last investigation to have been as prosperous as the most sanguine imagination can conceive, it never can be adviseable from the success of so short a period to break through the established laws of the Society to profit by it.

The report argued that, though persons assured since the year 1816 did not yet share in the profits, they had a prospective interest in the reserved third of surplus, which ought to be protected for their benefit by those who had the management of the Society.

In the grand debate on the proper mode of distributing the surplus, it is important not to lose sight of the actual business of life assurance. Primarily, a life office exists to pay the claims of those who die and some die unexpectedly soon.

Walter Raleigh Smith became assured for £1,000 on March 7, 1820 and died suddenly—a rare happening—three days later on March 10th. He was only 35 years of age and had been reported as being in good health, having had the smallpox and *not* the gout. It would be interesting to know the cause of death but unfortunately the records are silent; it was an illness, rather than an accident, because there was some doubt about the state of Smith's health at the time. He was Collector of H.M. Customs at Southampton and had been unable to appear before the Court of Directors in person at the time the assurance was made. The circumstances may have made the directors suspicious and they consulted Counsel about the claim, but they must have been satisfied, or at least found no grounds for action, because the claim was paid (W, March 14, 1821).

Smith's assurance was an exception. Usually, claims were recorded in full, including the cause of death. These 'causes of death', certified by medical men, were often mere descriptions of what had happened and were unscientific by current standards. As might be expected, 'old age' was the natural end of many members and is frequently recorded as being 'decay of nature', as for William Jones at the age of 72 on September 5, 1818. At older ages, the Rt. Hon. Lady Mary Mordaunt died at 82 on June 22, 1819 of 'extreme debility from age' and Martha Hoffman at 87 on June 29, 1820, of 'lethargy'. Where there was no obvious cause, the death was ascribed to 'visitation of God', as for Charles Nassau Thomas at the age of 69 on May 5, 1819, and George Harper at 83 on February 21, 1820. Harper, presumably, had his full faculties to the end; otherwise some kind of decay would have been mentioned.

A surprisingly large number of deaths were ascribed to apoplexy— about one-eighth of all deaths. Thus Charles Newmarch died of apoplexy at the age of 41 on January 10, 1823, and the Rev. Henry Pengelly at 54 on June 25, 1823. Possibly, these deaths reflect the social conditions of the time, especially the relatively high consumption of alcohol. They would include all deaths in coma, not merely those that would now be attributed to a stroke. The death of Daniel Harper, at the age of 48 on March 6, 1819, from 'exhaustion by fatigue of business' implies a stress which appears more suitable to our own age—but it probably conceals a condition such as coronary thrombosis, so prevalent nowadays. He was a coal master of Tamworth in Staffordshire.

Looking back, it seems unkind to attribute the death of William Jardin Alcock, at the age of 58 on August 24, 1819, to 'general debility by the climate of Canada', as also the death of Major-General William Mudge, at the age of 58 on April 17, 1820, to 'water in the head'.

Tuberculosis, of course, claimed many victims at all ages in active life. Consumption was the recorded cause for about one-fifth of the deaths under the age of 40 and one-tenth of the deaths between the ages of 40 and 60; some of the remainder may also have been due to tuberculosis, though recorded under another cause. A typical case was John Cooper Harries who died at the age of 35 on February 5, 1823; one wonders what family he left. There is the pathetic entry for a little girl, Maria Phillpotts, who died at the age of 11 years on January 10, 1822, of a rapid consumption. Her assurance had been effected by her father three years earlier, when she was only 8 years old.

Violent deaths were fairly common. Traffic had its problems; thus Laurence Williams died at the age of 54 on October 11, 1823, of an accident in a carriage, and John Nash, who died at 60 on June 15, 1820, was run over by a horse. Viscount Ingestre was drowned at the age of 24 on May 22, 1826, by a fall from his horse. He had been travelling on the continent for nearly two years— perhaps on the 'grand tour' usual to complete a young man's education. While he was riding on the Prater at Vienna, his hat was caught by the bough of a tree and fell upon his horse, which bolted. Horse and rider plunged into a pit or quagmire and were suffocated. By a curious coincidence his younger brother was hurt by a riding accident at home on the same day.

A tragic story lies behind the death of Sir Charles Warwick Bampfylde, Bart., on April 19, 1823 at the age of 70. He was wounded by the husband of one of his servants, who then killed himself with a second pistol. As it happened, the ball lodged in Sir Charles's ribs but carried with it a piece of brass wire from his braces, which could not be extracted. The wire corroded and the wound became gangrenous. Since Sir Charles was separated from his wife, the story is presumably one of a suspicious or a jealous husband. Sir Charles was descended from the Poltimore family.

In 1821, William Morgan published a table[1] showing the numbers dying of the various disorders.

Up to this time, the premium had to be paid either in one sum (a single premium) or by annual payments over the whole period of assurance, that is to say for life if the assurance was arranged for the whole continuance of life. A few years earlier, George Kirkpatrick of the Atlas Assurance Company, had had the happy idea that the premiums might be calculated so as to cease after a certain period of years though the assurance was to continue for the whole of life (now known as a 'limited premium' policy). This system has a considerable advantage for those who expect a lower income in later life, when retired. When the question was discussed on December 6, 1821, the directors so liked the plan, 'which greatly conduces to the comfort and convenience of different persons', that they decided to permit existing as well as new assurances to come under the new arrangements, with, of course, an appropriate adjustment of the premium.

'The late temporary rise in the public funds' proved as it happened to be more lasting than was expected. The trouble was that the relatively high prices of Government stock in which most of the Society's money had been invested (at much lower prices) gave an exaggerated impression of the wealth of the Society. Actually, the benefit of high prices for the existing investments tended to be off-set by the correspondingly low rate of interest at which new money could be invested and, in a growing fund, the rate for new money was at least as important as the market price of existing investments. The change in the investment climate demanded, too, a reconsideration of investment policy.

In the period between the close of the American War of Independence and the opening of the French wars, while the public funds stood at relatively high prices, the opportunity had been taken to invest part of the Society's money in mortgages. The largest total advanced on mortgage in any one year in the eighteenth century was £81,480 in 1798. In the opening years of the nineteenth century the amount lent on mortgage did not amount to much more than the re-lending of money which had previously been lent on mortgage and had been repaid. Indeed, one of the members proposed that the

[1] v. Table on pp. 170 and 171.

TABLE, SHEWING THE DISORDERS OF WHICH PERSONS ASSURED BY THE EQUITABLE SOCIETY HAVE DIED DURING THE LAST 20 YEARS, FROM 1800 TO 1821 [sic]

| Disease | 10 to 20 | 20 to 30 | 30 to 40 | 40 to 50 | 50 to 60 | 60 to 70 | 70 to 80 | 80, &c. | Total |
|---|---|---|---|---|---|---|---|---|---|
| Angina Pectoris | — | — | 5 | 11 | 12 | 9 | 4 | 3 | 44 |
| Apoplexy | 1 | 3 | 19 | 38 | 69 | 69 | 38 | 5 | 242 |
| Asthma | — | — | — | 2 | 19 | 19 | 11 | 2 | 53 |
| Atrophy | — | — | 3 | 4 | 6 | 11 | 1 | — | 25 |
| Cancer | — | — | 1 | 4 | 10 | 8 | 1 | 1 | 25 |
| Child Birth | — | — | 2 | 2 | — | — | — | — | 4 |
| Consumption | 2 | 9 | 34 | 31 | 44 | 28 | — | — | 153 |
| Convulsion Fits | — | — | 3 | 4 | 1 | 3 | 5 | — | 11 |
| Decay (Natural) and Old Age | — | — | — | — | 5 | 72 | 127 | 58 | 262 |
| Diabetes | — | — | — | 2 | 2 | — | 1 | 1 | 6 |
| Dropsy | 1 | — | 7 | 28 | 38 | 41 | 20 | 2 | 137 |
| Dropsy in the Chest | — | 1 | 3 | 18 | 34 | 28 | 16 | — | 100 |
| Dysentery | — | — | 1 | 1 | 2 | 4 | 4 | — | 12 |
| Disease of the Stomach and Digestive Organs | — | — | 5 | 4 | 8 | 8 | 1 | — | 26 |
| Diseased Liver | — | 2 | 5 | 24 | 23 | 21 | 4 | — | 79 |
| Disease of the Bladder and Urinary Passages | — | — | 2 | 4 | 15 | 23 | 15 | — | 59 |
| Epilepsy | — | — | 2 | 3 | 2 | 1 | 2 | — | 10 |
| Erysipelas | — | 1 | — | 2 | 3 | 2 | 2 | — | 10 |
| Fevers, General | — | 6 | 18 | 33 | 33 | 39 | 15 | 2 | 146 |
| Fevers, Bilious | — | 1 | 4 | 8 | 9 | 4 | 1 | 1 | 28 |
| Fevers, Nervous | — | 3 | 3 | 13 | 6 | 8 | 3 | — | 36 |

| | | | | | | | | | |
|---|---|---|---|---|---|---|---|---|---|
| Fevers, Inflammatory .. .. .. .. | — | — | — | 4 | 6 | 3 | 2 | — | 15 |
| Fevers, Putrid .. .. .. .. | — | 2 | 7 | 4 | 6 | 7 | — | — | 26 |
| Gout .. .. .. .. .. | — | — | 1 | 4 | 4 | 11 | 6 | — | 26 |
| Inflammation of the Bowels .. .. | 1 | 2 | 11 | 13 | 15 | 25 | 9 | 1 | 77 |
| Inflammation of the Lungs .. .. | — | — | 9 | 4 | 24 | 22 | 12 | 2 | 73 |
| Inflammation of the Brain .. .. | — | 3 | 7 | 5 | 5 | 3 | — | — | 23 |
| Inflammation of the Chest, and Peri-pneumony .. .. .. | 1 | 1 | 1 | 1 | 6 | 7 | 4 | 1 | 22 |
| Palsy .. .. .. .. | — | 1 | 3 | 8 | 26 | 42 | 34 | 2 | 116 |
| Quincy .. .. .. .. | — | — | — | 1 | 1 | 1 | — | — | 3 |
| Rupture of a Blood Vessel .. .. | — | — | 7 | 14 | 13 | 12 | 3 | — | 49 |
| Slain in War .. .. .. | 1 | 1 | 1 | 1 | — | — | — | — | 4 |
| Stone .. .. .. .. | — | — | — | — | 1 | 2 | 4 | 1 | 8 |
| Suicide .. .. .. | — | 1 | 2 | 3 | 7 | 2 | — | — | 15 |
| Water on the Brain .. .. | — | — | — | 1 | 3 | 1 | — | — | 5 |
| | 7 | 37 | 166 | 299 | 458 | 536 | (345 .. | 82) | 1,930 |
| | | | | | | | 427 | | |
| Number assured during the last 20 years | 1,494 | 8,996 | 33,850 | 45,429 | 36,489 | 19,042 | 6,454 from 70, &c. | | 151,754 |

171

sum of £400,000 more or less, then upon mortgage, should as soon as possible be called in, and the sums as received laid out in the purchase of 3 per cent Consols (G, June 2, 1803). He evidently felt that investment in stocks at the comparatively low prices then current was more profitable than investment in mortgages.

This history is unconcerned with the glamour of the year 1815 and hard-fought Waterloo; the behaviour of markets reflected the economic turmoil in the period of readjustment which followed it, rather than the power and the glory of politics. The winds of change which blew upon the Equitable were economic storms and the sails had to be trimmed to the prevailing weather in the investment markets. The prices of the public funds tended to rise after the close of the wars and, by the spring of 1817, the directors felt it was worth while to lay out more on mortgages. They decided to lay out £1,000,000 in this way but it was one thing to decide the policy, another to find the mortgages. Five years later, the total was still short of £1,000,000.

The wars left England with a depreciated currency; there was some argument about the extent of the depreciation but there could be none about the fact. The one solution acceptable to the thought of the day was a return to the gold standard (abandoned in 1797) and this was accomplished in the years 1819 to 1821. The return to gold was achieved only at the cost of deflation, the discomforts of a fall in prices of goods and a contraction of the note circulation in the years 1820 to 1822. Trade slumped and England passed into the first of the great economic upheavals of the nineteenth century—depression, recovery, boom, crash.

By 1822, the directors felt that a more aggressive mortgage policy should be pursued and they began to encourage mortgages by accepting a lower rate of interest than the legal maximum of 5 per cent per annum, provided the interest was paid within sixty days of its becoming due (S, July 3, 1822). It was five years since the decision had been taken to invest more in mortgages and though the amount in mortgages had grown substantially, the proportion had actually fallen slightly.

The rise in the prices of the public funds was partly responsible for this situation. Even the Bank of England itself began to lend money on mortgage in 1823, though it did not continue long in this market.

Recovery in the economic life came in the years 1823 to 1824 and passed into a wild boom. Parliament, by way of encouraging trade,

| Stock in funds | March 30, 1817 | | September 30, 1822 | |
| --- | --- | --- | --- | --- |
| | Amount | Value | Amount | Value |
| | £ | £ | £ | £ |
| 3 per cent Reduced bank annuities | (2,835,000) | 2,027,035 | (3,975,000) | 3,219,750 |
| 3 per cent Consolidated annuities | (3,160,000) | 2,291,000 | (4,340,000) | 3,558,800 |
| 4 per cent Consolidated annuities | ( 400,000) | 358,000 | ( 400,000) | 392,000 |
| | (6,395,000) | 4,676,035 | (8,715,000) | 7,170,550 |
| Laid out on mortgages | | 571,833 | | 834,436 |
| | | 5,247,868 | | 8,004,986 |
| Proportion in mortgages | | 11 per cent | | 10.4 per cent |

passed an Act (6 Geo. IV, *c.* 91) in 1825 which removed all restrictions on joint-stock trading—not yet, of course, with limited liability except by specific grant of Charter or Act. There was a tremendous eruption of joint-stock promotions, a period of feverish speculation. A count made soon afterwards showed that, out of some 600 promotions in the years 1824 and 1825, three-fifths were still-born and nearly another fifth, which at least got as far as the opening of a market in their shares, were soon abandoned. The remaining one-fifth of the promotions were still in existence in 1827, but the capital of these companies was then worth about 60 per cent only of the £15,000,000 that had been subscribed.

One of the big flotations during the boom was £5,000,000 for the Alliance Assurance Company (of which sum, only £500,000 was to be subscribed in cash) and the circumstances are amusingly illustrated in cartoons of the time. The promotions in 1824 included fourteen life offices, of whom five were dead within five years and only four now exist. One of the most colourful was the Asylum life office, which confined its business to unhealthy lives and to those who would, for one reason or another, be rejected or charged heavy extra premiums by other life offices. Its inglorious career ended in 1857 when it was absorbed by the London Assurance Corporation.

After the boom came the crash, at the end of 1825. Many of the bubbles burst and there was a run on the banks. On April 12, 1826, William Jones of Llanarth wrote to Sir Charles Morgan at Pall Mall about 'the money plethora of Mr Baring . . . ; I fear the effects of the late revolution in money matters are only beginning to be felt . . .'.

During the boom the Bank of England's cash fell to an alarmingly low level. Afterwards, in the late 1820s and the early 1830s, the Directors of the Bank of England aimed at keeping their liabilities covered roughly in the proportion of two-thirds by securities and one-third by bullion. How did they arrive at these proportions? It is interesting that the one-third reserve kept in bullion is a similar proportion to the 'reserved third' of surplus which had been the special feature of the Equitable for a quarter of a century. But the proportion of one-third was most likely adopted in each case as being what was considered a substantial reserve, rather than by any linking of ideas between one and the other.

Such was the economic background to the extraordinary events of the years 1824–25, when a determined attempt was made to enforce the realization of the Society's invested funds at the then relatively high prices, notwithstanding that it might, in effect, lead to the closing of the office for the benefit of the existing members. The fever in the business world was also at work within the respectable walls of the Equitable. It was just at this time that Arthur Morgan came into a responsible position.

William Morgan completed fifty years' service early in 1824; he was in his seventies and was naturally anxious to ensure that the management of the Society should be in competent hands after he had gone. In March 1824, he wrote a letter to the President recommending his youngest son, Arthur Morgan, for promotion and in June 1824 Arthur was elected Joint Actuary. The letter is worth quoting for the light that it throws on them both:

Having now been engaged above half-a-century in the service of the Society and having completed the 73rd year of my age, you will, I doubt not, agree with me in opinion that it is high time for me to look forward to the termination of my active labours. I am induced therefore to address myself to you on the present occasion not only as my friend which I am happy to acknowledge with gratitude but as the President of the Society, to request the favor [sic] of your communicating my sentiments to the Court of Directors and of assuring them of the regret I feel in being obliged to submit to any event which has a tendency to lessen my connection with a body of gentlemen from which I have for so many years experienced uninterrupted civility and kindness. Tho' formerly disappointed in the hope I had indulged of seeing this connection continued by a son whose integrity and abilities, if his life had been spared, afforded the prospect of his becoming highly useful to the Society, I have great reason to be thankfull [sic] to the Directors for doing what lay in their power to alleviate the grief and disappointment I felt on his premature death, by chusing [sic] his brother to succeed in the situation originally created for him.

I am sensible that the partiality of a father renders him a very unfit judge of the merits of his son and consequently that anything I can say on the subject ought to be received with caution. Still, however, in justice to my son now in the office, and perhaps to the Society, I ought not to be altogether silent on the present occasion. As far therefore as regards the strictest integrity and a knowledge more than sufficient to conduct and to determine upon the affairs of the Society I can honestly vouch for him, and I am confident that he will never be wanting in diligence or zeal to promote its interests. During the course of the last four years he has fully acquired a knowledge of the principles on which I have always proceeded in ascertaining the real state of the Society, and if the knowledge of these should be considered of any importance, he will possess it with a partiality in its favour on account of the individual from whom he derived it.

Should he be chosen to a more responsible office than he holds at present, I hope if my life is spared a few years to continue my assistance so that when my entire resignation takes place, I shall have the pleasure of knowing that the Society will have reason to place that confidence in him with which they have so long honored [sic] his father.

The rise in the market prices of stocks had continued; the 3 per cent stocks, which had been around 60 in 1815 and 1816, had risen to a level of about 80 in 1822 and 90 in 1824. Soon after Arthur Morgan's appointment, the attack was renewed. Joseph Bushnan gave notice of a motion that, in consequence of the great increase in the value of public funds, 25 per cent of the capital stock (i.e. the invested funds) of the Society should be divided amongst the members and paid either in cash or in stock in proportion to the bonuses already attaching to the policies; the idea was that part of the bonus which was payable with the sum assured at death should, in fact, be paid at once. The motion gave rise to a fierce argument though the minutes merely record the decisions. First, a motion *not* to include the proposal in the notice of the next General Court was defeated; then, one *to* include it passed in the affirmative. The proposal aroused great interest, for 420 members attended the next meeting on December 2, 1824. Such was the interest that it brought the affairs of the Society into the public notice and *The Times* inserted full reports of the next few meetings.

The directors had just three months for preparatory consideration of the question at issue and they used the time for a careful and thorough probe into the whole situation. They closely questioned Morgan on the facts and he convinced them that there was no extraordinary surplus; the claims had been much as expected and the rise in the public funds had tended to retard the accumulation of surplus. The older members had derived every advantage that they were entitled to (S, December 1, 1824).

The scope for differences of opinion is illustrated by divergencies between the opinions of two different Counsel. Charles Wetherell, the Solicitor General, gave his opinion, succinctly, that any change would be contrary to good faith; James Scarlett gave his opinion that changes could be made in general meeting and that such changes would be binding on members of the Society. However, the members entering since 1816 had no vote and a general meeting cannot bind a class without votes. The Society had assumed something of the form of a proprietary body. Morgan's technical knowledge and the legal opinions convinced the directors that no change should be made.

The meeting on December 2, 1824 was crowded to excess and there was a considerable hubbub. At 11 o'clock the Recorder of London, one of the Vice-Presidents, took the chair and started to tell the meeting that the directors had prepared a report but, before he could continue, Bushnan rose and tried to speak, amid loud cries of 'Order!'. He managed to explain that it was upon the point of order that he meant to speak and silence was obtained. He said:

> I wish to explain that I would like to withdraw the notice of motion which I have given and which has, I believe, led to the assemblage of such an unexampled attendance of members; I submit, therefore, is there any necessity of hearing the directors' report read as a preliminary part of these proceedings? . . . I have unwillingly withdrawn the notice of motion which I have given because I am advised that the object of it cannot, consistent with the bye-laws of the Society, be legally carried into effect.

As he sat down, another member, Samuel Sweet, rose, evidently by pre-arrangement, to make a proposal:

> The intention of my motion is simply this—that it should be referred to the Court of Directors to consider and report whether it would be advisable to open a new system for the new members who may be acquired, without prejudice to the present members, and having regard in their pecuniary arrangements to the existing price of the public funds. In giving notice of this motion, I refrain from pronouncing any opinion which is likely to lead to premature discussion, all I desire being to have the attention of the directors brought to the specific consideration of a new arrangement.

13. Income tax, when first imposed in 1799, a cartoon (British Museum 9280)

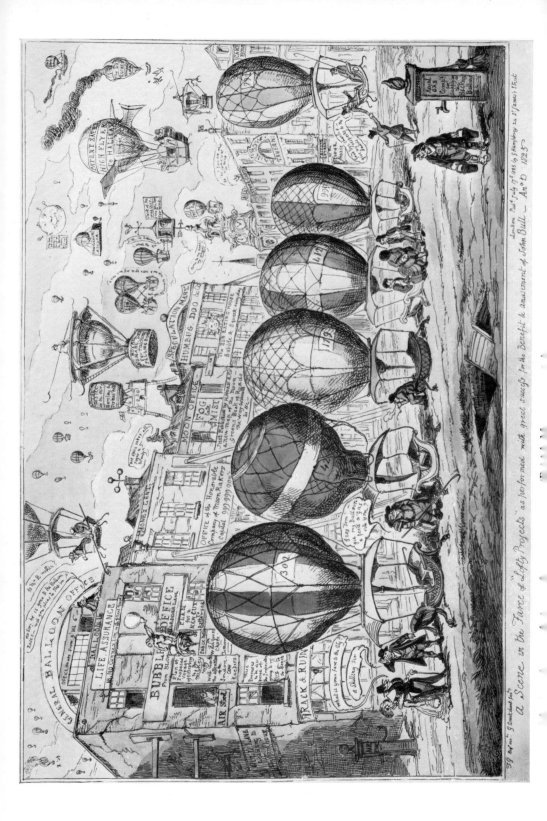

A Scene on the Farce of "Lofty Projects" as performed with great success for the Benefit & amusement of John Bull — Anno D 1825

After a very long discussion upon points of order, and after extra-ordinary meetings had been convened for December 16th and 23rd, the Recorder said it was for the meeting to consider whether the report by the directors should be read. But the meeting would not even hear the directors' report and the reading was postponed until the next meeting.

The agitation at the meeting called forth a letter to *The Times* of December 7, 1824, from 'Your constant reader, Bury St Edmund's':

> In common with many thousands of proprietors resident at a distance from town, I have to thank you for your communication of the late meeting of this highly respectable institution. As so many of your readers may be interested, allow me to suggest the expediency of reverting to the old rules of the Society, under which a division of profits was allowed to take place, whenever the excess capital might admit of such a division. Such was the plan till within a few years, when a resolution was adopted for making a division every tenth year. The injustice of this resolution towards the older policies is manifest. . . .
>
> If any new regulations are to be proposed, I would take the liberty of recom-mending a reduction of premium upon all policies of a certain date; as it appears an injudicious plan to be taking a considerable premium from the old proprietors, to be invested in the 3 per cents at par, for the purpose of a division to take place when they may be 30 per cent lower.

The interest was sustained; on December 16, 1824, 375 members were present and Sweet's motion was carried with only two dis-sentients. At the second confirmatory meeting, Joseph Bushnan dropped a bombshell by suggesting that the Society should, for the time being, cease to grant any new assurances for the whole of life. 'It must be obvious that by letting in new insurers we are . . . defeat-ing our own proposed object (Hear, hear!).' John Poynder objected that notice ought to be given of such a proposal; it tended to tie the hands of the directors. A long and irregular discussion showed the divergent points of view. Some members were afraid of the 'inrush of new members'. Others thought that the fears were unreasonable; the members ought to trust the directors—'it was unnecessary and ungracious to shackle the consideration of the subject'. James William Freshfield thought the existing members ought not to be called upon to admit 'a host of new proprietors who have incurred none of the past risk, though they were naturally enough ready to hurry in and partake of a distribution of well-applied capital'.

In response to appeals on questions of order, William Morgan rose to speak:

I assure the proprietors that the Court of Directors are prepared to meet the general question in the most calm, deliberate and unprejudiced manner. . . . Members ought to bear in mind the great importance of their decision to a Society like this, which might be called a national establishment as well as one of individual benefit. I think it would be much better to leave the whole subject, suspension and all, to the dispassionate judgment of the Court of Directors.

Mr Bushnan rose again:

I repeat that I merely mean my motion as a suggestion. I must deny, however, that this Society is a national one or any other than one established and supported for individual benefit and to be regulated by individual control. If a contrary notion gets abroad, and we are to be considered as a national society, the Government might give us their aid in nationally disposing of the ten and a half millions of capital which is under consideration. (A laugh, and cries of 'Hear! hear!')

Eventually the motion was carried in the crowded court with only seven dissentients. The substance of Bushnan's motion meant that the existing members would have put an end to the Society for their own benefit. The proposal needed to be scotched before the main questions were considered and, at the next meeting, the directors gave their considered view that the circumstances did not justify the suspension of the regular business of the Society. There was clearly a strong current of opinion against the directors, because the formal motion that their report be 'received and approved' was amended so that the report was merely 'received' by the General Court, not 'approved' by it.

The way was now clear for the consideration of the main questions at issue:

That it be referred to the Court of Directors to consider and report—*whether* it would be advisable to cease effecting assurances upon the footing of the existing Deed of Settlement, Regulations, Bye-Laws and Premiums; *and whether* it would be advisable to form a new Deed and new Regulations, to be signed and observed by new Members, having due regard to the interest of the present Members; *and whether* any and what measures would be advisable to be adopted, in order to benefit the present Members, either by a declaration of additional profit, or by a reduction of their Premiums, or by more frequent Rests and Additions, or otherwise, having regard to the price of the Public Funds. . . .

The views of the members who were backing the motion are explained by a letter to the directors, dated January 10, 1825, and signed by Samuel Sweet, George Brown, Joseph Bushnan and R. Slade:

Believing that you are anxious to receive any suggestions . . . we beg to offer to your attention some ideas which we know to be entertained by a large proportion of the Society. . . .

*First,* as to ceasing to insure under the present regulations and forming a new Deed. The original Deed of Settlement was drawn up in 1762, at a period when the subject of Life Assurance was by no means so well understood as it is at present, and the subsequent regulations have been framed on principles different from the Settlement and of each other. Hence it is not surprising that the Deed and Regulations should be subject (as they undoubtedly are) to considerable objections. . . . We therefore strongly recommend that all future assurances be effected under a new Deed, which Deed will of course embrace all the improvements introduced of late years into Deeds for the government of similar societies.

An idea seems to have gone abroad that it is contemplated by some Members of this Society to put an end entirely to the present Association, and to make an immediate division of the existing profits among the present Members. We do not believe that any such wish or intention is entertained by any individual in the Society and for ourselves we totally disclaim it.

We consider the Society to be a great co-partnership of which all the persons assured in it continue Members so long (and no longer) as their respective Policies of Assurance remain in force. We therefore apprehend that the whole legal and equitable interest in the present funds of this Society is vested in the present Members and that the holders of the Policies dated previously to January 1, 1817, have an *actual* and the holders of subsequent Policies a contingent interest in the existing surplus, both which interests it is right to provide for, in any new arrangement that may be formed. At the same time we beg it to be distinctly understood that we by no means wish the whole benefit of the present surplus to be divided among the present Members. We look upon the Society as an 'Institution of National Importance' and inasmuch as an advantage has been derived by the Society from the flourishing state of its affairs before the present Members belonged to it, so we wish to hold out to future Members a liberal participation in benefits to which we ourselves have contributed.

*Second,* we . . . consider what measures it may be adviseable to adopt in order to benefit the present Members.

From what we have already said, it is clear that in the appropriation of the present surplus, the present Members of the Society are fairly entitled to a preference over the new Members hereafter to be admitted. The present Members have mainly contributed to produce that surplus. They have the whole legal interest and, if they give up a part of their interest to future Members, it is to be understood in the light of a liberal concession to the public, which concession, while it forms an inducement to new insurers to prefer the Equitable Society to any other, obtains its equivalent in the increased business of the Society by which, as it has justly been said 'Old Members derive the greatest benefit' but which is in fact beneficial to all. . . .

The specific suggestions made in the letter are sufficiently indicated by the motion and the review of them in the directors' report.

It was natural that those who took part in these arguments should have been lawyers. Samuel White Sweet was a solicitor (of Basinghall Street, in 1814). It is difficult to identify George Brown with certainty. Joseph Bushnan was on the staff of Guildhall as City Solicitor 1797–1803 and Controller of the City Chamber 1803–31, a position which his father had held before him. Robert Slade was described in 1792 as being 'of Doctor's Commons, Proctor', i.e. he was an official of the civil courts. James William Freshfield, who had spoken at the meetings, was a solicitor (of Swithin's Lane, in 1802). He was a partner of the firm of Freshfields whose members have, since 1743, been legal advisers to the Bank of England—as was Sir William Leese, a recent director of the Society and a partner in that firm. John Poynder was also a solicitor (of Bridewell Hospital, in 1807).

Reading between the lines, it seems likely that the directors were faced with a confusing complex of suggestions in the General Court and invited the letter so as to clarify the issues and give a firm basis for their rejoinder. The writers of the letter would not face the consequences of their own logic; their arguments pointed to a disruption of the fabric of the Society, with a view to benefiting the then existing members, but they carefully disclaimed any intention of such an object.

The day appointed for the reception of the report of the Court of Directors upon the proposed plan of reorganizing the Society was March 3, 1825. The attendance was the greatest ever remembered; 383 were actually recorded as being present. Soon after 10 o'clock the spacious chamber in which the Courts were held was crowded to excess; the folding doors had to be thrown open and other members crowded the lobbies and the staircase, though they could not hear much of the proceedings. The President and Directors had great difficulty in getting to their seats at the table. After introductory remarks by Sir Charles Morgan and some of the members, the Recorder was able to proceed with the directors' report and Morgan's written exposé of the affairs of the Society, which occupied him nearly two hours. The report appears on the whole to have been favourably received because it was interspersed with 'Hear, hear'! At the conclusion a formal motion of thanks to the Court of Directors for their able report started a long discussion upon the propriety of introducing the world 'able', which involved approbation. The report said:

The Directors, in the exercise of the duty of their situations, have, individually and collectively, felt that they have a primary obligation, which is above all personal considerations; and that is to preserve, firm and unshaken, the foundations of that fabric which has been raised to their hands, and to guard it by all the means in their power from every measure, however specious or plausible, which, according to their judgment, can in the remotest degree tend to hazard its stability. And in the exercise of this particular duty they have adopted the utmost prudence and caution, because they are convinced of the extravagant expectations of some, and the fallacious notions of others; and they have endeavoured to perform . . . that duty by a strict, honest, vigilant, and impartial administration of the Society in reference to all its Members.

If any obstacles interfere with the accomplishment of the expectations of any Members, they are not raised by the Directors, for *they* would derive individually an equal benefit if those expectations could be realized; but they arise out of the circumstances and constitution of the Society. In suggesting that there may be such obstacles, the Directors do not intend to encourage any feeling of dissatisfaction, or to excite any idea that principles different from those by which the Society is constituted, would be more advantageous. There are numerous Institutions which profess to attain the same ends by different means; to those any speculative questions would more properly be addressed. But this noble Institution stands towering above all others; its stability is greater; its benefits have been larger, and it has administered comfort to the families of thousands, and will continue so to do, if the same principle of justice, and the same procedure and caution are persevered in, which have hitherto guided its counsels. It has stood the test of experience, and no better proof can be given of the excellence of any plan, than to try it by that test.

The report came down decisively against 'any departure from the essential principles of this Society' and against any new deed and regulations. Modifications were not excluded but:

In an Institution which has been so uniformly successful, and which has in its effects more than answered the reasonable expectations of every individual under the existing practice . . . the adoption of any new regulation . . . cannot be too warily considered.

This part of the report was clearly prepared in advance and the second part was added in reply to the specific questions which the directors were asked to consider. They were fortunate that the questions were asked

during the life of a man to whose opinion this Society cannot too much defer by whose prudence, ability, and exertions it has risen from infancy to maturity who has nurtured it with the most prudent caution, guarded it with the most anxious care, and guided it, by his pre-eminent talents, to its present state of prosperity and of national importance. It has been supposed, that he is influenced by prejudices arising from long-formed notions and opinions, but the Directors think, that well considered opinions, confirmed by experience, are much better for the guidance of this magnificent Institution, than speculative opinions, which, if they were adopted, really might very soon make this large, yet easily managed Establishment, a most unwieldy and unmanageable concern.

Were there any measures which could be adopted with a view to the benefit of the existing members? The answer was:

The Directors . . . are of opinion that there is *no power*, without unanimous consent, to alter any regulation which existed on January 1, 1817, if the alteration would in its operation have the effect of depriving *any* Member of present or expectant profit; but this result can only be determined by calculation. . . .

A 'declaration of additional profit', or the declaration of bonuses more frequently than once in ten years, would deprive recently admitted members of some part of their contingent interests; a reduction of premiums would prevent the accumulation of surplus and could not be applied in due proportion to every member. There was, therefore, *no power* to adopt these proposals. Many other suggestions had been made both by way of explanation of the object of the motion before the General Court and in numerous 'plans for the future management of the Equitable'. But before discussing some of these, many of which were wholly impracticable, the report went on:

The great and the leading principle of this Society has ever been its *Equity*: it has persevered for sixty years in a 'regular course', by which its security and stability have been confirmed: it has answered all its engagements, and afforded greater benefit than any other Institution of a similar nature; and it will continue so to do, if the same prudent and beneficial course is pursued. Why then should any doubts be suggested, any wavering in principle be excited, or any *new plans* of management be proposed, which cannot offer such experience, and which may require to be altered as speedily as they might be adopted? Let us not then lower the dignity or reduce the benefits of this Society, by a surrender of its mature and venerable character, for any charms which a more modern garb may display.

The general utility of the Society, the advantages it realizes, and the good faith with which its engagements have been performed, and which have induced and still induce new Members to join and to support it, might be destroyed if any essential principle were to be altered, without considering the risk of legal, or perhaps of parliamentary interference. . . .

Before the Directors proceed to state their opinion upon specific *suggestions* brought under this consideration, they earnestly entreat the attention of every Member of the General Court; and they wish to impress on their minds what was the origin of this Society, what its distinguishing feature from almost every other Society, and what has been *their* inducement for joining it; and, they believe, that of the majority at least, if not of all its Members. It has been an anxious desire to provide for the comfort of others, to extend blessings and protection to the widow and the orphan, and to assist, as far as pecuniary relief would afford it, to lighten affliction and relieve distress, and to procure support for those who may have lost their natural guardians and protectors. It never could have been the intention, as it never has been the practice, to make it a subject of speculation, or an object of personal and selfish advantage; and if any have joined it in that expectation, it is the duty of those who are actuated by *superior* motives, to rally round their standard, and to support and protect its proper principle, and its most important object.

The wording of the report carries its own sense of the urgency of the occasion. After such a powerful opening, the directors disposed speedily of various suggestions. To allocate bonuses in stock instead of in monetary additions to the sums assured would be complicated and impracticable. A new class of member with a lower reserved surplus would be of no advantage. Both the suggestions of a reduction of premiums and of more frequent allocations of bonus had already been rejected. The directors then turned to various suggestions 'for the purpose of realizing the present high price of the public funds'.

They scarcely felt themselves at liberty to hold out inducements for the surrender of an interest which they wished to see every member preserve for the benefit of those for whom it was designed. Apparently, a market in the Society's policies had sprung up; in several instances more than twice the office value had been obtained by public sale. The office value was the full reserve, less a small deduction. How was it possible upon just grounds of calculation 'to take into account the value of stock at the time of the surrender, or the contingent interest which the insurer has in the accumulating surplus of the Society's fund?' It would be practicable to permit the surrender of the bonuses already added to the assurance, on the condition that there was a corresponding reduction in the number of years ranking for bonus thereafter.

The proposal that the Society should lend money on its policies would 'interfere with every intention and object of the Society, and would occasion great additional expense, and most probably produce repeated litigations'. It is now common practice, but most would agree that it is a relatively expensive service, having regard to the smallness of the amounts usually borrowed.

If more money could be lent on mortgage, it would be an advantageous investment. But if more mortgages were secured by reducing the rate of interest, it would be necessary also to reduce the rate on existing mortgages. A reduction from 4 to 3½ per cent would be 'an object of serious importance'.

Assignments had never been recognized, except for the payment of claims. If they were to be registered, it might create a doubt whether the Society's contracts were *shares* instead of *joint assurances*; there had been legal decisions with regard to the legality of societies formed without charter or Act of Parliament, if the shares were transferable.

The Tredegar papers preserve a draft of the report and the deletions in this copy show that the original draft was even stronger in tone:

> No one can contemplate a dissolution of this important and beneficial establishment without alarm; it can only be effected by the power of a court of equity . . . (with) individual consent of everyone.

Such a procedure would be likely to confer the greatest benefits on the members of the legal profession engaged in the case,

> whilst it would leave widows and orphans to lament and repine at the folly and imprudence which had induced such consequences. . . .
> This is not a Society for experiment; we have experience of the happiest kind— let us continue to preserve it.

Morgan put the whole force of his powers of argument in support of the report and concluded:

> What reliance can be placed on the permanent value of a property so fluctuating as the public funds? Were the peace of Europe to be disturbed, or were any unfortunate event to take place which should lessen the confidence of the public in Government securities, this additional surplus would soon vanish; and it may be well, perhaps, should the mischief extend no further. If the late war, which began with a debt of less than 300 millions, sunk the three-per-cents in the course of it from 97 to 47 per cent, what limit shall be assigned to their depreciation should another war commence, with a debt of 800 millions? or from what source can the deficiency in the Society's capital be supplied, when, in addition to this depreciation, a considerable part of that capital had been alienated on the vain presumption of its always maintaining its present value? It should be recollected that five years only have passed since two millions were apportioned among the Members, which added to the annual amount of all the claims above £175,000 a year, and in some instances increased the sums assured to more than four times their original amount. . . . These are benefits of such magnitude as to admit of no parallel in any institution of the same kind, and are sufficient, it might be reasonably hoped, to satisfy the most extravagant expectations for some years to come. But, unfortunately, very different views have lately been entertained by

some Members of the wealth and resources of the Society, and propositions have been made for still further benefits, either by more frequent additions to the claims, or by an immediate reduction of the premiums. . . .

In a body composed of so many thousand Members it is hardly possible that its concerns should not be viewed in a wrong light by some of them and lead to injudicious motions. In the few instances which have occurred of this kind, more prudent councils have uniformly prevailed; and so far from deviating from that wise and temperate course which it has pursued from its earliest existence, the Society on all occasions has been anxious rather to raise new barriers for the preservation, than to form any measures for the premature alienation, of its capital. It would indeed be a matter of severe disappointment and mortification to behold the Society, regardless of those barriers, diverted into a different course. Certainly no recent events ought to have this effect. The capital must continue to increase with the increasing number and amount of the assurances. The temporary rise in the Funds, which of late has so violently inflamed the minds of the public, and generated such a multitude of delusive and visionary speculations, instead of accelerating, retards the accumulation of the surplus in the present circumstances of the Society; and the experience of former years exemplified in the prosperity and credit of the Society, far from justifying any new course, affords the strongest motives for avoiding every step that leads to it, and particularly for guarding against the contagion which unhappily prevails at this time and threatens such serious consequences hereafter.

In all my Addresses to the General Court it has been my principal object to moderate the too sanguine expectations of some of its Members, and thus guard them against the danger of too hastily adopting any measures that should directly or indirectly tend to invade the capital. On the inviolability of that capital depend the good faith, the honour, and ultimately the existence of the Society. To my former Addresses therefore I must now beg leave to refer the General Court, being well aware that if they shall have lost their effect, I can have but little hope of succeeding by any new arguments, were I possessed of health and spirits to advance them.

It is interesting that The Reversionary Interest Society Ltd., (founded in 1823) put a considerable proportion of its funds into Equitable policies in the early days. In the year 1825, about 40 per cent of its purchases of reversionary interests consisted of policies of insurance, 'principally in the Equitable office'. By a strange chance, quite unconnected with this, the Reversionary Interest Society became allied with the Equitable in 1919. The attraction of Equitable policies as investments was the speculative value which might be attached to the contingent interest in the 'reserved third' of surplus. The value allowed by the Equitable on surrender naturally took account only of the bonuses already added (including the interim bonus that would be payable at death) and could not anticipate the bonuses which might be declared at a later time.

As has been related, the directors' report was merely read at the meeting on March 3rd and so first came up for consideration at a special meeting on April 28, 1825. The directors brought forward two modest proposals but they were swamped by a series of propositions by members, mainly for more frequent rests and additions. After considerable discussion, these further proposals were withdrawn and the whole question was left to simmer until the quarterly meeting on June 2, 1825.

At this stage a comic incident relieved the severity of the discussions. The Rev. John Gardiner, DD of Bath (then close on 70 years of age) caught the eye of the chairman and addressed the Court at considerable length in a speech which was scarcely relevant to the question at issue; he was heard out of respect to the 'reverend and venerable' gentleman.

My complaint is that if I were to die before 1830, my executors would not receive, by a great deal, an equivalent for the sums I have contributed towards it, calculated at compound interest (Some expressions of dissent). I know that my children would receive far more than the sums insured; but hearing that there is a surplus or floating capital of about ten millions, they might naturally be tempted to ask if they could not receive a small portion of it. . . .

Dr Gardiner was under the misapprehension that the whole of the funds represented surplus! He reinforced his point with an amusing imaginary conversation:

No, that is all you are entitled to, you cannot touch this capital.
And why may not we be benefited by it?
It appears your father contributed more towards it than almost any individual.
And may we be so bold as to ask for whom this capital is intended?
Why for those who have a better claim to it than you, to be sure—or generations yet unborn (A laugh). A father, a predecessor, sows; and successors who have no affinity with him, strangers from the clouds, are to reap.

Dr Gardiner proceeded:

Suppose there are 10,000 members (which is about the present number) who paid £1,000 each on the average. This would give £10,000,000 capital owned by the Society. Might not two and a half millions, or 25 per cent, of this money be divided among the present members as a bonus in proportion to the sums they have respectively paid?

William Morgan called the proposition made by the reverend gentleman 'extraordinary' and

founded upon an erroneous view of the true interests of the Society. I most positively deny the assertion that, were Dr Gardiner's policy to be now due, he would have paid more money to the Society than his executors would receive for it. . . . There is only one member . . . who would not receive more than he has paid . . . computing all his payments at compound interest.

Dr Gardiner took up this challenge in a letter to William Morgan (published in *The Times*, June 8, 1825) in which he said that he had not the least doubt that Morgan was perfectly right in what he stated about the single member. The later part of the letter shows that Dr Gardiner was thinking of the loss that would be sustained if he were to die just before a decennial bonus and he included a calculation which showed that in order to produce a loss he had to accumulate all his premiums with 5 per cent interest.

Thomas Newell, MD, of Cheltenham, had prepared a report which for one reason or another he was unable to submit; he published it in July 1825. The report appealed to experience which 'is more to be depended upon than the strict computation made use of in the affairs of the Society'; the truth of his conclusions 'cannot fail to be seen by those who will take the pains to contrast his (William Morgan's) predictions during (the last thirty years) with the events as they have afterwards taken place'. The last was a sneer which might have had more substance had Newell himself any real understanding of the situation. But his report was a farrago of ill-digested ideas that were unworthy of any attention. The main burden was that the great caution, which had been shown in the early years of the Society's existence, was no longer necessary and that the Society would do better to revert to the original concept of dividing the whole of the surplus at once, whenever and so often as the stock was found to be more than sufficient for the Society's needs.

When, at the next meeting on June 16th, Samuel Sweet tried to return to the attack, it became apparent that there was a general desire to get rid of the resolutions at one sweep by affirming the propriety of the course taken by the directors. Francis Baily asked:

Have not all the topics mentioned by Mr Sweet been already considered and decided upon by the Directors? In fact, have they not been fully answered by the report?

*The Chairman:* They were considered and are fully answered.

*Mr Baily:* Have the directors, since the making of that report, had any reason to alter, or wish to revise, their opinions?

*The Chairman:* I am empowered to answer positively in the negative (A nice conjunction of opposites!).

*Mr Baily:* Then, were these resolutions submitted to the directors we should only have to go over the old ground again, and receive an answer corresponding with that already conveyed by the report.

*The Recorder:* There is no question among the directors but that the same answer would be returned.

*Dr Babington:* It is enough for me to know that unexampled prosperity has attended our present course and therefore we should be cautious of meddling with the basis of a system so practically approved. If a patient came to me for professional advice under such circumstances and with some partial desire of good, perhaps not clearly attainable, wished to risk a sound constitution by experiments, I would entreat him to forbear (A laugh and cries of 'Hear! hear!') and so I say to this motion (Hear! hear!).

There were now loud calls for the question to be put to the test of the vote. The amendment affirming the directors' report was carried by a show of hands. A division, however, was called for and produced 96 votes in favour of the amendment and 62 against it, the majority in favour being 34.

Thus the democratic process, by a none too large margin, stilled the voices of criticism for a while. Perhaps the critics were more vocal than numerous because Joseph Bushnan and Robert Slade both stood as candidates in the next election of directors on May 4, 1826 but got no support from other members. Both of them merely received one vote; presumably they voted for each other.

One change of practice of some importance emerged from the welter of ill-digested reforms proposed in the course of the debates. Up to this time a member who wished to realize some cash from his policy had to surrender the whole or a proportionate part of the assurance, including bonus additions. It was decided to permit the surrender of the existing bonus additions without affecting the assured sum itself or the future entitlement to bonus additions.

Much was published on the affairs of the Equitable and the public debate helps to show the Society's problems in perspective. George Farren, a solicitor and a founder of the Economic Life Assurance Society, which was intended to transact life assurance business at lower rates than other offices, expounded his ideas in a *Treatise on Life Assurance* (1823). He referred to the Equitable in glowing terms as 'the most flourishing Life Institution that ever existed in this or any other country . . .'. The praise, however, was followed by a note of criticism:

The imperfections of the Northampton Table are in no respect a reproach to

Dr Price, who did as much as the nature of his materials would allow. . . . That great errors have existed in the calculations founded on such imperfect materials may not excite surprise; but that they should be persisted in, after the experience of half a century has proved the extent of their inaccuracy, and when more perfect data can be obtained, is certainly a reproach to that Institution, which, having taken the lead in success, ought to have been the foremost in prosecuting the improvement of science.

When the Law Life Assurance Society was established, a committee invited, in May 1823, 'the opinions of several scientific gentlemen' on the question of the correct, equitable method of distributing the surplus of a life office. According to Farren:

No two of the gentlemen consulted agreed on the mode of making such distributions, so as to do justice to the several parties concerned, though they were unanimous in declaring (and Mr Morgan himself was of the number) that the mode adopted in the Equitable Institution is certainly not the correct mode.

William Morgan probably regarded the Equitable system as a good, practical working rule, which did rough justice to the various conflicting interests, and not as a scientific method which could be demonstrated to be the best mode in theory.

The number of life offices in the United Kingdom rapidly increased in these years so that, by 1825, sixty-two life offices had been formed and fifty-seven were still open for business.

NUMBER OF LIFE ASSURANCE OFFICES IN UK[1]

| Period | Number formed | Number discontinued | Number remaining at end of period |
|---|---|---|---|
| Before 1800 | 8 | — | 8 |
| 1801–10 | 13 | — | 21 |
| 1811–20 | 9 | — | 30 |
| | | | |
| 1821 | 2 | — | 32 |
| 1822 | 1 | 1 | 32 |
| 1823 | 6 | — | 38 |
| 1824 | 14 | 1 | 51 |
| 1825 | 9 | 3 | 57 |
| 1826 | 3 | 5 | 55 |

Charles Babbage, FRS, the well-known Lucasian Professor of Mathematics at Cambridge, who through his 'difference engine' (designed in the years 1823–33) and his analytical engine (begun in

[1] Table produced from a chart by Morrice Black.

1833) is acknowledged as a pioneer of modern electronic computors, decided that the time was ripe for a competent analysis of the practices of the various life assurance offices and he brought out his *Comparative View of the various Institutions for the Assurance of Lives*. The preface was dated December 26, 1825 from Devonshire Street, Portland Place, but the book was actually published in 1826.

Babbage adopted a rather professorial attitude, freely criticizing the life offices where he thought it justified; though the comparisons were mostly to the advantage of the Equitable, the tone of the comments roused Morgan's ire. Babbage stated that only two offices (he was dealing with English, not Scottish offices) 'have yet assigned a bonus to the assured, by adding a certain percentage to the policies, . . . the Equitable and the Rock; the latter in the year 1819 (it was founded in 1805) made its first septennial dividend of profits'. Babbage accused these offices of misrepresenting the facts about their bonuses, saying that less than the stated two-thirds of surplus was actually divided. He was certainly wrong about the Equitable; he had misunderstood the system.

Babbage included tables showing the amounts payable by the Equitable when bonuses were added:

From these tables the folly of assuring at any of the offices, where no additions are made to the policies, and where the same or nearly the same rate of premium is charged is perfectly apparent.

It would not, however, be reasonable to presume that the same sums can be added continually for a long period of years, because . . . there are causes in operation which will naturally diminish what may be called the mercantile profits of that Institution (i.e. the Equitable); and they will receive a considerable check from the great reduction in the interest of money, should it remain at its present rate for several years longer.

It is said, however, that they possess a large undivided capital, of which the public, from want of sufficient information, have very vague, and perhaps extravagant ideas. The legitimate use of such a capital is to equalize the fluctuations amongst the various circumstances on which the system depends; and it would be wise to allow some portion of that capital to be absorbed during the time in which interest is unusually low, as it has been created when it was unusually high.

In dignified language, Babbage was surely saying that, in his opinion, the Equitable should declare higher bonuses, whereas what William Morgan desperately needed was help, from those who were qualified to give it, in his resistance to unreasonable demands.

William Morgan knew that his days in the Equitable's service were numbered. He hoped that his son Arthur would succeed him and how should his son fare, if he were assailed by critics from outside who were looked up to as being well informed on the subject? He picked up his quill, determined to scotch these new critics, and wrote his own defence of the Society whose history was so largely his own, *A view of the Rise and Progress of the Equitable Society* (1828). The pamphlet is a living history by a man who made the history, though (regrettably) it is inaccurate in detail. As Morgan deals with his critics, the pages are full of righteous wrath. After answering Babbage's criticisms point by point, Morgan continues:

> I shall proceed no further in my remarks on Mr Babbage's publication. I cannot, however, conclude them without expressing my surprise and regret that he should be so free in censuring a Society which has conferred such benefits on thousands, without taking a little more trouble to inform himself how far he was justified in those censures.

Morgan defended, at length, the right of the members in 1816 to have made the bye-laws adopted in that year. He flung back at his critics:

> the gross misrepresentations by which the Society has lately been assailed . . . the Society has acquired a degree of credit and prosperity unknown to any institution of the same kind. So far, therefore, from being a fit subject for censure, the Equitable Society deserves the applause of the public and, with the hope that it may always continue to deserve it, I shall now take my final leave of a subject which has occupied the greater part of a long life—but I trust not altogether in vain.

At the time when the pamphlet came out, Charles Babbage happened to be on a tour of the continent, but Francis Baily immediately wrote to *The Times* in defence of his friend (June 26, 1828). Baily had read Babbage's manuscript and he mentions (what was true) that Babbage commented for the most part favourably on the practices of the Equitable, which 'so far from being censured . . . is everywhere held up (as it deservedly is) as the best institution of its kind in existence . . .'. Morgan replied briefly that Baily had taken the passages wrongly and reproached him with not understanding the situation better, though a member of the Equitable Society of long standing. In defending what he held so dear, Morgan, at 78 years of age, had been unconcerned with niceties of feeling; he had laid about him vigorously, with no respect to persons.

The blows fell more or less indiscriminately and started a lively controversy.

George Farren, who claimed to have started the transaction of life assurance on sub-standard lives, felt himself personally slighted by Morgan's passing reference to 'the quackery' of trying to assess such risks and angrily replied in *The Times* of July 1, 1828:

> Mr Morgan . . . is now declining into the sear and yellow leaf bearing all the honours which mental capacity, considerable attainment, persevering industry, and unimpeachable integrity must always obtain for their possessor; let him not, at the end of a well-spent life, underrate and stigmatize the exertions and humble attainments of men as honest and industrious as himself.

Henry James Brooke, FRS, reached conclusions which 'are entirely at variance with the opinions entertained by Mr Morgan'. His main conclusion was that 'an annual reduction of premiums . . . may be a preferable mode of disposing of surplus'; it was, of course, Brooke's own method.

The well-known medical man and scientist, Thomas Young, MD, FRS, found it difficult to interpret the figures produced by William Morgan and in a letter to him published in the *Philosophical Magazine* for 1828, wrote: 'you will be desirous of vindicating yourself from all possible suspicion of ambiguity and of inconsistency'. Morgan must have longed to get rid of all 'ambiguity and inconsistency' in the interminable debates.

15. Ralph Price, by J. P. Knight

16. Sir George Hayter's two sketches of meetings in 1849

# CHAPTER XIII

# AUTUMNAL GLORY (1829–1830)

As William Morgan looked back over more than half a century spent in the service of the Society, what memories crowded upon him? His early days could have afforded no glimpse of the later splendour that came upon the Equitable. It was weak and had been rocked by opposing factions. Life assurance was in its infancy; the business was virtually unknown. The directors and even the members who had originally elected him as Actuary had all passed away.

Morgan's office was, at first, also his home for by the terms of his original appointment he received a salary of £120 a year and was required to live in the Society's house. This was in the tradition of the merchant who lived over his shop. The Society moved to Chatham Place just before he was appointed and the house was then a fine, new building whose south wall looked across the newly-built Blackfriars Bridge.

Jenkin Jones, in a letter dated July 31, 1818 (printed by Thomas Bignold), wrote:

Small beginnings, particularly with the active and industrious part of the community, make great endings. The greatest man at the Equitable Life Office, at its commencement, kept a school; but are his exertions the less meritorious?

The reference is clearly to William Morgan, but is it true that he kept a small school? His brother George did so at Southgate but there is no evidence of William's school.

As has been mentioned, Morgan received a medical training and his academic interests were always wider than the mathematics which he used in his business life. His first publication, in 1779, expounded the mathematical theory of annuities and life assurance on the general lines laid down by his uncle, Richard Price, but he was spending part of his time in scientific experiments and they soon led him into print

N 193

again. In those early experiments he was obviously influenced by his uncle's friend, Joseph Priestley, the well-known discoverer, or, more exactly, re-discoverer of oxygen. The Swedish scientist, Karl Wilhelm Scheele (1742–86) had published the results of his observations and experiments on air and fire, his conclusions concerning the constituents of air being similar to Priestley's findings. Scheele wrote in German. At the urgent request of Priestley, an English translation was made and when it appeared, in 1780, Morgan obtained a copy, which he signed and dated. In the following year, Morgan published the results of his own experiments in *An Examination of Dr Crawford's Theory of Heat and Combustion.*

Another interest of Priestley's had been electricity and both William Morgan and his brother George studied the subject. William's next experiments were designed to try the effect of passing an electric current through a vacuum. When there was no air in his glass tube, no electric current could pass. When he admitted a very minute quantity of air, he observed 'the colour of the electric light . . . appears in this case of a beautiful green, and what is very curious, the degree of the air's rarefaction may be nearly determined by this means . . .'. As more air entered the tube, the air began to glow in a series of colours from green to blue and so on to purple and violet. From his description of the experiment (in a paper to the Royal Society in 1785), we may conclude that the green light was a fluorescent green glow of the glass of the tube, indicating the production of cathode-rays in the electrical discharge. It is probable that X-rays were also produced, though Morgan had no means of detecting them. On this evidence scientists have claimed that 'William Morgan must be given the credit of being probably the first experimenter to produce X-rays'.

The study of the fluorescent tube was continued by famous scientists over the next century but it was not until 1895 that Röntgen observed the effects of X-rays outside the tubes, from the fogging of photographic plates stored near to them. The tubes he used did not differ in principle from the apparatus used by Morgan in 1785. Röntgen's discovery of X-rays has led on to the study of radiation, its use and misuse.

The cathode-rays, which would have been responsible for the effect that Morgan observed, are used in the cathode-ray tube of a television receiver as the vehicle for 'painting' the picture elements.

But the production of such a cathode-ray tube required further steps in the development of the apparatus which were far beyond the means available to William Morgan.

His experiment was forgotten, but it was brought to light again, on January 19, 1925, by V. E. Pullin in his Cantor lectures[1] to the Royal Society of Arts.

For calculations involving survivorships on two or more lives, the standard works on life contingencies had used a conventional rule as an approximation which was convenient for calculation but too wide of the mark to be permissible when the subject became better understood. In the years 1788 to 1800, Morgan produced for the Royal Society a series of papers in which he placed the evaluation of survivorships upon the firm footing of calculation from the actual probabilities of life. These papers were valuable contributions to the subject though, as might be expected in pioneer work, there were flaws in some of his solutions. The value of this work was recognized by the Royal Society by the award of the Copley medal on November 30, 1789 and his election as a Fellow on May 6, 1790. He served twice on the Council, from November 30, 1798 to November 30, 1800, and from November 30, 1810 to November 30, 1812.

For the first seven years in Chatham Place, his sister Anne kept house for him. She was there in June 1780 during the Gordon riots, when the Society's house was threatened by the mob. It must have been a frightening experience—she was never tired of re-telling it—though no attack was actually made on the premises.

In 1781, William Morgan married Susannah Woodhouse, the daughter of John Woodhouse, a London merchant and a friend of Mrs Price. The family came from Staffordshire and Susannah inherited a small estate at Portway. Anne Morgan was no longer wanted to keep house, as she had with considerable success for she was good company; she returned to Bridgend where she married her cousin in the following year.

In the early years of his marriage, William Morgan built one of the first of the houses on Stamford Hill, then quite a rural neighbourhood. A pleasant walk through the fields led to his brother's home at Southgate. There was ample space for good kitchen and flower gardens, lawns and paddocks. The home was just what was

---

[1] There is a fuller account in *X-rays past and present*, by V. E. Pullin and W. J. Wiltshire (1927).

needed for the family of six children, who grew up in happy surroundings.

Some notes written in 1857 by Richard Rees of Alltycham,
Pontardawe, Glamorgan, give a picture of the family between fifty
and sixty years earlier—a home where 'almost every member of the
family might, at all times, feel assured of a hearty welcome'. Richard
Rees arrived in London from Wales in March 1796. He was in
business with two of his brothers in Paternoster Row; a fourth
brother was also in business in London. Sunday was their only
'Holyday', which they usually spent in William Morgan's home at
Stamford Hill.

The family were close friends of the family of Samuel Rogers, the
banker and man of letters, a man of liberal opinions, whose poetry
was then rated very high though now ranked as a minor muse. When
Theodore Hook was editor of the Tory weekly paper *John Bull*, he
printed all kinds of vulgar, personal abuse of Rogers. The following
verses appeared on March 7, 1824 and refer to Rogers's appearance;
he was very pale and bald.

HUMAN LIFE

Cries Sam, 'All human life is frail,
   'E'en mine may not endure.
'So lest it suddenly should fail,
   'I'll hasten to insure.'

At Morgan's office Sam arrives,
   Reckoning without his host—
'Avaunt!' the affrighted Morgan cries,
   'We can't insure a ghost.'

'Zounds! 'tis my Poem, not my face—
   'Here, list while I recite it.'
Cries Morgan, 'Seek some other place,
   'We cannot underwrite it.'

The house on Stamford Hill became a meeting place for persons of
liberal opinions, such as John Horne Tooke, Sir Francis Burdett and
Tom Paine. On one such occasion when Samuel Rogers and Tom
Paine dined with William Morgan, Rogers noted in reference to
Morgan 'a strong silent man but very emphatic in his language'.
This must have been between 1787, when Paine returned to England,
and 1792, when he was indicted for treason.

There were lively gatherings on Sunday evenings. The shutters would be drawn against intruders and songs such as 'The trumpet of liberty sounds through the world', would be sung. The coming of war, in 1793, altered the situation for the various groups of radicals. Violent pressure for change, looking to France as a model, could be regarded as being treason against the King's government. When, in 1794, the radicals appealed for a national convention, a challenge to the authority of Parliament, the leaders of the various radical societies were indicted for high treason. Among them was Morgan's friend Horne Tooke. The leaders in Scotland received severe sentences but those tried in England were acquitted and so the minor figures in the movement escaped further trouble. However, Morgan received a warning from the authorities at this time.

Soon after his election as Actuary of the Equitable, William Morgan began to build up a reputation as a consultant on all matters connected with annuities and reversionary interests. At the time of Morgan's marriage in 1781, Dr Price noted that his nephew 'already adds to his income by answering annuity questions'. His work on survivorships added to his reputation and his practice as a consultant grew. There is no evidence that the offices established up to about 1800 consulted Morgan though they paid him the back-handed compliment of using his published calculations and his scale of premiums.

When the Rock Life Assurance Company was founded in 1806, Morgan probably played some part in the election of William Frend, M A, as the first Actuary. Frend was Second Wrangler and Smith's Prizeman in 1780 and had been elected a Fellow and Tutor of Jesus College, Cambridge. However, he soon came to hold unitarian views which lost him his post as college tutor and a pamphlet of his, published in 1793, led to his removal from the University. From 1793 to 1806, Frend lived in chambers in Middle Temple, occupying himself with scientific and statistical work. He was friendly with Sir Francis Burdett, Horne Tooke and others of the same liberal circles as William Morgan. It is not known when their friendship commenced, but Morgan and Frend were associated, e.g. in advising friendly societies, and Frend modelled the practices of the Rock upon those of the Equitable. Frend's daughter married Augustus de Morgan.

When the National Debt Office began the granting of life annuities in 1808 (as a means of redeeming the public debt), the tables were prepared by William Morgan. He used the Northampton table of mortality, which he had been accustomed to use for life assurance calculations. He thus assumed too high a mortality, and as a consequence the National Debt Office's prices for annuities were too low, at least at the younger ages.

At the start of the Sun Life Assurance Society in 1810, the managers went to Francis Baily for advice on the premium scale. However, they consulted Morgan and Frend as well as Baily, concerning suitable candidates for the post of Actuary of the new society and they chose Joshua Milne, who had been recommended by Morgan. Milne's text-book published in 1815, and the Carlisle table of mortality which it contained, were lasting memorials to Milne's worth.

Early in the year 1813, a deputation of three—David Wardlaw, Patrick Cockburn and William Wotherspoon—came from Edinburgh to London to consult William Morgan. David Wardlaw was the originator of the idea which led to the formation of the Scottish Widows Fund and Life Assurance Society. Patrick Cockburn was an accountant who had made the actuarial calculations and Wotherspoon became the first manager of the new office. The journey by stage coach was a long one in those days but the three Scots were amply satisfied with their cordial reception by William Morgan and the valuable help he gave them. The facts were given in an address by the manager, John McKean, in 1829 and he sent an autograph copy to Morgan 'with most respectful compliments'.

In the years 1817–18, a Parliamentary Committee on the Poor Laws sought advice of an actuarial character from William Morgan and Francis Baily. In the light of this, it is significant that the Bill which was introduced in 1818 provided that the tables of payments or benefits of friendly societies should first be submitted to a committee of five persons, to be appointed by the Treasury, of whom at least two would be 'professional actuaries or persons skilled in arithmetical calculations'. Government policy was to counter problems of indigence by the encouragement of thrift, especially through friendly societies, and Morgan's help was sought as the leading member of the profession. The Bill became law in the following year and, though the proposal for a committee was dropped, the Act contained the first official reference to 'professional actuaries'.

Benjamin Gompertz, FRS, read his first paper on life contingencies to the Royal Society on June 29, 1820. In it he said that 'Messrs Morgan, Baily and Milne, of the present age, are among the number of mathematicians to whom this department (of science) is greatly indebted'. Thus he put Morgan first among the three leading names.

The portrait of William Morgan by Lawrence shows a man of strong character and considerable mental ability. He was a good conversationalist. The smile about his lips would give him a charm in conversation with his friends but a mordant wit might well turn the smile to a sneer if he were provoked by lesser men. Such a man could scarcely escape criticism.

Francis Baily attributed to Morgan the Royal Society's rejection of tables by George Barrett, demonstrating a new method of calculating life contingencies. Morgan was on the Council of the Royal Society at the time. It is true that he did not see the full value of Barrett's method, which is now in general use, but—to be fair to Morgan—we have not seen the paper that was rejected.

A more important criticism is that he was much too fond of using Dr Price's tables of mortality and sickness, and that he gave too little weight to current experience; he usually argued that the statistics were too few or too unreliable to construct a table from them. There seems to have been some personal animosity between him and John Finlaison, the first Actuary of the National Debt Office and later the first President of the Institute of Actuaries. The clash of views came to a head in the evidence given to the Parliamentary Committee of 1825 on the subject of friendly societies and two years later a mass of statistics was produced to give as much information as possible about actual experience. His attitude to the use of the Northampton table for the sale of life annuities by the National Debt Office was really indefensible, though there was some truth in his comment:

> By the assistance of these tables (Finlaison's tables of the mortality experience among government annuitants), the notable discovery has been made of the loss sustained by the public of many thousands every week. . . . With the least knowledge of the subject, it might easily have been seen that the use of the Northampton table could not possibly be attended by such a loss, and that the extent of any loss (if it really existed), instead of six years, did not require as many hours to ascertain it.

The 1820s, when Morgan was in his seventies, were years in which he had to meet much criticism. It may be that he should have quitted the stage earlier. But there was much that he, and only he, could do. What the directors of the Equitable thought of him is shown by their steady support throughout and the warmth of affection that shines through the minutes—for example, the 'good fortune' of the Society in their Actuary which 'has derived from his unrival'd talents and undeviating attention and integrity a success unexampled in Europe' (G, December 7, 1826). Now, as an old man nearly eighty years of age, he had to face his last challenge.

The debate 'outside the walls' had the effect of drawing attention to the favourable mortality experience of the Equitable. Both Charles Babbage and Griffith Davies had produced tables from the scanty information given by Morgan. Rather naturally, there were inconsistencies between Babbage's and Davies's figures, which Morgan pointed out (S, November 14, 1828). He argued that it would be wrong to use the Equitable experience instead of the Northampton table which he had been accustomed to use in the decennial valuations because it would increase the apparent surplus and tend to benefit the older members at the expense of the younger members: 'But one class of the Society has no right to benefit itself at the expense of the other class in direct violation of its own engagements to the contrary.'

Samuel Sweet was quick to follow up the new line of attack. Whereas in the previous year, he had been pestering the directors to disclose their plans for 1830, and putting forward again (S, December 6, 1827) the rejected ideas of more frequent rests and the distribution of the whole of the profits, he suddenly shifted the attack with proposals (G, December 4, 1828): (1) that the Equitable experience should be used in the valuation; (2) that the assurances should be classified by age, with a calculation of the average duration at each age; and (3) that a printed copy of the results should be sent to each member before the final decision was taken.

Morgan commented to the directors:

> During the many years in which I have been Actuary of this Society, I have seldom witnessed such an entire disregard to its laws and so little knowledge of the subject of Life Assurances as are displayed in these resolutions.

The craftiness of the proposals was explained by the directors in a report to the members, which said:

> The expectation of a future participation in our profits has been, unquestionably, one of the principal inducements to persons (assuring since 1816) to become Members. Repeated acts of the Society have sanctioned this expectation. We have made with the new Insurers, it is true, no specific contract, as to the amount or proportion of this participation; but, we have freely made known to them the Rules by which the Society had in this respect been guided, before they were

admitted into it. We have given to those Rules a subsequent and solemn sanction, by adhering to them on the only occasion on which they could have come into operation; and it would scarcely be consistent with good faith and fair dealing, even if it were lawful, to introduce a new Regulation less favourable to those who have relied upon our implied engagement.

The directors moved an amendment to Sweet's motion, but their amendment was defeated (G, February 19, 1829). Upon Sweet's original motion being put to the ballot, 125 votes were cast in favour and 80 against, but the President thereupon declared the motion to have been lost because the majority in favour was less than the four-fifths required for certain types of resolution. As could be expected, some of the majority objected to the ruling and it was agreed to take a legal opinion. Counsel did not support the chairman and, two months later, the Vice-President (who was in the chair) had to reverse the ruling and declare Sweet's motion to be carried.

Counsel's opinion had been obtained on the limited question concerning the exact nature of the motion. The directors counter-attacked by taking Counsel's (John Bell, Henry Brougham, Henry Bickersteth) opinion on the broad question of principle—whether changes could be made.

We are of opinion that the new Insurers have entered the Society and paid their Premiums under circumstances from which it must be implied that a contract subsists between them and the other Members of the Society, that the mode of calculation adopted for the purpose of ascertaining the profits of the Society, and the amount or proportion of their participation in such profits, shall not be altered so as to affect the relative interests of the new and old Insurers; and that while such relative interests may be thereby affected, it will not be legal to depart from the practice of the Society as it existed before the year 1817, by using any other Tables in calculating the profits than those on which the Premiums are calculated, or by reserving a less proportion of the surplus on each appropriation, or by altering the period of appropriating the surplus Stock of the Society. And we think that a Bye-Law or Order to be made by the General Court, if it involves a departure from the former practice in any of the above particulars, will be inconsistent with the principles of Law and Equity, and may lead to adverse legal proceedings.

So that the arguments regarding the use of the Equitable experience should be based on fact, William Morgan prepared his own table of the experience.[1] Calculations, making a comparison between valuations by the Northampton table (previously used) and this experience table,

[1] Printed in the appendix to the second edition of Morgan's, *View of the Rise and Progress of the Equitable Society.*

showed that the value of the liabilities would be reduced by about £700,000 if the Equitable experience were used and the immediate surplus would be enhanced by that amount, though, of course, no juggling with the figures could increase the total surplus in the long run. Armed with this information, the directors proposed that the valuation at December 31, 1829 should be conducted by the accustomed mode and that two-thirds of the surplus should be distributed according to the plan followed in 1809 and 1819. The opposition within the membership put up formal amendments to both motions, the first calling for a valuation by the Equitable experience and the second requiring the results to be printed and circulated before a decision was taken. However, both amendments were defeated and the directors' resolutions were carried (G, September 3, 1829). Another round had been won but the Society was being driven into a position which made change difficult, when change was necessary.

The results of the decennial investigation as at December 31, 1829 were ready some weeks earlier. There were 8,867 policies in force for sums assured of £12,417,630 and annuities of £5,617 10s. The surplus came out at £5,394,033. About 52 per cent of the assets was surplus, notwithstanding that the sums assured had already been increased by earlier additions by about one-fifth in the aggregate to nearly £15,000,000. The surplus was swollen by the high prices in the stock markets at that time. Well over £1,000,000 of the surplus must have come from the revaluation of the 3 per cent stocks at current prices (89 and 90) and this tended to mask the fact that surplus was accumulating at a slower rate than formerly, due to the low rates of interest at which new money could be invested.

Though Morgan had misgivings about the high prices, he felt bound to pursue the same methods of distribution as formerly. He and his son recommended a rate of £3 per cent for every year's premium due and paid before January 1, 1830 on assurances made before January 1, 1817. This actually took rather less than two-thirds and one of the directors proposed a rate of £3 3s which would have absorbed the full two-thirds. However, the Morgans' recommendation was adopted.

An assurance for £100 effected in 1790, on which forty years' premiums had been paid before January 1, 1830, would have been increased to £381 with bonus additions and would increase by £3 for each further year's premium paid up to January 1, 1840. Though the rate was a high one, the sum assured and bonus additions for a policy forty years in force was about the same as it had been in 1819 and 1809. The effect of spacing out the distributions to ten-year intervals was beginning to be felt and the exceptional profits which had been made in the earlier years were no longer available.

Assurances made since January 1, 1817 were still excluded from participation in this surplus. Had they been admitted to participation, the rate would have been substantially less. The reserved third of surplus was still a material benefit for the excluded policyholders; yet it is clear that the regulations of 1816 were operating more harshly than had been expected when the regulations were made and the wonderful results in 1829 gave probably the last opportunity for modifying the regulations to make them more equitable, if indeed modification were practicable at all.

Though the older policyholders had done so well, some of them were unsatisfied and managed to carry a resolution which kept open the door for the distribution of a larger part of the surplus at subsequent valuations. The temper of one of them is shown by a letter from 'Senex' in *The Times* (December 19, 1829). He argued that the funds of the Society were rapidly accumulating and said 'the proposed addition is now only 3 per cent!' But the point of view of the younger members is seen in the question asked by 'Number one' in a letter in *The Times* of December 8, 1829: 'Is it equitable to confine the benefits of such additions to policies commencing before 1817?' If 'Number one' was indeed the holder of the first policy effected in the new series, he was John Miles, of Throgmorton Street, Apothecary, aged 25 in 1817.

William Morgan was ailing and unable to attend the General Court on December 3, 1829; Ralph Price, Vice-President, had to read his speech. After a reference to the 'infatuation which so generally prevailed' some five years earlier, the speech continued:

The accounts now laid before the Court, while they exhibit the progressive improvement of the Society, afford a striking proof of the beneficial effects of those measures which were adopted in the year 1816, and to which are to be principally attributed the excess of the present, above all former additions. Had no such measures been adopted, so far from exceeding, the present additions would probably have fallen short of the preceding ones, notwithstanding the advantage which has been derived from estimating the funded property of the Society at more than 20 per cent higher than has been done in any former investigation.

That the Society may probably have a right (founded on its former practice) to estimate its Stock in the Public Funds at the price it bears at the time of determining its surplus, I do not pretend to dispute; but I think the prudence of exercising this right to its full extent is very questionable: and I very much doubt whether the Society could as easily be prevailed upon to exercise it to the same extent, should the Funds at any future investigation be reduced 20 per cent lower than they were in either of the two former investigations. The great fluctuation in the value of funded property will always render the Surplus very precarious. It might perhaps be desirable that the Stock in the Funds should be invariably fixed at some mean price, rather than that the amount of the Surplus should be suffered to depend on property perpetually changing in its real value. . . .

In the intervals of the former decennial investigations, it has not been uncommon, especially among the old Members, to witness some expressions of impatience, and an eager desire to have their hopes more speedily fulfilled. Without entering into the reasonableness of this anxiety to participate in the last farthing of the Surplus (for nothing short of this can satisfy such a disposition)—I am sorry to observe that in the present interval this anxiety has been greatly increased by the unreasonable expectations which have been entertained during the last four or five years. On what ground these expectations are founded, it is not easy to imagine. They are not supported by any events that have proved more than usually favourable to the Society. On the contrary, the probabilities of life have approached nearer to those in the Table, from which the premiums are computed; the interest on the Mortgages has been reduced; the purchases of Stock in the Public Funds have been made at a much higher price, and the Sums paid for the prospective additions have necessarily exceeded their amount in any former interval. The experience of the Society therefore justified no such expectation; and the excess of the present Surplus should be ascribed partly to the casual high price of Stock in the Public Funds, but chiefly to the wise regulations adopted in the year 1816. But it is not my wish to discourage the future expectations of the Society. My chief object has always been, as it is at present, to moderate, not to destroy those expectations: and I should be very sorry to take my leave of the Society with any other impression on my mind than that of a full assurance of its continued welfare and prosperity.

The President, Sir Charles Morgan, wanted William Morgan to continue as Actuary of the Society as long as he lived. But Morgan felt his powers declining and asked to be released. The directors were speaking for the members as a whole, when they recorded that they regarded his industry and ability 'as the principal cause of the prosperity of an Institution, which has afforded and will continue to afford blessings to thousands'. The terms of his appointment have been quoted. On retirement he was granted a pension of his full salary of £2,000 a year for life.

Arthur Morgan had 'given proof of great ability and industry' and the directors were 'perfectly satisfied of his integrity and of his entire competence to perform all the duties required by an Actuary of the Equitable Society'. He was elected in his father's place. William Morgan's speech on this occasion (G, December 2, 1830) was a moving one:

During the last two or three years, I have felt myself unable to attend the General Court; and it is with no inconsiderable degree of exertion that I now address you on a subject which has long agitated my mind, and which from its great importance to myself has rendered me very anxious to communicate it to this Court. The advanced age of Fourscore, of which more than fifty-six years have been engaged in the service of this Society, will, I trust, require no other reason for my wishing to retire from my labours, to enjoy the few remaining days of my life in ease and quiet.

In order to accomplish this end, the declining state of my health and spirits renders it necessary that the tie which has so long connected me with my present office should in a great measure be dissolved, and that I should no longer attempt to discharge the active duties of it. It is not without sorrow and a deep sense of the obligations I owe to the Society, that I resign my present office. To the Members to whom I am indebted for my original appointment to a situation in which I have enjoyed so many years of ease and comfort, I have it not in my power to express my grateful acknowledgements; for none of those Members are in existence to receive them. To their successors I am under equal obligation; and to them, with sentiments of equal gratitude, I now resign an office which during my whole continuance in it has been distinguished by so many instances of kindness and respect. I am far from meaning that this resignation should sever me entirely from the Society; on the contrary, I shall never cease to be anxious for its welfare, nor (while my mental faculties are continued) to devote them to its service. During the long series of years which have passed away since my first appointment, I have witnessed the progressive prosperity of this Society. I have witnessed it rising from a puny Institution, consisting of few Members and possessing a Capital of a few thousands, to a magnificent Establishment consisting of many thousand Members and many millions of Capital, diffusing its benefits to the families of its deceased Members, and holding forth the prospect of equal benefits to those of its living Members. With this view I am cheered under the pain I feel on the present occasion; and encouraged to express a hope in this my last Address to the General Court, that the Society may long continue to enjoy and deserve the approbation of mankind.

The death of William Morgan on May 4, 1833 is mentioned in a letter written by John Morgan to Richard Rees on May 12th. It is interesting that the letter was written from the Equitable Office and indicates that John was helping his brother there.

My dear Richard . . . father . . . died on Friday week, without pain or any other suffering, having fallen a victim to the prevailing influenza—Arthur has not yet been able to return to business but will do so tomorrow. In the meantime, I enclose your office receipt—My poor mother bears her affliction as well as we could expect. . . .

William Morgan's assurances for £2,500 yielded a total claim of £7,495 with bonuses.

John Morgan (1797–1847) became a 'plodding, hard-working and intelligent' surgeon of Guy's Hospital, whose judgments were regarded as important and whose operations were skilfully performed. Like his father, he had wider scientific interests, John Morgan's being in natural history and the Linnaean Society. He was like his father, too, in build—a thick-set, heavy man of middle height and phlegmatic temperament, taking snuff to excess, a man of great sincerity and warm heart.

A contemporary view of the Society's affairs is given by Augustus de Morgan, in *An Essay on Probabilities* (1838), one of the volumes in 'The Cabinet Cyclopedia'.

> I always consider (the Equitable) Society as a distinct and anomalous establishment, existing . . . under circumstances of an unique character. It is the result of an experiment which it was most important to try, but which, having been tried, need not be repeated. . . . The hazard having been run, and having turned out profitably, the proceeds belong to those who ran it, and to those who, by their own free consent, became their lineal successors. Nor is it the least remarkable circumstance connected with this Society that the immense funds at its disposal have been always opened, though under restrictions, to the public. . . . The general lesson taught by it (the history of the Society) is—be cautious; but . . . be cautious of carrying caution so far as to leave a part of your own property for the benefit of those who are in no way related to you. If there be a Charybdis in an insurance office, there is also a Scylla: the mutual insurer, who is much too afraid of dispensing the profits to those who die before him, will have to leave his own share for those who die after him. Reversing the fable of Spenser, we should write upon the door of every mutual office but one *be wary;* but upon that one should be written *be not too wary* and over it *Equitable Society*.

Clearly, Augustus de Morgan thought that too little bonus had been declared and too much surplus had been held back for the future. In this he was probably misled either by the size of the rapidly accumulating funds or, as seems more likely, by the increase in the *rate* of bonus at successive decennial distributions to the magnificent rate of 3 per cent per annum in 1829. However, this takes no account of the effect of spacing out the distributions to ten-year intervals and the figures already quoted for claims under assurances which had been forty years in force do not support his opinion (£390, £380 and

£381 for assurances of £100 effected in the years 1770, 1780, and 1790 respectively).

The relatively high prices of Government stocks at this time gave an appearance of great prosperity but, in fact, the outlook had been worsened. Credit had been taken for the full market value of the investments. The immediate surplus had been swollen but the margin for future surpluses had been lessened. The position would have been serious but for the use of the antiquated Northampton table—which overstated the value of the liabilities—and the reservation of one-third of the surplus.

Actuarial opinion, too, would not support Augustus de Morgan's argument that the funds of a mutual society belong exclusively to the members of the fund at the particular point of time. A mutual life assurance society is a continuing business. Ample funds are necessary for the credit and stability of the office and each generation of members comes into a heritage from the past; so in its turn, each generation should endeavour to pass on that heritage unimpaired to the generations that succeed it. William Morgan understood this and modern opinion would support him.

Augustus de Morgan's view of the Equitable as a unique institution, whose practices should not be adopted by other societies, was related to the rigid, inflexible methods into which the Society had been forced. Experience has shown that more flexible methods are desirable and the whole subject is now better understood. But the principles of mutual life assurance, with the policyholders sharing in periodical bonus allocations, are part of traditional practice in the United Kingdom and in many parts of the world; these were taught by the 'experiment' of the Equitable Society.

In the early days, life assurance offices published few figures which might show their size, so that it is difficult now to compare the Equitable's figures with those of other offices. Very few offices—the Equitable, London Life and Scottish Widows were honourable exceptions—published in their prospectuses the figures relating to premium income, funds and business in force. By the year 1837, when Queen Victoria came to the throne, there were eighty-two life offices established in the United Kingdom. David Deuchar, FIA, FFA, estimated[1] that these eighty-two offices had total funds of

[1] In his paper on 'The progress of life assurance business in the U.K. during the last fifty years', in the *Trans. Actuarial Society of Edinburgh*, Vol. 2, p. 137 (1887).

£27,700,000, excluding share capital, in 1837. The business in force consisted of assurances for about £102,000,000 subject to annual premiums of £3,000,000.

By comparison, the Equitable, at its peak some twenty years earlier, had had nearly 10,000 assurances in force for over £12,500,000 which by 1837 had been reduced to about £11,000,000, the premium income being £348,204. The assets had continued to rise over this period and stood at about £10,500,000 in 1837. Thus, at this time, the Equitable Society's invested funds were more than one-third of the total life funds of all offices in the United Kingdom—but the business in force had dropped to little more than one-tenth of the aggregate business in force.

That the other life offices were able to reap a golden harvest by reason of the Equitable's restrictions on new business could be illustrated in a variety of ways. The Norwich Union Life Insurance Society was quickly off the mark. Its pamphlet of 1820 included a long comparison between the two offices—it claimed to be 'still more cautious' than the Equitable:

> That valuable Institution . . . has since attained to such an extent both of insurance and capital that it has been found expedient to check its progress, lest it should grow too unwieldy for convenient management. . . . The effect of the regulation has been to bring a great increase of business to the Norwich Union, much of which had previously gone to the Equitable.

In the printed report of the annual meeting of the Scottish Amicable Life Assurance Society held on March 27, 1834, the results of the first septennial investigation (a bonus at the rate of 30s per £100 for each year in force) were given with a glowing tribute to its model:

> This Society is on the principle of mutual assurance, on the model of the Equitable of London. . . . The astonishing and unrivalled prosperity attending the Equitable . . . is a sufficient proof of the accuracy of the principle on which this Society is formed, a prosperity to the individuals holding policies absolutely unattainable in any proprietary institution whatever. . . . The Equitable . . . having altered their original plan . . . it must be many years before members now entering with the Equitable can derive the advantages which are immediately imparted to those who may insure with the Scottish Amicable Society.

The argument was superficially attractive and was no doubt effective in practice. However, since the Equitable's bonuses increased with the duration of the assurance, the 'immediate advantage' might be reversed long before the time when the assurance could be expected to become a claim.

In January 1830, one of the more colourful life offices, the Asylum, was inviting members of the Equitable Society to insure their lives against the loss of the next decennial bonus. Since the bonus might be as much as the original sum assured or more, the amount was substantial and would be added only to the assurances of those who survived to the end of 1839. There is a letter in *The Times* of January 16, 1830 from 'An Equitable Proprietor' which mentions this practice of the Asylum life office and complains of the 'cruel and unjust system of a life tontine'. The letter tells the story of a medical man who refused to submit to a surgical operation, because the day of the bonus was approaching; he actually died before the important day, for want of it. Two days later, George Farren of 70 Cornhill, Resident Director of the Asylum life office, replied to the letter and invited Equitable members to insure, as he himself had done before the 1830 bonus.

Many financial organizations have borrowed the name 'Equitable'. The word came into the Society's title as an adjective but it was used by others because it had a pleasant sound and rich associations. That they wished to borrow the name was a compliment to the Society. In Sir John Clapham's *The Bank of England* there is a brief mention of the Equitable Assurance Company of Calcutta under the date August 1789. This is intriguing but nothing else is known of this company.

The second instance of the use of the name 'Equitable' by an insurance office in the United Kingdom was the Essex Equitable Insurance Society, which was founded in 1802 in Colchester for fire insurance. It still exists (as the Essex and Suffolk Insurance Society Ltd.—'Equitable' was dropped in 1958), though now as a subsidiary office in a large group. This example is an interesting one because 'Equitable' came into this title also as an adjective. The office was founded as a mutual society 'upon the equitable principle of every insurer becoming a proprietor and participating in the profit or loss of the institution'. The idea may have been borrowed from the Equitable Society but there is no evidence of it. And when the fire office started life assurance in 1820, a proprietary form was chosen, under the title the Essex Life Insurance Society. As it happens,

o                                209

Mr John Oxley Parker, one of the Equitable's directors, is also a director of the Essex and Suffolk.

When the Scottish Widows Fund and Life Assurance Society was started, with the help of advice from William Morgan as has been seen, the promoters at first proposed to call the new office the Scottish Widows Fund and Equitable Assurance Society. However, second thoughts prevailed and 'Life' was substituted for 'Equitable'.

A number of the solidly founded life assurance societies paid the Equitable the compliment of borrowing its name. When at a meeting in Edinburgh on March 29, 1831, it was decided to found a new life assurance society 'on the model of the Equitable Society of London, and (the) Scottish Widows Fund Society of Edinburgh', the new office was called the Scottish Equitable Life Assurance Society. Its 'Reports and Proceedings' in 1837 contained the tribute: 'The London Equitable . . . is well known throughout the Empire and the profits which that admirable institution has divided are familiar to everyone at all acquainted with life assurance'. The British Equitable Assurance Company was founded in 1854.

Not all the borrowers of the name were so respectable. Some of the ephemeral life offices of this period used the name so that they might catch and reflect some part of the glory that surrounded the Equitable Society. Thus, the London Equitable appeared in 1855 and the New Equitable in 1851 after an abortive attempt in 1841; they had only short lives. The name was used for a number of short-lived offices in the late 1800s and also for regional offices transacting fire insurance, which have been absorbed into the larger groups.

'Equitable' is such a good-sounding name that it was naturally an attraction to speculators in concerns where the meaning of the word (as distinct from the name) could have little connection with the actual business being transacted. One of the bubble formations of the year 1824 was a disreputable financial project known as the Equitable Loan Bank Company, which occupied premises in Warwick Lane, near where Dodson had lived. A large sum of money was to be subscribed for the purpose of making loans on personal effects at rates of interest which would put pawnbrokers out of business. The capital was to be £2,000,000; the Duke of York was secured as Patron with twelve distinguished Vice-Presidents, including ten Members of Parliament. The Bill authorizing the establishment of the company was bitterly opposed by pawnbrokers and was thrown out by the House of Lords. Many of the original promoters took the opportunity of the bubble conditions of 1824–25 to dispose of their holdings at a profit. The unfortunate public were left with the resulting loss and the scandal reverberated in the correspondence columns of *The Times* for years afterwards.

An even more disreputable concern at this time was the Equitable Tea Agency, whose manager was soon arrested for fraud. Curiously, the name was also used by the philanthropist, Robert Owen, for the Equitable Labour Exchanges that he founded but, in this case, the name was probably unconnected with the Equitable Society; there is no evidence either way.

The modern building society movement began with small, local, terminating societies and operated on such a basis for about seventy years from 1775. The earliest permanent building societies date from the year 1846, though some terminating societies, founded earlier, made the necessary changes in their rules and became permanent. The inspirer of the permanent system for building societies was an actuary named Arthur Scratchley and it is not surprising that some of the building societies borrowed the names 'Amicable' and 'Equitable', which had honourable traditions in life assurance. The Bradford Equitable Building Society was founded in 1846 and the Second and the Third Bradford Equitables in 1851 and 1854. The Woolwich Equitable Building Society was founded in 1847. The first of the new building societies in Halifax was the Halifax Permanent of 1853; the Halifax Equitable followed in 1871 and they were amalgamated in 1928.

Abroad, there is the instance of the Equitable Life Assurance Society of the United States, which was started in 1859 by Henry Baldwin Hyde, then aged 25, and which rapidly became one of the largest life offices in the world.

Looking back, it is astonishing how widespread was the use of the name Equitable in the middle of the nineteenth century and it reflects the relatively large size and good repute of the Equitable Society.

# CHAPTER XIV

# THE EBB-TIDE (1830–1870)

RTHUR MORGAN took over the actuaryship of the Equitable at a most difficult time. The pressure of conflicting ideas amongst the members was like the turbulence of the sea; but the damage had been done on the incoming tide and now the tide was receding.

The staff at this time were six in number, with two supernumerary clerks—probably in preparation for Lovelock's retirement (S, May 24, 1832); Lovelock retired in 1833 at the age of 70.

THE EQUITABLE'S STAFF

|  | Salary £ | Gratuity £ | Christmas bonus £ s |
|---|---|---|---|
| Arthur Morgan, *Actuary* .. .. | 800 | nil | — |
| John Scott Martineau, *Assistant Actuary* | 500 | nil | — |
| Edward Lovelock, *Principal Clerk* .. | 300 | 200 | 78 15 |
| George Train .. .. .. .. | 250 | 50 | 47 5 |
| Thomas Butler .. .. .. .. | 250 | 30 | 26 5 |
| Edward Lovelock, jnr. .. .. .. | 150 | 50 | 26 5 |
| Samuel Brown .. .. .. .. | 100 | — | 10 10 |
| Peter Hardy .. .. .. .. | 100 | — | 10 10 |

The mathematical staff included Martineau, Train (who succeeded him as Assistant Actuary), Butler, Brown and Hardy. When the Institute of Actuaries was formed in 1848, Hardy, now FRS, became one of the original Vice-Presidents and helped to create its examination system. Brown (1812–75) was President of the Institute from 1867 to 1870.

As has been related, the mortality experience of the Society had assumed great importance and Arthur Morgan's first major task was to settle the question once and for all by a thorough tabulation of the facts. This he did by tracing the lives of all the members of the

Society from the time of their entrance into the Society (on the first occasion if more than one policy had been effected) until the member went out of the experience either by death or by withdrawal, or until January 1, 1829, if the life were a member of the Society on that day. The numbers involved were very large; 21,398 members had entered the Society and 5,144 had died. This mortality experience was a pioneer effort; such a task had never been attempted before and, though in some respects it is defective—modern ideas would require the experience to be tabulated in a rather different way—the work is a monument to the ability and industry of Arthur Morgan. The directors referred to 'the talent evinced by the actuary in forming such tables'. While the experience was being tabulated, there was an outbreak of cholera in the suburbs of London and some of the directors wished to stop granting new assurances until the epidemic was over (S, February 17, 1832). This was the first of the cholera outbreaks of the nineteenth century.

It had been customary to charge substantial extra premiums for persons who were resident overseas. Arthur Morgan had too few statistics to enable him to analyse the experience but he produced what figures he could, so that the extra premiums should be based on statistical evidence. The number of persons exposed to the climate of America (Canada and USA), north of Maryland and Virginia, was forty-nine, no less than thirty of them having gone there within the previous nine years. There had been twelve deaths, i.e. a fourth part nearly, and with one exception all the deaths had been at the younger ages—'before the middle period of life'. The extra mortality at that time, due to the severe climate, was substantial and justified the then charge of 20s per cent per annum (G, June 1, 1837). No figures were given for the East and the West Indies, but it was noted that a large proportion of the deaths were at ages under fifty, and that they were attributed to climate. The charge of £5 per cent per annum was to be maintained. On the other hand, the results were not unfavourable from such places as the Cape of Good Hope, New South Wales and so on; while the charge for the first year was maintained at £2 per cent, the charge in subsequent years was reduced from 20s to 10s per cent (G, December 7, 1837). Nowadays, these would seem high extra premiums but conditions were different then, especially in the less settled areas.

The Court of Directors was anxious to encourage mortgages and with this in view adopted a sliding scale so that a lower rate of interest than the legal maximum of 5 per cent would be charged when the price of Consols was high. For practical reasons, the price of Consols on the last day of April was to govern the rate at which interest would be charged for the half-yearly instalment due in the six months after the next October, and the price on the last day of October the rate in the six months after the next April (S, December 9, 1830):

| Price of Consols | Rate of interest to be charged on mortgages |
|---|---|
| 90 and upwards | $3\frac{1}{2}$ per cent |
| 90 – 86 | $3\frac{3}{4}$ per cent |
| 86 – 78 | 4 per cent |
| 78 – 70 | $4\frac{1}{2}$ per cent |
| under 70 | 5 per cent |

The maximum amount to be invested in mortgages was raised from £3,000,000 to £3,500,000 (S, April 15, 1835) and to £4,000,000 (W, May 2, 1838). To qualify for a mortgage, an estate had to show a rental of at least 10 per cent per annum (S, March 30, 1831)—presumably the gross rental, before charging expenses. The requirement was reduced to 8 per cent per annum in 1853.

The members were constantly urging upon the Court of Directors the advisability of encouraging loans and mortgages, so as to enforce the realization of as much as possible of the Society's holdings of public funds, at the relatively high prices then current. Someone suggested that the Society should make loans to members on the security of their policies, a practice which is now customary but which was then a new idea. William Morgan had been scornful and there may be some sympathy with his comment that the practice would 'perplex the accounts'. As a means of relieving a member in difficulty, 'this method of pawning his policy is neither so simple, nor . . . so effectual in the end, as that of surrendering his additions'. Counsel (E. B. Sugden, J. Campbell and A. R. Sidebottom) supported Morgan:

We think that the directors are not authorized to lend money on the security of their own policies, which are merely personal securities, and produce no income for payment of interest, and we think that a General Court could not confer such authority. If the plan were feasible, we could not advise the directors to act upon it, as we foresee much practical difficulty in the remedies that it might be advisable to adopt.

Counsel's opinion was against the tide of affairs but William Morgan's views help to explain why the refusal to make loans on policies was maintained for a quarter of a century.

Two members suggested that a large amount of stock should be realized and the proceeds put into Exchequer Bills—a proposal which should only be adopted as a temporary expedient. The Court of Directors kept the selection of investments in its own hands and rejected the proposal twice (S, August 24, 1836, and January 18, 1838).

Overshadowing these problems was the constantly recurring theme of the conflicting interests of members in the surplus. Immediately after the last declaration of bonus, the members had asked the directors to consider whether an arrangement with the new assurers would be practicable; obviously the older members were still hungry for a larger share of surplus. Before the directors could report on this question, an event occurred which heralded a new phase of the problem; the number of the 'old assurances', i.e. those effected before January 1, 1817, was reduced below 5,000 and the survivors of nos. 1 to 18 of the new series came within the privileged 5,000 (W, August 10, 1831).

That Arthur Morgan was well thought of was shown by his election as Fellow of the Royal Society on April 2, 1835, an honour conferred primarily for his tabulation of the Equitable's mortality experience. His sponsors included men who were prominent in various walks of life—Benjamin Gompertz and Griffith Davies (leading actuaries), John Pond the Astronomer Royal, Marc Isambard Brunel the engineer, Richard Twining, Benjamin Travers and Sir David Pollock, directors of the Equitable. Sixteen Fellows, altogether, added their names to recommend him.

While life assurance was passing through its growing-pains in the middle years of the nineteenth century, the Equitable was suffering pains of another kind. The Society had been, as it were, put into a strait-jacket from which it could not escape. The regulations of 1816 had been intended to stabilize the membership at about 5,000 assurances or rather more. But was it reasonable to expect growth to be arrested, without other injurious effects? In a period of long-continued stagnation, the Society might lose its power to attract new members. The system of adding bonuses to the sums assured, which the Society had developed, had proved to be a powerful attraction for new business. Conditions had been favourable and the results were magnificent. There now set in a period of low rates of interest when bonus rates were declining; conditions became less favourable for new assurances just when the restrictive regulations began to be felt most acutely.

At its zenith, the membership consisted of close on 10,000 assurances. There was a gradual fall at first to 8,867 in 1829; thereafter, the number declined rapidly so that it fell below 5,000 in 1855 and reached its lowest point round about the end of this period, the number of assurances being 3,785 in 1869. Though the membership declined, the assets went on increasing for some twenty-five years because the renewal premiums on the existing business and the income from investments exceeded what was required for the outgo on claims, etc.; the excess had to be invested. The total assets rose to a peak of nearly £11,000,000 but began to decline in the 1840s and fell to £4,600,000 in 1869. Even then the Equitable was one of the three largest offices, all with life funds a little in excess of £4,500,000.

The members themselves were, of course, concerned about the declining membership as, indeed, were the directors, but the latter also saw the difficulties of making changes. The older members had greatly increased advantages out of the arrangement of 1816, which, in the opinion of the directors, 'secured an amount of business which cannot, perhaps, be permanently secured under any other plan'. The fall in the number of new assurances could be attributed largely to the establishment of new offices. The Equitable could 'depend not only upon the number of 5,000 but also a considerable number beyond that limit'. If any individual member were to suffer from a change in the arrangements, he might defeat the whole—'a majority could not in this case bind a minority'. This report (G, June 7, 1832) did not satisfy the members and, by the narrow majority of 61 to 57, it was referred back to the directors to consider 'what are the relative interests in the surplus . . . of the old . . . and of the new insurers'. The directors thought that it would be 'equally difficult to define the surplus itself and the interests in it'. Arthur Morgan produced a valuation of the two sections of the business separately which showed that the assurances not yet within the 5,000 were about three-eighths of the whole, though the reserve accumulated for them was only half-a-million out of a total of £7,000,000. A year later the directors themselves were considering a number of different schemes, mainly for the benefit of the older members, but the various plans got no farther than the Court room.

In the 1830s the low level of new assurances gave such concern that Arthur Morgan was led to try to put their prospects in a better perspective (G, December 7, 1837):

> The Bye-Laws passed in 1816 have unquestionably secured to the members then existing a large share of the surplus stock of the Society; but those regulations do not operate in favour of the older members in a manner similar to . . . a tontine, as many persons have supposed or represented them to do; on the contrary, the interest (in the surplus stock) of the Members who have joined . . . since 1816 is gradually outgrowing the interest of those who were admitted prior to that year, and will at no very distant date . . . secure to the members assured since 1816 a very large share of the future profits of the Institution. . . . They (the Bye-Laws of 1816) were never intended to operate for the exclusive benefit of any one . . . class, but after securing the fulfilment of the just and reasonable expectations of the older members, . . . to continue its benefits to those that should succeed them. Framed in the same spirit which had led the Society in former years to extend its benefits and credit by . . . a moderate use of the advantages with which it had then been peculiarly favoured, these regulations will be found . . . to perpetuate the same system and to promise to the new insurer a share in profits derived . . . from the prudent forbearance of his predecessors, as well as from his own contributions.

When the time for the next distribution of surplus came round the directors felt that they ought to consider once again whether the method of allocating surplus should be altered, though the earlier proceedings might be thought to settle the question. They concluded that no new principle could be adopted 'with any regard to equity and security' which would give the existing members a larger share of surplus than they would receive by the 'accustomed mode'. When the results of the lengthy calculations were ready, Arthur Morgan addressed the members (G, December 5, 1839), as his father had done before him. He was concerned to prevent any possible misunderstanding:

> The . . . additions now proposed . . . exceed in amount any which the Society has ever been able to afford . . . I know not whether it may have been generally expected that the *rate* as well as the amount of the addition would . . . be higher . . . than in any former division . . . ; that it is not so is owing to the combined effect of the increased ages of the lives assured . . . and to their each taking an addition now in respect of ten more payments than . . . in 1829.

Actually, the surplus in 1839 was nearly £1,000,000 less than in 1829. Credit had been taken in full for the capital appreciation in

1829 and surplus was now accumulating at a slower rate. The cake, once eaten, could not be eaten again. Arthur Morgan quoted figures concerning the cost of bonus additions at the next valuation in order to guard the older members against 'immoderate estimates' and to encourage the younger members:

> Accustomed to behold a vast annual addition to the capital (i.e. the funds), and to associate with this accumulation the idea of increasing opulence and profits, many persons may be led to suppose from witnessing a contrary order of events that the Society's profits have ceased and that its surplus is . . . diminishing; . . . no accurate judgment can be formed . . . either from the increase or decrease of its capital. . . . For such a society may . . . be increasing in number and adding . . . to its capital, (yet) at the same time be proceeding in a course which must (end) in disappointment and insolvency; whilst . . . another and older society . . . may be decreasing in number and compelled to have recourse to its capital (to pay claims), yet be not only solvent but opulent. . . . How far is it prudent and safe to enter into fixed engagements, . . . as it is now proposed to do, on the security of a surplus depending so much . . . on the fluctuating value of the public funds? The practice of the Society in this respect has been thought objectionable and it must be admitted that to a certain extent it is so. But . . . it is considerably lessened on the present occasion by reason of the much larger portion . . . now invested on freehold mortgage.

Reporting these proceedings, *The Times* (December 24, 1839) commented that 'the concerns of a corporation so gigantic have something of national importance about them'.

By this time the Society had been driven into a situation from which it seemed impossible to escape. Of course, it was easy to devise new arrangements which were superficially attractive and all kinds of suggestions were made. One of the members, Henry Septimus H. Wollaston, was invited to the weekly meeting so that he could explain his scheme (W, November 16, 1842). The suggestion was to create another class of member, which would not be limited but would give up one-tenth of the premiums to the older members. One-tenth 'is far below the expenses incurred in other insurance companies and scarcely more than is paid by some offices to agents through whom insurances are obtained'. Actually, the new assurers would be worse off with such a scheme and it was rejected. A simpler suggestion was to alter the waiting period to a fixed term of years. Would such an alteration 'be inconsistent with the principles of law or equity or likely to lead to adverse legal proceedings?' (G, June 4, 1846). Any change of this kind was bound to affect different members in different ways and Counsel advised against it. Later in the year, *The Times* reported (December 4, 1846) that the Society had paid a claim of £16,560 on an assurance for £3,000.

The next step was a motion for a committee of five old and five new members to consider what plan could be adopted 'to place . . . the affairs of the Society on a more equitable footing'. Since a majority could not bind a minority on this question, a committee would not be of much use and the motion, though often repeated, made no progress. Thus, when a member tried to propose this motion on June 7, 1849, another member moved the adjournment, and the meeting broke up. When the time came round for the next allocation of bonus, the announcement of the results of the valuation produced a crop of motions for the remodelling of the Society. Also, Robert Knipe Cobbold ('late of Eye, now of Carlton, Suffolk') entered a protest against the adoption of the cash accounts so as to call attention to a grievance of his. Nine years before, he had claimed that the directors were acting inconsistently with the bye-laws in allocating bonus to his assurance from the date, only, of its admission to participation and not from the date of the policy. The directors had ruled (S, November 26, 1840) that his claim was 'founded in error and misunderstanding'; he had overlooked the word 'subsequent' in the 40th bye-law. How much lies in a word!

Arthur Morgan had the difficult task of persuading the members to continue in a course which had met fierce criticism and he had to contend with less favourable conditions. The rate of bonus (£2 per cent) was the lowest since 1800 but the actual amount of bonus added to each assurance effected before 1817 (with few exceptions) exceeded the amount added at any previous distribution:

The participation of the members who have joined the Society since 1816 . . . has . . . been more gradual than . . . was . . . expected or probable; nevertheless the system established in 1816 will . . . be found to have conferred benefits of considerable magnitude on these members, and . . . a prospect of . . . much more extensive benefits hereafter. . . . (They) possess an expectancy far greater than has been secured to the members of any other Institution of the same kind which has been established . . . during the last thirty-five years. . . . The limitation of the policies participating together in the profits to a constant number, is . . . peculiar to the constitution of the Equitable Society and . . . limits also the whole number of members of which the Society can reasonably be expected to consist; but it may confidently be expected to secure a sufficient number always to recruit the participating body with assurers of six or seven years' standing

. . . I have little doubt of (a total number of 7,000) being again attained when the operation of the 40th bye-law comes to be tested by further experience and more fully understood by the public. . . . It will be strange indeed if (the Society) should not now continue to increase and with an accelerated progression. . . .

In eighty-six years, the Society had received £19,000,000 in premiums, had paid £25,000,000 in claims and had in hand funds amounting to nearly £9,000,000. The expenses of management had amounted to only £400,000 in the whole period—about 2 per cent of the premiums. Had the Society resorted to the 'modern practice' of paying a commission of 5 per cent on the premiums, it would have cost nearly £1,000,000, 'a sum which, with . . . compound interest, would go far to provide for the additions on the present occasion'.

The proposed bonuses were to be discussed at two meetings on December 18 and 20, 1849; the number of motions on the agenda promised lively meetings and, fortunately, some sketches by Sir George Hayter (Principal Painter in Ordinary to Queen Victoria), who was present, give entertaining glimpses of the proceedings. Hayter has delightful sketches of the chairman, Ralph Price. On December 18th, the chairman has gavel in hand, ready to strike— suggesting a noisy meeting—the person on his right is whispering to him while the person on his left is reading, or is about to read, the minutes. At a guess, the chairman is being given a formal letter from Cobbold to be read to the meeting, which ran:

I hereby give you notice not to make any division of apparent profits until my claim . . . be decided either by the reference provided for by the Deed of Settlement or by the decision of the Court of Chancery. . . . Under my hand this 18 December, 1849.

The member who is crying 'I want Equity and I will have it' could be Cobbold. He seems not to have pursued his threat of legal proceedings.

On the proposal to allocate the bonus in the accustomed mode, a member moved an amendment to give the bonus for all premiums, without the restrictions of 1816, but the chairman declined to put the amendment to the meeting on the ground that it contravened the bye-laws and regulations. He was supported in his refusal by the Earl of Devon and Sir Edward Sugden, ex-Chancellor of Ireland, who were present. Hayter has drawn one member saying: 'If you made laws, you have the same power to unmake them.' The opposition were few in number because the directors' motion was carried by 132 to 28.

Two days later, the chairman is shown sitting back, hands folded on chest—above a large paunch, with an expression on his face which seems to say 'I will give a fair hearing but I will not give way'. The person on his right hand is indicating a place in the minutes and the one on his left is angrily pointing across him to them. The group is being addressed by a dumpy figure with a large head, curly hair, and spectacles, who is carrying a stick in his right hand and who has his left hand upraised, while addressing the chairman. On this occasion, the directors won over some members because the voting was 149 to 18 against.

The chairman on both occasions was Ralph Price (Vice-President), whose portrait shows an urbanity which must have been sorely tried. Some years earlier he had been given a piece of plate (G, December 3, 1840) and later the members asked for his portrait to be painted (G, May 5, 1859). They must have liked him. What impressed itself on the members was his 'upright and amiable character'—his 'judgment and urbanity eminently promoted the harmony and welfare of the Society'. Ralph Price was an oil merchant (of Charles Price & Co., William Street, Blackfriars) who served as a director for forty-five years, for most of which time he took the chair, as Vice-President, at the Weekly Courts as well as at the quarterly meetings of the General Court.

In the spring, Wollaston was again pressing his scheme for a new class of member, in effect closing the other classes. The scheme was short-sighted for the 'reserve . . . will eventually remain undivided after every policy now existing becomes extinct'. Richard Beddome with eight other members wanted a special meeting and the appointment of a committee to consider the causes that had led to the long, continued decline. He did not get his way but Morgan was asked to report on what changes could be made. Meanwhile, the directors themselves came to the conclusion that, when an assurance came within the first 5,000, it should share in bonuses from the date of the policy, not merely from the date of admission to participation; they consulted Counsel (John Romilly, Richard Malins, C. W. Christie) who advised on August 23, 1850, that

the effect of the proposed change would be to alter the relative shares of the policies prior to 1817 and of the subsequent policies . . . and . . . the alteration would be to the prejudice of the policies dated prior to 1817.

An increase of business might increase the divisible surplus

but this compensation is merely speculative and precarious and we think that the proposed alteration . . . would be open to question by any of the class who might be aggrieved by the change.

By this time there had grown up, amongst many of the members, the feeling that the regulations of 1816 had been 'injudicious' and had proved 'injurious to the general interests of both classes of member'. They felt that it would be advisable to revert to William Morgan's original plan. Arthur Morgan favoured this idea, which would first give the older members their accustomed share and then redistribute the share of the newer members on the original principle:

I have made a variety of calculations . . . but am constrained to report that, tested by calculation, it utterly fails. . . . It is, in my opinion, impossible at this time to alter the present mode of distributing the surplus among the present members, without injuriously affecting the interests of a great many of them. . . . On more than one occasion . . . it appears to have been contemplated either to close the office entirely or to declare the whole of the surplus stock to belong to the then existing members, but the legality of such a step appears to have been doubted . . . even before (1816) and certainly could not now be taken . . . without the consent of every existing member. . . . The true policy of the present members . . . still consists, as it did in 1796, 1810 and 1816, in restrictive measures and in retaining for their own benefit and security the greater part of the advantages in their actual possession. . . . I am not myself . . . prepared to suggest any alteration; and after much deliberation and . . . laborious calculations . . . am clearly of opinion that the safest and ultimately the most beneficial course will be . . . to proceed on the Society's present plan, possessing, as I am confident it does, the means of satisfying the reasonable expectations of every present member. . . .

Arthur Morgan included a numerical example which showed the progress and result of 3,000 assurances all commenced at the age of 35 years: but for the present purpose the financial effect of the arrangements can best be seen by looking at the outcome of assurances, a period of forty years being about the whole duration of the assurances, on the average. The following comparison[1] shows the claims paid on assurances for £1,000.

Notice the tremendous difference between the outcome of assurances effected before and after the changes of 1816. Yet an assurance taken out in 1820 had been increased by 86 per cent, an average of 43s per cent per annum, which would have been reasonably comparable with

[1] *v.* Table on facing page.

| Year in which assurance was effected | Year from which assurance ranked for bonus | Year in which fortieth premium was payable | Amount of sum assured and bonus to that year £ | | |
|---|---|---|---|---|---|
| 1790 | 1790 | 1829 | 3810 | | |
| 1800 | 1800 | 1839 | 3670 | | |
| 1810 | 1810 | 1849 | 3400 | | |
| 1820 | 1835 | 1859 | 1862 | 10s | |
| 1830 | 1843 | 1869 | 1910 | | |

the reversionary bonuses declared by other offices. Notice, also, the improvement for entrants in 1830, compared with those in 1820, due to the shortening of the waiting period. However, the great disparity between the results of assurances effected before and after 1816 was grossly inequitable; it could be justified only by the plea of some extreme necessity, which demanded extreme measures to ward off the danger.

The agitation continued throughout the 1850s, though some members tried to make the critics see that the agitation itself was injurious to the Society. To Arthur Morgan, 'it seems . . . to admit of no doubt that the continuance of the business of the Society upon the present terms must be beneficial to a large class of the senior members' (S, April 9, 1851). Yet some older members still felt that the new business was unremunerative. Others were anxious to increase the 'prosperity and usefulness' of the Society.

The directors brought forward a well-considered scheme for various alterations, including the transaction of new assurances without the right to participation in profits, where the lower scale of premiums for such a class was chosen by the proposer. However, Counsel's opinion was against all the changes (S, December 6, 1854). All that came of these efforts was the dropping of the charge for 'entrance money' and some relaxations with regard to payment of claims. Also, the maximum assurance on one life was raised to £10,000.

Wollaston, now a director, had been pressing his own pet scheme for new business for many years and, at last, Arthur Morgan was stung into a reply (S, January 17, 1855):

The proposal is . . . that the present Society become in a manner a proprietary body . . . and take as profit one-tenth of (new) premiums. . . . Neither of the principal advantages anticipated—the improvement of the interests of the old members and the acquisition of a large (new) business . . . are at all likely to result from this scheme. For what inducement is the Public likely to find in (the) scheme?

With the fall in numbers, the prospects for new entrants had improved, since they came into participation immediately after the first premium. This, however, made those who had been subject to the restrictions nervous lest their share of surplus should be encroached upon by the new members. For example, John Rodick Nicholls, of Grosvenor Lodge, St Bartholomew Road, Holloway, wrote two letters arguing for 'the protection of restrictive measures or of compensation to prevent new members from obtaining an unfair advantage over ourselves'. The second letter, dated November 1856, was printed as a pamphlet.

A more reasoned discussion of the situation was put forth in 'A letter to the members of the Equitable Society respecting the coming bonus and their prospects for the future' by Charles John Bunyon, who was both an actuary and a barrister. The letter was dated November 24, 1859, from 4 Queen's Terrace, Queen's Gate. Bunyon's letter rested upon two main arguments. The first was that the major part of the profits had been derived from the increased value of the investments in the public funds—'an increase sufficient in itself to account for bonuses unlikely ever to be equalled in the history of life assurance'. The second was that, since the total number of assurances had fallen below 5,000 and the waiting period was no longer effective, 'the accession of new members is a source of weakness rather than of strength'. Bunyon used what he considered to be reasonable estimates of future experience to calculate what bonuses the new assurances might be expected to earn out of their own premiums; he found it was considerably less than was then being allotted to existing members: '. . . the bonus of the whole body must ultimately be reduced to the same level'.

Bunyon suggested three possible remedies, all of which would (though he did not say so) lay violent hands on the reserved third of surplus, the feature which distinguished the Society from all its competitors. The first suggestion was the outright division of the reserved third among the existing members. The second was the closing of the Society to new assurances, which would have kept the 'reserved third' for the ultimate benefit of existing members; this 'might be carried into effect indirectly by largely increasing the rates of premium for new insurers'. The third suggestion was to bring the

17. Arthur Morgan, FRS

18. Chartists passing the office in Chatham Place, on the way to the meeting on Kennington Common

*[Illustrated London News, April 15, 1848*

method of calculating bonuses for new assurances into line with the methods of other offices, so that their bonuses would not increase with duration and the 'reserved third' of surplus would cease to be required for them—in essence the reserved third of surplus would be gradually distributed to existing members. The main trouble, however, was that the Society was no longer attracting sufficient new assurances and they could scarcely be won in greater numbers by making their terms less attractive.

The latter part of the letter returned to the subject of the investments in the public funds:

The rise in the values of stocks during the first half of the 19th century has been prodigiously beneficial to it (the Society); but, the benefit having been obtained, the hazard of the investment is very great . . . a fall of 20 per cent in the stock market would be sufficient to swallow up the whole of the surplus. Is such a depreciation impossible? Could it fail to follow a struggle of any continuance with either France or the United States? We are so accustomed to the range of high prices of the last 36 years, as to look at the low prices of the preceding 50 years as quite unnatural to the security, and unlikely to re-occur. . . . There are many causes why Consols should be . . . unsuitable for the investment of the bulk of the funds of an insurance company. . . . It is one of the imperative conditions of its existence . . . that the funds shall be invested at a certain rate of interest and that the capital shall remain intact, ever ready to be balanced against its liabilities . . . the risk that is run in the Equitable is well known and, among actuaries, is continually the subject of unfavourable comment . . . the policy of retaining such an investment is infatuation and is abundant reason for preventing any prudent man from joining the Society.

Arthur Morgan tried to make members see that the wisest course to pursue was to persevere with the regulations as they had been made by their predecessors. Alteration was exceedingly difficult and time would be a solvent of the problems. If the reduction in the waiting period attracted new members, that was what was required for the prosperity of the Society as a whole. His attitude is most clearly seen in his remarks (G, March 1, 1860) on the occasion of the next bonus, when some members proposed regulations which would hold back new members from participation for a minimum of five or six years. The Society had experienced 'all the evil of disappointed hopes and discontent from unequal distribution which has been experienced for twenty years past from the over-stringent provisions of the 40th bye-law and which there is every reason to hope is now subsiding . . .'.

The benefits secured by those members who entered soon after January 1, 1817, were in glaring contrast to the benefits of those who had assured earlier; the inequity having been created, it could not and should not be made good out of the pockets of new assurers. The relatively poor results for members assuring after 1816 were bound, in the long run, to be shown up by unfavourable comparisons with other offices. In 1865, when the Scottish Widows Fund was fifty years old, and there was a danger of similar restrictive measures being forced upon it, the Hon. A. Leslie Melville, who was a member of both societies, pointed out how much less favourable the results of the Equitable's assurance had been because he had effected his policy 'at the wrong time'. The Scottish Widows included his speech in the printed report of the meeting and Arthur Morgan challenged some of the assertions. A long, rather embittered, correspondence ensued with Samuel Raleigh, the Manager of the Scottish Widows Fund, which he published.

An arbitrary dividing line is thrown into sharp relief by any hard case. Unfortunately, Thomas Windus failed to pay his premium and let his policy lapse in 1816; it was replaced with a new one early in 1817 (but, of course, without the bonus rights of the earlier assurance). He did not become aware of the dire effect of the loss of bonus rights until 1839 but, on full investigation, the General Court decided there was no reason to alter the arrangement that had been made (G, September 5, 1839). Thomas Windus never accepted this 'denial of justice' as he called it and, when he died in 1854, his son brought an action in the High Court of Chancery. The case dragged on from 1860 to 1864 but all the courts, including the House of Lords, decided in favour of the Society. However, a victory is barren if it leaves dissatisfaction.

Members of the Equitable might wish 'to render its working more in accordance with its name, character and original principles' but legal advice was consistently against change. Thus, a few years later, when a proposal for bonus every five years, instead of every ten years, was being discussed, Counsel advised (August 5, 1868) that, though there was no contract in the bye-laws since they could be altered by general meetings of members, the representations which had been made since 1825 that the situation was unalterable did amount to a contractual right, which would be enforceable in a Court of Equity should any member feel aggrieved by a change in the regulations.

At the end of 1869, Arthur Morgan was able to congratulate the members on the 'continuing prosperity and success of this old and opulent Society'. But the decennial investigation and bonus was his last service. A sudden illness enforced his retirement on March 3, 1870, and he died on March 10th.

The office organization was still of a very simple character. The Assistant Actuary (John Ware Stephenson) answered all the letters on the general daily business of the office which naturally involved numerous calculations. Though the number of insurances in force was falling the 'correspondence is as great now as it has ever been'. He also had charge of the daily cash account which was balanced every day. The Principal Clerk (Edward Lovelock) was in charge of payments to policyholders; thus he dealt with all claims, surrenders of policies or bonuses and loans on policies. In addition he prepared the fair copy of the Minutes of meetings and made out the policies of new assurers. Much of the time of the Actuary, Assistant Actuary and Principal Clerk was taken by personal interviews with policy-holders. The Actuary had two clerks. The first clerk (John Coldicoate Dell) attended to the public at the counter, taking money and giving receipts, and also posted the ledgers. The second clerk (William Morgan—Arthur's nephew) prepared and despatched the renewal notices each month (about 4,800 yearly) and the summonses for General Courts (about 900 in all) five times a year; he was also responsible for taking money each day to the bank. On the Court day each week, William Morgan was responsible for the new assurances. This was the daily work of the office in 1858. In addition, there was the classification of all the assurances and the preparation of the decennial valuation and allocation of bonus, together with any special investigations that might be called for by the General Court. At this time there were fifteen directors—a large number compared with the smallness of the staff. Originally, as has been seen, they conducted the business of the office, but by this time it seems that the current business was managed by the office staff and the directors merely kept a general oversight of the business.

# CHAPTER XV

# THE SEETHING POT (1830–1870)

I N the 1830s, the 'condition of England' became a topic for serious public discussion. The structure of an industrial society had rapidly developed with the quickening tempo of inventions. Long hours of work and drab living contrasted with the wealth that was being created by capital projects. The age had little time for the graces of life. G. K. Chesterton aptly called the conditions 'flimsy and degraded'.

In the earlier years of the industrial revolution, public feeling had expressed itself primarily as a movement for political reform, which came to a head with the first Reform Bill in the spring of 1831. Three Bills and a general election were needed for success but the third Bill passed the House of Lords on June 4, 1832, a historic date.

Working-class politics produced the People's Charter, published in 1838, the mainspring of agitation for some ten years at least and a potent ideal for a much longer period. The six points of the petition seem ordinary now, though then they were strange, revolutionary claims—annual parliaments, universal male suffrage, removal of the property qualification for Parliament, secret ballot and payment of Members of Parliament. A Convention of the Industrious Classes (an imitation of Parliament in some respects) met in London on February 4, 1839 and the petition was presented on May 6th; the House of Commons refused even to consider the petition. A second national petition was brought to the House of Commons on May 2, 1842 but was rejected by a large majority. This time the leaders had threatened a general strike, but it fizzled out. For a third attempt, deputations met on Kennington Common on April 10, 1848 with the plan of marching on Westminster.[1]

[1] The picture facing p. 225 (*Illustrated London News*, April 15, 1848) shows the Chartist demonstrators going south across Blackfriars Bridge to attend the mass

The drabness of the industrial revolution should not be over-stressed. Agriculture was still the largest industry and the factory was still something of a social experiment. Many industries were conducted at home or in small workshops and there was a rapid rise in the professional and commercial occupations. The urban population sprawled in ugliness but not necessarily in squalor. The murky view of Britain, seen through the eyes of a Carlyle, was a protest against the Britain that was being created, precisely because its ugliness contrasted with fairer parts of Britain elsewhere.

Underlying many of the difficulties of the time, were the rapid growth of the population and the need to find adequate employment for it. Numbers in England and Wales rose by about 2,000,000 each decade between 1830 and 1860, and the rise would have been greater had the natural increase not been reduced by emigration. Although the wealth of the country increased, it was not until after the mid-century that employment grew sufficiently to enable increased real wages to affect large sections of the working classes. Until then, the growth in well-being was limited to relatively small sections of the population, but even this small improvement was reflected in the rise in savings and in savings-bank deposits. Expansion of the economy was interrupted by recurrent commercial crises, the manifestation of the 'trade-cycle', about every ten or eleven years. Each was marked by speculation, when the economy got out of balance, but each by speculation of a different character.

Just why there should have been intense speculation in the promotion of life offices is an interesting question to which there is no sure answer. The market prices of the public funds (the principal investment) were high throughout this period. In the economic sense of the words, there must have been a plentiful supply of 'savings' available for 'investment' in at least some of the various enterprises which needed capital expenditure. An economist might match the unused 'savings' with the unemployed workers, the waste of human resources which was a feature of the times. If this were so, the question would still remain—why should the available capital have gone into the promotion of weak and speculative life offices?

The increase in the number of salaried employees in professional and commercial occupations was amongst a provident section of the

meeting. The Society's office is the building on the corner of Chatham Place which projects at the back of this picture.

community and created a demand for the protection which life assurance could give. Experience had shown that life assurance was a profitable business; if the profits were not passed on to the policy-holders, the business could be very rewarding to the proprietors. For the business to be sound, what was required was restraint in expenditure and a careful husbanding of resources. But the scope for spending money tended to attract the dishonest; the successful starting of a life office was a quick way of raising money which appealed to the speculator and the absence of official control left free play to all who would enter this field—governmental control of life assurance was delayed too long.

For a complete view of the question, it would be necessary to survey the alternative enterprises open to speculators and life assurance was not the only one. The trouble was that life assurance was treated as a commercial activity like any other commercial enterprise.

Arthur Morgan's career covered a curious period in the history of life assurance. It was a period of intense development, which saw the beginnings of life assurance in many parts of the world, the firm establishment of the business and its professional organizations, yet a period that was disfigured by the worst evils of company promotion, some the froth of bubbles soon blown away, and some the frauds of scamps.

Up to the year 1830, sixty-six offices had been formed, fifteen discontinued business and fifty-one remained open for business in that year. In the period 1830 to 1869, 321 offices were formed and 262 discontinued business, a net increase of fifty-nine to a total of 110 offices open for business at the beginning of 1870. In the period from 1837 to 1870, the aggregate of the life assurance funds in the United Kingdom increased about three-fold, an increase which would surely have been achieved, with less loss to the public, if most of the newer companies had never started business.

The life assurance world was mirrored in the *Annals, Anecdotes and Legends* of John Francis (1853). As history, it is unreliable in detail; as a portrait of speculation, it faithfully represented one side of the business. But John Francis believed in life assurance and his words in his preface still speak to us:

Men toil, work, slave, nay almost sin for their families; they do everything but insure: and should this volume induce any one to avail himself of the benefits of life assurance . . . the writer will not deem his labour entirely in vain.

New ideas are in ferment in such a time. From the earliest days of the Equitable, life assurance took two major forms (*a*) an assurance payable at the death of the assured life within an agreed period of years and (*b*) an endowment payable on the survival of the life assured to the end of the agreed period. The two types were now fused into an 'endowment assurance', whereby the sum assured is payable either on the survival of the life assured to the end of the agreed period or at the death of the life assured, if earlier. Endowment assurances have become by far the most popular type of life assurance but their origin is obscure; they were first announced (so far as can be traced) by an ephemeral office, the British Empire (No. 1) which was founded in 1839 and had a life of five years only. It is interesting that this pioneer contract included an option to buy an annuity.

One effect of the promotions was to offer life assurance to sections of the community that had been passed over by the older life offices. The service was expensive and the business tended to be transient. Another innovation was the half-credit system, introduced by an office called the United Kingdom[1] which was founded in 1834 and had a life of twenty-eight years.

One of the difficulties was the primitive state of company law; incorporation was still reserved for the comparatively few. The legal problems were reviewed in a report, dated March 1, 1837, made by H. Bellenden Ker of Lincoln's Inn to the Board of Trade. Among the distinguished men who gave evidence in this inquiry, it is interesting to see the name of Samuel White Sweet, who had been such a severe critic of the Equitable. The report notes that Hudson Gurney, in debates in Parliament, had advocated the registration of joint-stock companies; while this could give them the benefit of incorporation, the responsibility for granting it would be placed upon Parliament, acting through the officially appointed Registrar. The report was not implemented at once but formed part of the evidence to the Select Committee on Joint-Stock Companies.

In the year 1836, the promotions of life offices reached a peak of eleven, of which five had been discontinued by 1842. The story of one of them, the Independent West Middlesex, was told in full in the report of the Select Committee. It was started by a tallow-chandler named Hole, subsequently a house agent; he had been bankrupt in

---

[1] A different office from the United Kingdom Provident Institution, founded in 1840, an active mutual life office of the present day.

1827 and had been frequently in the King's Bench prison. All the persons concerned in the project were 'in a mean and indigent condition of life'. Hole's principal collaborator was his assistant, Knowles; Hole's brother-in-law, the porter, was named as auditor and a journeyman bell-hanger was named as manager. The so-called capital was in the names of fictitious shareholders, whose signatures were obtained on various pretexts for 7s 6d or 5s 6d each. The prospectuses gave the addresses of offices in London 'opposite the Bazaar, Baker Street, Portman Square', and in Edinburgh, Glasgow and Dublin. They mentioned 'fire, lives and annuities—on equitable principles'; about £96,000 was collected by the sale of annuities on apparently favourable terms, quite uneconomic, by indefatigable advertising and by the activity of agents.

Despite outspoken and courageous public criticism by Peter Mackenzie, the editor of the *Scotch Reformers' Gazette* of Glasgow, the public did not find out that the whole concern was a swindle. Its managers took him before the Court of Session in an endeavour to frighten him, but he stood up to them in a 'manly and gallant' way. The edifice collapsed when the parties could not agree about the division of the money. They divided the wine in the cellars of the office and absconded in December, 1840, said the *Scotch Reformers' Gazette*, with about £200,000 of their victims' money; yet the press, in too many places, continued to publish the specious advertisements of the swindlers, and even to puff them, and hence the swindlers succeeded in pillaging the public to the above enormous extent.[1] At his trial in January 1841, Hole put forward the impudent defence that there is no offence in starting a company which is unsuccessful; the failure was the result of mistaken calculation. Some of the directors and managers of the respectable life offices so admired Peter Mackenzie's stand that they recommended their offices to contribute towards his costs at the Court of Session.

Rather naturally, a substantial part of the evidence to the Select Committee on Joint-Stock Companies concerned life assurance companies. Four leading actuaries were called to give evidence on May 25, 1841 and their evidence gives a picture of life assurance

---

[1] It is said that Charles Dickens took this scandal as the basis for his 'Anglo-Bengalee Disinterested Loan & Life Insurance Company' in *The Life and Adventures of Martin Chuzzlewit*. Since the book was originally published in monthly numbers from January 1843 to July 1844, i.e. within two years of the scandal, there is every reason to believe the story.

practice and opinion at that time. They were Charles Ansell of the Atlas Assurance Company, George Kirkpatrick of the Law Life Assurance Society, Griffith Davies of the Guardian Assurance Company and Arthur Morgan of the Equitable. Charles Ansell (1794–1881) acted as spokesman; he was a few years junior to Griffith Davies (1788–1855) in age, but senior to him in length of service in a life office. Ansell afterwards became the leading spirit in the formation of the Actuaries' Club and Davies in the formation of the Institute of Actuaries. Arthur Morgan was relatively junior in age but represented the largest life office in terms of funds.

Many of the newer offices held out the attraction of well-known names by way of support to their ventures. Ansell remarked . . . 'the largest office ever founded, namely the Equitable . . ., was established by persons of sound sense . . . but . . . they were persons not at all in elevated stations'. He suggested that at least £10 per cent of capital should be paid up in proprietary offices. However, 'ultimate security depends on the sufficiency of the premiums'. He was against requiring scales of premium to be approved by a Government officer. 'If . . . six . . . actuaries (were asked) . . . what they believed to be a perfect scale, you would not get two of them quite to agree.' The best safeguard was to publish statistical evidence of soundness.

By way of showing what they had in mind, Arthur Morgan handed in the General Cash Account of the Equitable for the year 1840, the valuation balance sheet, and a classification of the business in force for each year of age. The ideas expounded by these four actuaries in 1841 have coloured the framework of British legislation ever since. They pointed the way to the Committee, but it takes time to translate discussion into action.

In the autumn of 1841, the Government fell and the ensuing general election brought Peel into power. His government of 1841–46 was one of the most memorable administrations of the century, when industrial conditions, the work and livelihood of the people, came to be a central concern of government. The great statesman, William Ewart Gladstone, took control of the Board of Trade, first as Vice-President and from May 1843 as President. The Board then covered a much wider field, but the position brought Gladstone into the problems of company organization and when the Select Committee next met, Gladstone was in the chair.

The same four actuaries were called to give evidence again on

July 10, 1843 and confirmed their earlier evidence. Ansell made the specific recommendations that the deeds of settlement of life offices should be registered and that 'a return should be periodically made by each assurance office . . . in the general form adopted by the Equitable Assurance Society'. Morgan thought that methods were capable of improvement but there had been no changes in the last ten years—'there are various schemes which recommend themselves to the public, who have different views in making assurances'. In reply to a question whether the life offices were more numerous than could be carried on with a profit, he said, 'No', adding that the number of insured lives was surprisingly small.

The evidence showed that most offices had followed the Equitable's example in increasing their sums assured by allocations of bonus, rather than in reducing the premiums. Ansell mentioned that a 'vast number' of offices quoting lower rates of premium had broken up. No office that had been in existence any length of time had adopted much lower rates than the Equitable's. Ansell estimated that there were about 100 offices with 100,000 policies in all (an average of 1,000 only per office) and said that, in his opinion, there could not be sufficient business to keep all those offices afloat.

The Select Committee recommended that joint-stock companies, including those in insurance but excluding banking companies, should be registered and this was embodied in the Act of 1844. Although this piece of legislation was a great step forward in the legal recognition of joint-stock companies, it did not achieve all the success that was hoped for in protecting the interests of shareholders and company creditors. This was partly due to the fact that the penal powers given to the Registrar of Companies in the Act were not sufficiently stringent. As a result, many fraudulent companies formed after 1844 claimed to be 'empowered by Act of Parliament', or some such phrase, so deceiving the public into thinking that there was much greater public supervision than actually existed.

The number of life assurance company promotions rose to a fresh peak of eleven in 1840 and, in a further wave of promotions, forty-eight were formed in the four years 1845 to 1848. No fewer than forty-five of these have ceased to exist, most of them after a very few years; their average life was less than ten years. The lush growth of new companies was a most serious problem which was repellent to the actuaries of some of the older and more respectable companies.

Under the leadership of Charles Ansell, they kept themselves apart when the Institute of Actuaries was formed in 1848 and formed their own association in the Actuaries' Club.

Arthur Morgan stood aside and took no part in this controversy and it is interesting to ask why. He was regarded with some affection because a special toast was drunk in his honour (he being absent) at a dinner at the London Coffee-house on October 14, 1848 following the first general meeting of the Institute; Arthur Morgan was there described as 'not a supporter but not an opponent of the Institute'. It is clear from his evidence to the Select Committee in 1843, that he thought there should be room for the newer offices. Leadership from the Equitable (at that time the largest office in terms of funds) would have counted for much; but Arthur Morgan gave no lead and the Institute was the loser. Nineteen years passed before he permitted his name to be put up for membership of the Actuaries' Club.

Another eruption of companies occurred in the years 1851–55. In these five years, no fewer than ninety-two life offices were established, the peak being reached with twenty-six in the year 1854. Most of these had a very short life; seventy-nine of them had an average life of less than five years and only two of the whole ninety-two still exist.

Some thoughtful articles on 'Life Assurance in England' appeared anonymously in 1851 and 1852 in the *Assurance Magazine*.[1] The articles were signed with the Greek letter X; they were written by Charles Jellicoe who had, with Samuel Brown, founded the magazine in September 1850. Jellicoe was one of the original Vice-Presidents of the Institute and was President from 1860 to 1867.

It cannot be considered that the business of life assurance in England is . . . in a satisfactory state. There is reason to believe that not a year now passes in which the average expense of it to the assured is not increased. . . . (The) business transacted by the newer companies is to a great extent taken from the old ones and . . . the total quantity is very little, if at all, increasing. . . . Not so, however, the aggregate expenditure. . . . Is any one to blame for this? We cannot say that the projectors are, at least in the early stages of their undertakings. . . . But they are to be blamed for carrying on a fruitless struggle, when it is proved to be one. . . . More than all, we think the Government, by the apathy with which it regards these proceedings, is incurring a heavy responsibility.

The articles advocated the requirement of a deposit, as security for

[1] Adopted in the year 1852 as the official *Journal of the Institute of Actuaries*.

the proper conduct of new offices, and the production of proper accounts.

Jellicoe's original article brought into the open the doubts that many sincere people had about the unhealthy condition of life assurance at that time. He was followed by the publisher of the *Post Magazine*, William Slater Dixon Pateman, who produced a candid and fair survey of the field in the spring of 1852. The Equitable has a copy initialled by Archibald Day and dated March 8, 1852, which would be soon after publication. Pateman left no doubt of his own views:

> The facility with which new assurance offices are set on foot, the tempting promises with which each new scheme is baited, . . . have . . . converted a scheme of infinite utility and philanthropy into one of the greatest speculative projects of the present day.

Pateman warned that, though open failures might be rare, the real snare lay in the 'undetected poverty of a necessitous institution'. In his opinion, the severest blow to the security of the life offices had been the popular cry for reduced premiums and he pointed his remarks with a nice analogy.

> Should we be considered in possession of our senses, were we to risk our necks by travelling on a railroad, the engineer of which . . . promised to put the engine to its extremest speed, with the comfortable assurance that, however great the pressure in the boiler might become, it should be preserved just short of an actual explosion?

Material evidence of the high expenses of conducting many of the newer companies was forthcoming in the second report of the Registrar. Using these facts, Robert Christie, Manager of the Scottish Equitable Life Assurance Society, fired a broadside designed to sink the newer flotations; from the distance of Edinburgh, criticism could be outspoken. In an open letter to the President of the Board of Trade, on July 19, 1852, Christie condemned most of the newer companies root and branch; his 'impression, nay my entire conviction, . . . is that they are rotten; and are, in effect, though not perhaps in design, fraudulent'.

A question asked in the House of Commons showed that the disquiet about life assurance had spread to Parliament. The time was ripe for statesmanship and William Thomas Thomson gave the lead in another open letter to the President of the Board of Trade, a very different letter from Christie's. Thomson wrote from Edinburgh, on August 12, 1852, a well-reasoned plea for government action. The trouble lay in England rather than Scotland: 'it is to be lamented that England should . . . have become so prolific a mother of a very heterogeneous offspring . . .'. Life assurance was important to the community and life offices 'require the watchful attention of a paternal government'. Thomson advocated six points for legislation, which were far ahead of his time. Much of what he wanted has, ultimately, come about in one way or another, though it has taken about three-quarters of a century. However, he preferred to rely upon government supervision rather than upon publicity and, in this matter, opinion followed Charles Ansell rather than Thomson.

It is noteworthy that all the protagonists in the battle of words in 1852 were senior members of the Institute and all, except Christie, held high office in it. The debate was not (as might have been expected) between members of the Institute on the one side and members of the Actuaries' Club on the other. It was a debate between fellow members who were striving to bring the life assurance business on to a sounder foundation.

The public disquiet could not be ignored and the House of Commons appointed a Select Committee to inquire into Assurance Associations, which reported on August 16, 1853. Charles Ansell was the only one of the four actuaries, who gave evidence in 1841 and 1843, who also gave evidence in 1853. Kirkpatrick had died or retired and Griffith Davies was close on retirement. But why did Arthur Morgan stand aside? The reason may have been that the older offices were represented by senior members of the professional organizations. Thus Charles Ansell, James John Downes, Samuel Ingall, John Adams Higham and Thomas Rowe Edmonds were all members of the Actuaries' Club. The Scots were represented by William Thomas Thomson. The official witnesses included John Finlaison of the National Debt Office and William Farr, MD, of the General Register Office. Thomson, Finlaison and Farr were all members of the Institute but Charles Jellicoe, the senior Vice-President, acted as its spokesman. Samuel Brown, later the third President of the Institute, also gave evidence as did several Institute members from the junior or weaker offices.

Pateman, with the freedom of the Press, was able to produce some colourful stories of what had been going on. Perhaps the worst was of a certain Richard Wilsdon Morris. He had been tried at the Old Bailey for forgery in August 1848 and had been sentenced to be transported for ten years, but he was 'unfortunately for the public' set at large after a year's imprisonment. Taking the name of G. R. Herbert Denison, he promoted a whole series of fraudulent insurance schemes. The first, registered July 9, 1851, was 'The Reciprocal Life Assurance Company' which issued a large number of life policies. Four of its directors could not be found; others were an usher in a school and the promoter's father-in-law. In quick succession there followed 'The Hope Reversionary Life Interest Company' and the 'Reciprocal Fire Insurance Company'. The latter issued a large number of fire policies, though it had no deed of settlement and when a claimant came to collect his insurance money he found no office in existence. Denison could not be found and his so-called office had been shut up for twelve months. Denison continued his schemes with 'The Absolute Security Life and Fire Assurance Company'—which belied its title—and the Newport branch of the National Friendly Society, which had thirteen directors whose names had been used without their knowledge and consent. Denison did not scruple to use names similar to or even the same as those of other offices.

A high-sounding title was that of the 'European Alliance Full-pay Insurance Company', registered September 21, 1852. But (said the witness):

> On enquiry I found that the office consisted of one room over a milliner's shop in New Oxford Street, containing only two chairs, a broken table and a large number of prospectuses printed on foreign notepaper. . . . The manager decamped shortly afterwards.

There were more than a dozen fraudulent offices; not all of them had been registered but all described themselves as 'empowered by Act of Parliament'.

The interplay of opinion at the time can be savoured from the evidence given before the Committee. One thread runs through it all; the respect in which the Equitable was held and the firm example it had set to other offices. The remarks of William Farr on June 30, 1853 may be quoted as an example:

> The admirable manner in which on the whole the business of assurance was conducted by the Equitable Society was no doubt an important element in establishing the assurance business of this country. . . . The Equitable has published a form of account which enables you to determine exactly the condition

of that office . . . the other offices do not give you all the data you require. No other office has followed the excellent example of the Equitable.

The stresses which were apparent within the actuarial profession in these years were merely symptoms of the unhealthy condition of life assurance business at the time, but economic forces were at work. Possibly, the report of the Select Committee acted as a catalyst for, soon afterwards, insolvency or absorption into other groups began to reduce the numbers of offices. The number of life offices ceasing to exist was fourteen in 1854 and reached a total of sixty-six in the three years 1856-58. Meanwhile, legislation tarried.

Amalgamation did not necessarily produce stronger groups. The take-over terms might be extravagant and the offices which sought to buy business in this way might be those which sought to expand at all costs. The affairs of two such groups eventually stirred the Government to action—the Albert and the European. Both offices had absorbed vast numbers of offices by the 1860s and both were viewed with some suspicion. In the end, trouble was touched off by a run on the Albert. There were so many requests for surrender of policies that payment of cash for surrendered policies had to be stopped. A petition for winding-up the Albert was presented in 1869. Nervousness about the European led to a similar petition for that office a few weeks later but the European managed to ward off the attack until early in 1872, when it finally crashed.

As a direct consequence of these failures, the Government at last acted. The Life Assurance Companies Act, 1870, put in force the main proposals of the Select Committee of 1853, though the strengthening of the powers of supervision had to wait for many years longer. The basic idea was the 'freedom with publicity' recommended by the four actuaries in 1841 and the required returns closely followed what had been the practice of the Equitable for some seventy years—but brought into line with current accounting practice.

# CHAPTER XVI

# THE ENDING OF THE RESTRICTIONS
## (1870–1912)

I N a living city there is always change. A scheme for a new road to be cut from the Mansion House to Blackfriars (Queen Victoria Street) meant that the Society would have to move its house. Good warning was given and the Metropolitan Board of Works offered compensation for the house in Chatham Place (S, December 9, 1863) and an exchange for a building site in the new street. But the whole question was handled in a far too hesitant manner.

The first reaction was to try to obtain a building on the other side of Chatham Place or two houses in New Bridge Street and temporary offices in Simpson's Hotel were suggested. No decision was taken, however, because it seemed premature. Later, the Metropolitan Board of Works offered a choice of sites in the new street and the directors liked one at the corner of St Andrews Hill (S, August 15, 1866) but they boggled at the terms. The premises in Chatham Place had a site area of 4,200 square feet valued at £5 a foot. The building plot in the new street was 4,500 square feet at £6 a foot. The premises in Chatham Place had to be given up at Lady Day 1868 but there was still good time for building. What seems a fair exchange was rejected by the Court of Directors, who preferred to secure a site either in New Bridge Street or to the westward.

The time came when the office in Chatham Place had to be given up and the Society moved to temporary premises at 11 New Bridge Street on the other side of the road. The Metropolitan Board of Works paid £29,000 in compensation. Nothing had been done about a new office. The Court of Directors would not pay the price for property in New Bridge Street; Nos. 35, 36 and 37 were offered at £25,000, later reduced to £22,000, but the Court would not pay more than £20,000. A suggestion that the Society should take

19. View of Mansion House from the doorway of the office in Mansion House Street, by Hanslip Fletcher

20. Plaster cast of gold medal (by Gilbert Bayes) presented to Sir William Elderton in 1937 by the Institute of Actuaries and the Faculty of Actuaries

Farrance's shop, then vacant in Spring Gardens, also fell through. Meanwhile, the Society was 'deprived of its long-accustomed offices'.

The problem dragged on, with various sites being inspected, but nothing definite done, when Arthur Morgan fell ill. At this point, one of the Vice-Presidents, James Spicer, found what he thought suitable accommodation in the heart of the City. This was a lease of offices on the first floor, over the Union Bank in Mansion House Street, opposite the Mansion House. The lease cost £22,000 and £100 a year for sixty years (S, January 7, 1870). It is, perhaps, unfair to job backwards in criticism of the arrangement.

Arthur Morgan's successor was another member of the staff with a long connection with the Society. When a former Assistant Actuary, John Stephenson, died in 1828, he left a widow and three children, the eldest being a boy of ten. This son, John Ware Stephenson, spent all his working life in the service of the Society, becoming Actuary in 1870. The connection with the Morgans was maintained by the promotion of Arthur Morgan's nephew, William Morgan, the son of John Morgan, to be Assistant Actuary.

On his appointment Stephenson was elected to membership of the Actuaries' Club so that the Equitable was by then in the camp of the older offices who held aloof from the Institute of Actuaries. However, the time was approaching when the breach would be healed and Stephenson was one of those who were, by the terms of the charter, made Fellows of the Institute in 1884.

Stephenson was a Fellow of the Royal Astronomical Society but his chief scientific interest was in microscopy. In all he contributed 18 papers to the Royal Microscopical Society (Treasurer, 1872 to 1881). The year 1870 was his great year in several ways because it was in that year that he designed the binocular microscope which is known by his name. He took a leading part in this branch of science for many years and showed an intelligent and inventive mind in his published work.

The story goes that when electricity was first introduced, the shares of gas companies fell to a low level because investors thought that the gas industry was finished. Stephenson had confidence in the outlook for the gas industry and made a considerable amount of money by buying gas company shares at low prices.

Time brought another change, the end of the 'remarkable and honourable connection between the House of Tredegar and the Equitable Society'. Sir Charles Morgan Robinson Morgan, Bart., MP, the third of his family to be President, had been created the first Baron Tredegar in 1859. When he died in 1875, father, son and grandson had presided over the Society for 102 years. Lord Tredegar had been a member for fifty-two years.

The new President, elected in 1875, was a member of a well-known legal family, Sir (William) Frederick Pollock, Bart., Queen's Remembrancer and Senior Master of the Supreme Court. He was the eldest son of Sir Jonathan Frederick Pollock, Bart., FRS, who had been senior wrangler and Smith's prizeman in 1806 and who became Attorney General under Peel. Father and son were educated at St Paul's School and Trinity College, Cambridge. Pollock was at Cambridge at the same time as the poet Tennyson and, though junior to him, was one of the circle of the poet's friends celebrated in *In Memoriam*. He had wide interests and many friends, among them Macready, the actor. His entertaining *Personal Remembrances* shows how various were his accomplishments; his literary work included a translation of Dante.

The surviving assurances effected before 1817 were now rapidly dwindling in number but the comparatively few that were left blocked any change in the restrictive regulations. Whether this was justified remains an open question. The weight of legal opinion was against change; yet the feeling remains that a more adventurous spirit would have found a way round the barrier. Arthur Morgan had hoped that the Society would gain in popularity as the real advantages of new assurers entering with no waiting period were appreciated. But as the years passed, it became clear that the increase in business would be trifling.

The concept that nothing could be done until all the assurances effected before 1817 had died out seems a strange one. Those effected subsequently also had conflicting rights; they had endured waiting period of all lengths up to about sixteen years and those who had suffered most were naturally concerned that later assurances, with shorter waiting periods, should not encroach upon their rights. The concept seems to have been that the regulations of 1816, in effect, closed one membership and opened another, by means of a gradual transition rather than an abrupt closing of one fund and opening of a new fund. For the twenty years following 1870 the Society remained in the uneventful routine of large funds, comparatively few new assurances, the business stagnant.

Traditionally, the Society had invested its moneys in British Government stock and in mortgages. The pattern of investment was, however, changing with the growth of the economy. In the early days of the industrial revolution, mortgages had been a sufficient and appropriate form of finance. The landowner mortgaged his estates, sometimes to effect improvements in agriculture, sometimes to promote industrial ventures on or near his estates and sometimes to finance younger sons in business or industry, leaving the estates to be managed by the eldest son. The development of large-scale industry at home, and in India and the colonies abroad, demanded other forms of finance. As company organization evolved, debentures and fixed interest stocks became available, yielding higher rates of interest than the public funds. Life offices responded to the new opportunities though the evidence in 1853 showed that railway debentures were then considered to be too speculative for respectable life offices.

The Society took the first step towards a wider policy in 1860, with the adoption of new Bye-Laws to permit investments in British India Stock, East India Stock, and bonds, mortgages and debentures of companies incorporated by special Act. A start was made with £150,000 in the East Indian Railway Company at 5 per cent interest. As the years went by more and more use was made of these powers and they were extended from time to time. Loans were encouraged. By 1879 the list of investments included many stocks of railways and public boards; the public funds had been reduced to about 10 per cent only of the whole investments. Later still, the power was widened to include the prior charges of any company either incorporated by Act of Parliament or registered under the Companies Acts, subject to a dividend qualification (S, April 24, 1889).

The search for wider fields of investment was dictated by the need to obtain a better rate of interest than was yielded by investments in the public funds. The figures for the market price of Consols[1] at the successive decennial valuations are remarkable.

In the year 1888 Stephenson retired after nearly fifty-one years of service and the President, Sir Frederick Pollock, died—remembered for his 'dignity and efficiency'. The old era ended in 1892 with the

[1] v. Table on p. 244.

| Year | Market price of Consols at end of year |
|------|----------------------------------------|
| 1829 | 90 |
| 1839 | 90⅝ |
| 1849 | 93⅝ |
| 1859 | 96 |
| 1869 | 93⅜ |
| 1879 | 97½ |
| 1889 | 96⅞ |

death of the last of the members assured before 1817, and the retirement of William Morgan in the same year ended the formal connection with the family who had served the Society for 118 years.

The Court of Directors had to look outside for a successor to Stephenson and they turned for help to Archibald Day, who was the London Secretary of the Scottish Widows Fund and at the time President of the Institute of Actuaries. He recommended three young actuaries, all afterwards leading members of the profession, Arthur Francis Burridge of the Equity & Law, W. J. H. Whittall of the Clerical, Medical & General and Frank Bertrand Wyatt of the Clergy Mutual. The directors chose Burridge, then aged 35, whose task was to carry through the re-organization of the Society. Burridge was a dapper man; later, the younger men of his day said that he wore the tightest stays of any actuary. He died at the early age of 51.

The President elected in 1888 was John Alldin Moore, but he served only four years and resigned in 1892; he died the next year, when his assurance for £5,000 yielded with bonus a total of £15,975. His place was taken by Richard Twining, a tea and coffee merchant (Twinings in the Strand).

No time was lost when the last of the old members had died. The Society at once applied for registration under the Companies Acts, so as to gain the benefit of incorporation. The directors also consulted Augustus Hendriks, President of the Institute of Actuaries at the time, to find out whether there were any objections from an actuarial point of view, to alterations in the Equitable's methods of distribution of surplus, especially the more frequent allocation of bonuses. He asked Ralph Price Hardy to make some calculations and together they reported that there was no sufficient objection to change:

We are of opinion that there could be framed from time to time a sound method of valuation which would completely safeguard the interests of the members and preserve to them the same order of security they now enjoy. . . .

The drawing up of suitable Articles of Association took more time because, rather naturally, members wanted to discuss the draft with the directors and a committee was appointed. The Memorandum and Articles were adopted January 12, 1893, and registered June 16, 1893. They preserved the general character of the Society—'the features of large reserves and low expenses, of mutual assurance with complete security, will continue unimpaired'—but gave the requisite powers to the Board of Directors, acting on the advice of the Actuary, thus giving a centralized authority which had been so banefully lacking from the original constitution. The official title of the office became 'The Equitable Life Assurance Society'.

In 1893, Burridge was recalled to the Equity and Law Life Assurance Society to take up the actuaryship and again the directors had to look outside the office for a replacement. The choice fell on Henry William Manly, then aged 49, the Actuary of the Mutual.

Manly's first tasks were to put the Society's affairs on to an adequate scientific basis and to expand the Society's activities into new kinds of life assurance that were being developed. The way was clear for the transaction of endowment assurances. Another type of contract, introduced by Manly, enabled a parent or friend to begin an assurance for a child who, on coming of age, would take over the assurance at a much lower premium than would be required for a new policy. Such assurances for children have been popular with successive generations of policyholders, each enabling their children to become members of the Society. Manly also introduced a special pension policy which happened to meet the needs of a pension scheme started in 1902; it must be about the earliest scheme arranged by means of life assurance policies.

Bonuses had been declared every tenth year for a hundred years. The last was in 1899 and Manly arranged that, thereafter, a valuation should be made every fifth year, as was the general custom with other offices.

Manly became a great authority on pension funds and was President of the Institute of Actuaries, 1898–1900. A remark of his, that his family considered he kept a good head of hair because of his habit of rubbing his head with his pipe when thinking out a problem, inspired some 'after dinner' verses (quoted by R. C. Simmonds), which began

Does your hair begin to fall
Like to autumn leaves when ripe?
Maiden, heed it not at all,
Rub your head with father's pipe.

Unfortunately, failing eyesight hampered Manly. He lost the sight of one eye in 1900 or 1901 and the sight of the other eye began to weaken; there was a lack of discipline among the clerks who took advantage of his shortness of sight. A legal case which the Society lost in the year 1904 was a disappointment to him and he retired in the following year at the comparatively early age of 61. At his last Board Meeting, the directors recorded a tribute to the 'great services' he had rendered the Society.

His place was taken by a very distinguished actuary, George James Lidstone who, in his comparatively short period with the Society, pulled the staff together and thoroughly revised the office methods and books. He left in 1913 to be Actuary of the Scottish Widows Fund.

Forty-three years had elapsed since Arthur Morgan's death and twenty years since the modernization of the Society. Its business had begun to grow but little effective progress had been made in putting the Society back into a competitive position. Lidstone left his successor a legacy of a printed report to the directors, dated August 13, 1913, which gave an interesting review of all kinds of problems in the Society. But the chief burden of the report was that such new business as had come had been through special schemes; there had been little increase in the standard classes. In the twenty years between 1889 and 1909, the number of policies in force increased by 70 per cent and the total amount of assurances in force by rather more than 40 per cent, including some annuities.

The President of the Society in 1912, when it was 150 years old, was Sir Samuel Hoare, Bart., the banker. He was Member of Parliament for the City of Norwich, 1886–1906, and took an active interest in farming as well as in cricket, golf and athletic clubs.

# CHAPTER XVII

# EXPANSION IN MODERN TIMES
## (1912–1962)

———

WITH the last fifty years of the Equitable's history, a period of tremendous expansion has begun. The funds have increased sevenfold and the premium income has grown to sixteen times its level half a century ago; the assurances and annuities in force are more than ten times larger in total. The Society has been transformed into a modern, vigorous mutual life office which transacts all classes of life assurance business, and this has been achieved without the payment of a penny of commission for the introduction of business.

While many hands have contributed to this growth, all would agree that the inspiration and driving force has been one man, Sir William Palin Elderton, KBE, whose career has dominated the whole period. He was Actuary and Manager from 1913 to 1942; he has been a director since 1940 and was President from 1947 to 1953. This remarkable man and brilliant actuary has a diversity of talents and achievements. The Institute of Actuaries (whose President he was in the years 1932 to 1934) and the Faculty of Actuaries in Scotland have made only two joint awards of gold medals for services to actuarial science—to Lidstone in 1929 and to Elderton in 1937.

A formative influence in his early years was his friendship with Karl Pearson, Galton Professor of Eugenics in the University of London and the creator of the Galton Laboratory. Pearson was laying the foundations of mathematical statistics and the association developed in Elderton a power of analysis and interpretation of statistics which is gained by few men. An impression by one who knew him from these years is of Elderton at work upstairs, calculating the mathematical constants of 'curve-fitting', while his friends downstairs were dancing.

During the first World War, he added advisory work at the Ministry of Shipping to his duties with the Equitable and, during the second World War, he rendered similar service to the Ministry of War Transport. This was only one way in which he gave as much to statistics as to actuarial science.

When he came to the Equitable, Lidstone wrote to him a letter which also reveals something of Lidstone's own personality:

> . . . You will find some problems that are quite worthy of your great powers, but at least you will find that they have been considered and stated . . . though the complete practical solution of them—having regard to past history and vested interests of a cantankerous body of mutual policyholders—has to a great extent baffled me.

Though, no doubt, all societies have their difficult members, the word 'cantankerous' seems unfair because, from the time of William Morgan onwards, those engaged in the management of the Equitable testified to the steady support of both the directors and the majority of members. The support of its policyholders is an abiding source of strength to the Society.

In the course of his working life, professional and business organizations delighted to honour Elderton, both for his business acumen and his personal qualities. A keen eye and a love of walking have given him a store of knowledge about the country-side, especially the churches and cathedrals, which make him a good companion and his charm of manner has brought him many friends. A talent for sketching and a taste for genealogy find him a member of unexpected societies to which he has contributed some part of his energetic spirit. And his brotherly character, a help to many young men starting in life and to older men suffering misfortune, has been a strong support in all kinds of ways to the old boys of Merchant Taylors' School, as indeed to many others.

Elderton served under four Presidents. The first, Sir Thomas Lane Devitt, Bart. (President, 1912–20), was a shipowner, the senior partner of Devitt & Moore, who was the dominant influence in that firm for many years. He was well thought of in the shipping world and served as Chairman of Lloyd's Register of Shipping and as President of the Chamber of Shipping; also, he had a year of office as Chairman of the London Missionary Society. The second, Sir Evan Spicer (President, 1920–30), the head of the paper firm, was a man of benevolent character but rather rigid, uncompromising principles, which might, on occasion, clash with purely business judgments. He was Governor of Dulwich College, became Chairman of the London County Council and had been President of the British and Foreign Bible Society. At his home at Dulwich, the grounds occupied the whole of the triangle between the road and two railway lines, so making an oasis of open country in the midst of London streets. During the general strike of 1926, he opened his home to those of the staff who could not get home each day. The third, Herbert Leslie Melville Tritton (President, 1930–40), was a Director of Barclays Bank and Chairman of Barclays Bank (D.C. & O.). His portrait is a character study but it does not, perhaps, sufficiently bring out the kindly spirit of the man, generous to those who served him. The fourth, Mr Desmond Abel Smith (President, 1940–47), is still a director of the Society.

The Equitable has fortunately been able to rely upon its members for much help in making the Society better known and this is still its best source of new business. It has always had strong family connections as could be illustrated from the directors as well as the members. Bringing together the names in alphabetical order helps to illustrate this feature, though some with the same surname are un-related, and others with different names may be related by marriage. Thus the Spicer family has had a long connection with the Equitable; Sir Stanley Unwin is a grandson of James Spicer.

The Oxley Parkers have a distinctive name which it is easy to pick out through successive generations of members. They claim descent from the ancient family of Parkers in Suffolk, whose head in the reign of Edward IV was Sir William Parker. The first John Oxley Parker (d. 1826) was the son of Samuel Parker and Mary Oxley (both d. 1758). His grandson, John Oxley Parker (1812–87), JP, DL, of Woodham Mortimer Place, Essex, joined the banking firm of Sparrow, Tufnell & Co., and wielded an influence far beyond his estates—a genial, hospitable man who loved the round of his farms, with hunting and cricket as his principal amusements. He was Chairman of the Essex Equitable Insurance Society. The family has tradi-tionally used the Christian names of John Oxley and Christopher William; both have been represented on the board of the Equitable.

The great-grandfather of Mr John Henry Bevan, CB, MC, the present President, was David Bevan (1774–1846) of Fosbury, Wiltshire, and Belmont Park, Hertfordshire, a member assured in the early nineteenth century. He was a banker and his portrait hangs in the head office of Barclays Bank; his grandson, David Augustus Bevan, became the founder of the firm of stockbrokers which bears his name, and a Vice-President of the Society. It is interesting that the crest in the Arms of this family includes a griffin, which is the creature chosen for the supporters in the Arms recently granted to the Society.

Another Equitable director is the grandson of Sir Roundell Palmer (1812–95), first Earl of Selborne, PC, LLD, DCL, FRS, Lord Chancellor in 1872–4 and 1880–5, and a member of the Society in its troubled days.

The connection with the Abel Smiths does not go so far back, though the family has given two directors to the Society as has also the Walters family (of *The Times*) who are related to them by marriage. The John Abel Smith who was a member of the Select Committee on Assurance Associations of 1853 was Treasurer for many years of the Benevolent Fund associated with the Provident Mutual Life Assurance Association in its early days.

Twinings, the tea and coffee merchants in the Strand, supplied many members and three directors of the Society, including one who became President at the age of 84 years and served ten years. He was a partner in Twinings[1] for 68 years, retiring in 1897. He died at the age of 99 in 1906, when his assurances for £5,000 yielded with bonus a total of £25,452 10s, compared with premiums paid of £8,339.

An unusually long connection is with the Talbots of Kidderminster, who have been members of the Society through six generations, beginning with William Talbot (1806–87), a solicitor who started in practice in 1828 and who founded the Kidderminster Permanent Benefit Building Society in 1851. His grandfather, Samuel Talbot, was appointed a Commissioner of the Court of Requests in 1772 and since that time the family has an unbroken record of public service to Kidderminster and Worcestershire—approaching 200 years.

Another long connection through five generations is with the Harpur Michells of Penzance. It is said in the family that the first of them in the early nineteenth century paid his premiums out of the proceeds of smuggling, which was, in those days, regarded as a fair game with the revenue officials.

It is possible to refer to a few examples only of such connections but

[1] There is a charming account of the firm by Stephen H. Twining, MBE.

some well-known names may be mentioned. Four generations of the Chamberlains were members of the Society, including Joseph Chamberlain and his son, Neville Chamberlain. Several generations of the Trevelyans have been members. Charles Babbage, FRS, the well-known mathematician was a member as was also William Gilbert Grace, the cricketer. The father and grandfather of Ethel M. Dell, the novelist, both served the Society as clerks. John Galsworthy was a member.

For the greater part of the Equitable's history, its legal advisers have been drawn from members of one family firm—the Brays and Warrens of Shere, whose practice was originally in Great Russell Street and is now at 5 Bedford Square. The Brays trace their ancestry to Sir Reginald Bray, a statesman of the reign of Henry VII, Lord Treasurer of England, who directed the King's great building operations at St George's Chapel, Windsor, and at Westminster. The connection with the Equitable started with William Bray (1736–1832), the historian of Surrey, whose diary first mentions the Equitable in May 1774. At the age of 70 in 1806, he noted that his eye-sight was still so good that he could use his eyes in reading or writing till 10 at night; he could walk or ride for four or five hours together 'but I do not ride fast'. Obviously, he was well liked by everyone—at times dining with the directors, or going to Sir Charles Gould's chambers, or inviting the William Morgans—father and son—to dine with him. When he was 82 in 1818, he happily recorded,

19 Nov. My granddaughter Harriet was married to Mr Warren, my partner, very much to my satisfaction, having that opinion of them both, that I think there is every prospect of happiness for them.

This was Augustus Warren (1790–1853) who succeeded William Bray as the Society's solicitor. The last of the family to act for the Society was Bertram Reginald Warren (1868–1952).

The Society did not make a formal appointment as Chief Medical Officer until comparatively late in its history. It has been served by four distinguished physicians, beginning with Sir George Johnson (1818–96), MD, FRCP, FRS, Professor, successively, of materia medica, medicine and clinical medicine in King's College, London, and Physician to King's College Hospital (appointed Physician Extraordinary to Queen Victoria in 1889). Sir George Johnson was a man of outspoken views. He was an authority on kidney diseases and cholera, and is said to have been the first insurance examiner who

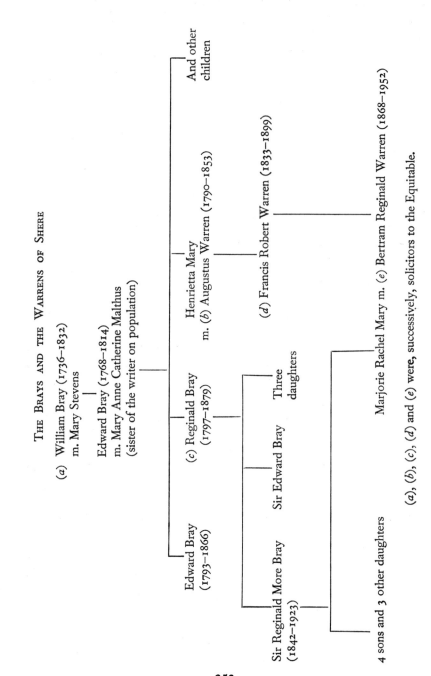

The Brays and the Warrens of Shere

(a) William Bray (1736–1832)
m. Mary Stevens

Edward Bray (1768–1814)
m. Mary Anne Catherine Malthus
(sister of the writer on population)

Henrietta Mary
m. (b) Augustus Warren (1790–1853)

And other children

(d) Francis Robert Warren (1833–1899)

Edward Bray
(1793–1866)

(c) Reginald Bray
(1797–1879)

Sir Edward Bray

Three daughters

Sir Reginald More Bray
(1842–1923)

4 sons and 3 other daughters

Marjorie Rachel Mary m. (e) Bertram Reginald Warren (1868–1952)

(a), (b), (c), (d) and (e) were, successively, solicitors to the Equitable.

insisted on testing the proposer's water. The other three physicians were all trained at St Thomas's Hospital: William Miller Ord (1834–1902) FRCP, Physician of Guy's Hospital, Seymour Taylor (1851–1931), author of the well-liked *Index of Medicine*, and John Forest Smith, FRCP.

The Equitable has had a close connection with the City of London and it is interesting that no less than five of its directors in the eighteenth century held the office of Lord Mayor: Sir Richard Glyn in 1758–9, Nathaniel Newnham in 1782–3, Thomas Wright in 1785–6, Thomas Sainsbury in 1786–7, William Gill in 1788–9. A number of the directors held office in the City, e.g. as Recorder, Chamberlain and so on.

The Equitable is proud of the good name it has built up over the long course of its history and this has given it a distinctive place amongst life offices, which they are glad to acknowledge. Many highly respectable institutions have borrowed the name. It is all the more distressing when the name is taken by a less worthy organization as it was by the City Equitable, an office which was founded in 1908 and was wound up in 1922. The office may be ephemeral but the damage it does may be more lasting.

The Equitable has recently been honoured by the grant of Arms. The crest incorporates the pelican which has been the Society's traditional emblem from the seal device adopted by the trustees in the early days. The pelican is set in a civic crown, which marks the Society's long connection with the City of London. The pelican is fabled to feed its young with its own life-blood, a fable which also has relevance to the choice of a heart (as a symbol of life) for the central device of the shield. Surrounding the heart are six quills, an association with the 'Hand and Pen', where James Dodson lived, and a reminder that the Equitable originated the use of the title 'actuary' in the context of life assurance, though in the sense of 'secretary', then the customary title of the chief official. The supporters are griffins, the traditional guardians of the treasure. On their necks, they bear collars with three thistles and three roses, which were part of Sir Charles Gould's insignia and were incorporated on chevrons in the Morgan arms, when he became head of the family. The wavy bend on the wing of each griffin is borrowed from the Arms of the Institute of Actuaries, which bear a wavy bend (argent) as a symbol of the river of life, referring both to the connection with life assurance and the stream of life in a continuing society such as the Institute or the Equitable.

There is little doubt that the symbol of the pelican and the motto, 'Sic nos non nobis', were chosen by Edward Rowe Mores. The motto harks back to a pleasing story about the poet Virgil. An unsigned couplet of his about the Emperor Augustus was, much to his annoyance, claimed by a minor poet named Bathyllus. Thereupon, as a challenge to Bathyllus, he put up the words 'sic vos non vobis' which were to be the opening words of each line of a quatrain. Bathyllus being unable to complete the verse, Virgil then put up his original couplet with the completed verse which reads (in a translation by the Rev. Gifford H. Johnson, MA):

I wrote these verses, another took the credit:

Thus ye, not for yourselves, build nests, O birds.
Thus ye, not for yourselves, carry fleeces, O sheep.
Thus ye, not for yourselves, make honey, O bees.
Thus ye, not for yourselves, draw ploughs, O kine.

In the form 'sic nos non nobis' produced by Edward Rowe Mores for the Society the motto is especially appropriate since the members of the Society become members in order to provide for their dependants.

Assurances for the whole of life have been a feature of the Society's business from the earliest days and it still operates the bonus system which has given such remarkable results. The system recognizes the need for large reserves; since the older members have contributed most to the reserves, the system allots bonuses which increase with the number of years that the assurance has been in force.

Manly began the practice of listing all the claims under whole-life assurances; the lists form an interesting part of the annual report and accounts. These show good results for assurances of all durations and spectacular results for those which are longest in force. In the sixty-eight years for which these lists are available, the Society has paid fifteen claims where the amount with bonus was more than five times the original sum assured, two of them being over six times. Of what other life office can this be said? Earlier claims would increase the number but unfortunately the records do not enable them to be traced, except in individual instances.

These remarkable results were achieved for assurances which had been well over seventy or even over eighty years in force. The lives had assured at young ages and survived to a good old age. Though comparatively few can look forward to so long a life, the results for all assurances have been wonderfully good. Year in, year out, for many years the claims under 'whole-of-life' assurances have been more than doubled in total; all such claims since 1800 have, on the average, yielded more than twice the amount originally assured.

The high rates of death duties since the first World War have operated to discourage these assurances, because the larger bonuses have tended to benefit the Chancellor of the Exchequer rather than the beneficiaries for whom the assurance was intended. It cannot be too widely known that the Finance Act, 1960, has largely done away with this problem. Assurances given to a husband, wife, or child under the Married Women's Property Acts are now treated in a comparable way to other gifts; if the premium is no more than a reasonable provision out of income, the policy would escape death duties altogether.

Expansion has come in many ways. With the growth in business, it has been possible to expand the number of the staff engaged in actively seeking new business. These are salaried officials whose job it is to see, to the best of their ability, that policyholders' needs are met and that the Society's activities are made better known. The first branch office was secured with the acquisition in 1919 of the University Life Assurance Society—a chartered corporation founded in 1825 which transacts life assurance amongst university men and women and persons of a similar educational standard. The opening of other branch offices has enabled both societies to cover the country more adequately by officials stationed locally.

Reversionary and life interests in trust funds of various kinds can be both suitable investments for the funds of life offices and a useful source of life assurance business. The Equitable's place in this field was strengthened by the acquisition of The Reversionary Interest Society Ltd., in 1919 and The Equitable Reversionary Interest Society Ltd., in 1920.

A popular way of buying a house is by means of a loan from a life office combined with a life assurance policy which will repay the loan at the end of the agreed number of years or at the death of the life assured, should he or she not survive to complete the payments. Many Equitable policyholders are buying their homes in this way. The Society also has an interest (with three other life offices) in the

255

Standard Property Investment Company Ltd., of Edinburgh, which transacts a similar type of mortgage business.

A feature of the Society has been the encouragement of staff pension schemes. It has been associated with the Federated Super-annuation System for Universities since the commencement of that scheme fifty years ago and has taken a leading part in the organization of the panel of offices which operate the scheme. The Society also has pension arrangements for many employees, which are operated by a section of the head office at Aylesbury. The Equitable has been a pioneer in the application of profit-sharing to pension arrangements, which has helped those whose main interest is in pensions to have a share, also, in the prosperity of the Society.

The expansion of the Society has taken place in a world shaken by economic storms and darkened by the two world wars of 1914–18 and 1939–45. Inevitably, there were stresses and strains but perhaps the personal losses were least easy to be borne. However, the experience of these years has been that low rates of interest and high rates of taxation can be at least as damaging to a life office as more obvious signs of physical loss.

What the future will think of outstanding interest in current developments is always a speculative question to which no sure answer can be given. What seems important at the time of writing is the greater freedom of investment which the life offices have felt both necessary and desirable, in the current economic climate, for the purpose of giving their policyholders some share of profits from the expansion of industry and some protection against the possible effects of further inflation, should it recur. In this movement, the Equitable is ready to play its part as it has been in other developments of life assurance in the past.

Whether there are new forms of life assurance contract yet to be developed is unknown. But the tremendous increase in pension arrangements made by employers for their staffs may well lead back to popularity the traditional forms of life assurance which have receded into the background in past decades. For when the head of a family can look forward to adequate superannuation at the end of his working life, he more than ever needs life assurance to protect his dependants should he not survive to take care of them himself. This was the earliest form of life assurance granted by the Equitable and is commended to every reader of this book.

# NOTE ON THOMAS SIMPSON (1710–61) FRS, AND THE FOUNDATION OF THE SOCIETY

An error which is constantly repeated is difficult to counteract because mere repetition tends to give it the weight of authority; this is especially true of historical errors. It has been said many times that Simpson was lecturing on insurance when the Equitable Society was formed and he has been credited with some share in the foundation of life assurance. Cornelius Walford, in his *History of the Equitable Society* (1875) (reprinted from the *Insurance Cyclopedia*), set out the evidence at length and came to the conclusion that Simpson was lecturing on insurance when Dodson, acting independently, called the meetings in the year 1756. This was an error. Further evidence has come to light since 1948, when the question was discussed in the *Proceedings of the Centenary Assembly of the Institute of Actuaries*, vol. III, p. 364. It has now been possible to trace the origin of the error.

The *First Lecture on Insurances* was written by James Dodson early in 1756 and contained the material required by the committee formed for the purpose of petitioning for a charter for the Equitable Society. The accounts of this committee show that Richard Jenkinson (afterwards a clerk in the Equitable's service) was employed for the purpose of copying some of the documents, which may well have included Dodson's lectures.

Soon after the Society was formed the directors thought that it would be useful to have a copy of Dodson's tables and one of the directors was instructed to apply to Dodson's executor, William Mountaine, for them (W, January 17, 1764). A week later the tables had been obtained from William Mountaine who 'left the same with and for the use of the Society'. He evidently intended this to be merely a temporary loan of the tables because, six months later (W, July 24, 1764), it was arranged that Dodson's tables should be copied by his son. This was in the year before the son was elected Actuary of the Society.

The copies of the lectures and tables may have been temporarily mislaid in the course of changes in the staff, especially when the dispute was at its height, and in 1768 William Mountaine sent James Dodson's lectures to the directors 'giving some of the foundation principles on which his tables were formed . . . they were extremely welcome to take a transcript'. John Edwards, the Actuary of the Society, was instructed to take a copy of the lectures (W, December 13, 1768).

William Mountaine died in 1779 and bequeathed the lectures to the Society. On the occasion when his executors handed them over to the Court of Directors, the minute reads: 'The Actuary laid before the Court by the desire of the executors of William Mountaine sundry tables of premiums of assurance computed by the late Mr Dodson and also a copy of lectures on the method of establishing a society for making assurances on lives by the late Mr Simpson, which Mr Mountaine had

R

by his will bequeathed to this Society' (W, November 24, 1779). The minute was clearly wrong in attributing the lectures to Simpson. There is no reason why Mountaine should have had any lectures by Simpson and the lectures that were handed over must have been those written by Dodson. William Morgan, who was the Actuary of the Society at the time, must be held responsible for the error.

The first three editions of Richard Price's *Observations on Reversionary Payments* refer to Dodson and do not mention Simpson's name in connection with the founding of the Society. The fourth edition, which was published in 1783, brought in Simpson's name and was evidently based upon the erroneous minute of 1779; Morgan would have helped his uncle in the preparation of this edition. Later writers have copied the error from this source.

The Society has two copies of the *First Lecture on Insurances*. One of them, which has been in the possession of the Society continuously, was probably made by Richard Jenkinson before the foundation of the Society, though it could have been made by James Dodson's son in 1764: the copies of the lectures and the tables seem to be in different handwritings. The other, which was owned by Cornelius Walford and passed from him to the library of the Equitable Life Assurance Society of the United States and from them to the Old Equitable, would be the copy made by John Edwards in 1768. The actual lectures which were given to the Society in 1779 have disappeared.

*Note:* There is no mention of any lectures of this kind in *Thomas Simpson, FRS and his times* by Frances M. Clarke (1929).

## SUPPLEMENTARY NOTES

*Page* 22: The development of the concept of a probability law in the seventeenth century is an illustration of the general change in mental attitudes that was then taking place: e.g. see Chapter 7 of *The Origins of Modern Science*, by Herbert Butterfield, M A.

*Page* 97: The French Revolution engendered a spirit of idealism at first, which it is difficult now to re-capture, knowing what came later. The feelings of a radical in 1791, the year in which Price died, are well expressed in the poem by William Blake, published in that year: 'The dead brood over Europe . . . the loud voice of France cries to the morning . . . the Commons convene in the Hall of the Nation . . . the prisoners look up and assay to shout . . . visions of sorrow leave pensive streets . . . ancient darkness and trembling wander thro' the palace'.

*Page* 113: On the west wall of the Painted Hall at Greenwich, Thornhill depicted one of the daughters of George I as Prudence, holding a mirror. He used the same symbolism for prudence in his paintings for the ceiling of the Old Aldermen's Court Room in Guildhall. It is possible that the mirror on the gold cup was intended as a symbol of prudence, which would be in keeping with Gould's character.

*Page* 172: The hatred of paper money, behind the urge to return to a gold standard, is forcibly expressed in a group of political poems written by Shelley in 1819. 'Paper coin—that forgery of the title deeds . . . of the inheritance of the earth' (*The Mask of Anarchy*). Shelley's ideal was not merely political freedom but also spiritual and economic freedom—'clothes, and fire, and food' and a 'neat and happy home' for the labourer.

*Page* 229: The 'bitter discontent of the working classes' in the 1830s and 1840s could be described as the seed-plot of some modern political ideas. Carlyle's main specifics were education and emigration (*Chartism*, 1839). The really evil conditions were, of course, local to the manufacturing centres. Southey, the poet, wrote to Lord Ashley in 1833: 'They who grow cotton (i.e. the slave-owners) are merciful taskmasters in comparison with those who manufacture it'. Thomas Arnold was trying to form a society to collect information about the poor and wrote to Carlyle in January 1840: 'The Society should broach no theories, and propose no remedies; it should simply collect information, and rouse the attention of the country to the infinite importance of the subject'. What comment is more apt than Ebenezer Elliott's about the condition of the people?—'Their heritage a sunless day'. It was a tragic problem; the economy needed the capital which was wasted in speculation in life assurance projects that came to nothing.

# PRESIDENTS OF THE SOCIETY, PERSONS WHO HAVE HELD THE POSITION OF ACTUARY, AND THE ORIGINAL SUBSCRIBERS

## (A) Presidents

| | | *Portraits* |
|---|---|---|
| 1762–1764 | Right Hon. Lord Willoughby of Parham (died 1765) .. .. .. .. | None known |
| 1764–1769 | Sir Richard Glyn, Bart. (1711–72) .. | J. Zoffany —(at King Edward's School, Witley, Surrey) |
| 1769–1773 | John Spencer Colepeper (1712–88) .. | None known |
| 1773–1806 | Sir Charles Gould (1726–1806) .. (from 1792, Sir Charles Morgan, Bart.) | T. Gainsborough |
| 1806–1846 | Sir Charles Morgan, Bart. (1760–1846) .. | (*a*) W. H. Pickersgill (*b*) William Owen |
| 1846–1875 | Sir Charles Morgan Robinson Morgan, Bart., cr. 1859, 1st Baron Tredegar (1792–1875) .. .. .. .. | R. Buckner[1] |
| 1875–1888 | Sir (William) Frederick Pollock, Bart. (1815–88).. .. .. .. .. | W. W. Ouless |
| 1888–1892 | John Alldin Moore (1817 or 1818–93) .. | None known |
| 1892–1902 | Richard Twining (1807–1906) .. .. | A. S. Cope |
| 1902–1912 | Sir Samuel Hoare, Bart. (1841–1915) .. | A. S. Cope |
| 1912–1920 | Sir Thomas Lane Devitt, Bart. (1839–1923) .. .. .. .. .. | R. G. Eves |
| 1920–1930 | Sir Evan Spicer (1849–1937) .. .. | Hugh C. Riviere |
| 1930–1940 | Herbert Leslie Melville Tritton (1870–1940) .. .. .. .. .. | R. G. Eves |
| 1940–1947 | Desmond Abel Smith, MC .. .. | Maurice Codner |
| 1947–1953 | Sir William Palin Elderton, KBE .. .. | Harold Knight |
| 1953– | John Henry Bevan, CB, MC .. .. | In conversation piece by Edward Halliday |

[1] This portrait is to be presented to the Society by President Oates of the Equitable of the United States at the bi-centenary celebrations.

# APPENDICES

## (B) Actuaries

*Portraits*

The first and principal promoter of the Equitable
    James Dodson (*c.* 1710–57), FRS        ..    None known
The salaried director named in the deed of settlement
  (voted out 1770)
    Edward Rowe Mores (1731–78), MA, FSA    P. van Bleeck
                                            engraved, J. Mynde
                                            —(at the Society of
                                            Antiquaries)

Consultant for about 15 years from 1768
    Richard Price (1723–91), DD, FRS    ..    Benjamin West

| | | |
|---|---|---|
| 1762–1764 | William Mosdell (or Mosdale) (*c.* 1709–64) | None known |
| 1765–1767 | James Dodson (1742–   ) .. .. .. | None known |
| 1767–1773 | John Edwards (1729 or 1730–73).. .. | None known |
| 1774–1775 | John Pocock (1743–75) .. .. .. | None known |
| 1775–1830 | William Morgan (1750–1833), FRS, (Assistant Actuary, Feb. 1774).. .. | Thomas Lawrence |
| 1830–1870 | Arthur Morgan (1801–70), FRS, (Clerk, 1820; Joint Actuary, 1824) .. .. | Unknown artist |
| 1870–1888 | John Ware Stephenson (1817 or 1818–1901), FIA (Clerk, 1837; Assistant Actuary, 1852) .. .. .. .. | Photographs in album of Actuaries' Club |
| 1888–1893 | Arthur Francis Burridge (1852 or 1853–1904), FIA .. .. .. .. | |
| 1893–1905 | Henry William Manly (1844–1914), FIA.. | |
| 1905–1913 | George James Lidstone (1870–1952), LLD, FIA, FFA, FRSE .. .. .. .. | Frank Eastman —(at Institute of Actuaries) |
| 1913–1942 | Sir William Palin Elderton, KBE, FIA, FFA, PHD (Oslo). (Also, President and Director) .. .. .. .. .. | Harold Knight |
| 1942– | Henry John Tappenden, FIA (first appointed 1922) .. .. .. .. | —— |
| 1948– | (Joint Actuary) Maurice Edward Ogborn, FIA, FSS (first appointed 1924).. .. | —— |

*Note:* Edward Halliday painted a conversation piece of Mr John Henry Bevan
with the last three named.

## (C) ORIGINAL SUBSCRIBERS

| Name of subscriber | Description in petition (or from other sources, where not a petitioner) | Subscriptions £1 | £2 | Total £ | How disposed of | Number of shares in Article 59 of Deed of Settlement (nominal value £5 each) | Subscribers whose shares were acquired |
|---|---|---|---|---|---|---|---|
| John Ashton | of Christ's Hospital, London | 15 | — | 15 | Sold | — | — |
| John Bedford | of London, Vintner | 15 | 20 | 35 | — | 7 | — |
| Jane Bonham | of London, Spinster | 15 | 15 | 30 | Consolidated | — | — |
| Sarah Newton (afterwards Bonham) | —(Wife of William Bonham) | 15 | 20 | 35 | — | 7 | Jane Bonham (6) |
| William Bonham | of London, Packer | 15 | 20 | 35 | — | 19 | Richard Martin (6) |
| George Bowser | of London, Embrosser [sic] | 10 | — | 10 | — | 2 | — |
| Richard Bridgman (senior) | —(Master Deputy, Citizen and Grocer) | | | | | — | — |
| Richard Bridgman (junior) | —(Citizen and Grocer) | 15 | 20 | 35 | Consolidated | — | — |
| James Brooks | of London, Attorney | 15 | 15 | 30 | Died about August 1762 | — | — |
| Edmund Chantrell | of London, Grocer (spelt Chauntiel) | 5 | — | 5 | Declined to continue | — | — |
| John Coulson | of Bermondsey, Brewer | 15 | — | 15 | Consolidated | — | — |
| George Coulton | of London, Taylor | 15 | — | 15 | Consolidated | — | — |
| James Dodson | of Christ's Hospital, London, FRS | 15 | — | 15 | Died November 1757, shares held by executor | — | — |
| Richard Emans | of London, Fire Smith | 15 | 20 | 35 | Consolidated | — | — |
| Sir Richard Glyn | Kt. and Alderman of London | 15 | — | 15 | — | 3 | — |
| William Gollop | of London, Esq. | 15 | — | 15 | Died about 1757 | — | — |
| George Hale | — | 15 | — | 15 | Declined to continue | — | — |
| John Huntridge | of London, Scrivener | 15 | — | 15 | Sold | — | — |
| Benjamin Johnson | of London, Accomptant | 10 | — | 10 | Sold | 2 | — |
| Charles Lucas | of London, Wine Cooper | 10 | — | 10 | Sold | — | — |

| Name | Description | | | | | | Nominees |
|---|---|---|---|---|---|---|---|
| Richard Martin | of London, Ship Chandler | 15 | 15 | 30 | Sold | — | — |
| Edward Rowe Mores | of London, Esq. | 15 | 20 | 35 | — | 23 | { Richard Bridgman (sen.) (7); Richard Bridgman (jun.) (6) } |
| Elizabeth Mosdell | of London, Spinster (spelt Mosdale) | 15 | 15 | 30 | — | 6 | John Huntridge (3) |
| William Mosdell | of Southwark, Brewer (spelt Mosdale) | 15 | 20 | 35 | — | 17 | { Richard Emans (7); George Coulton (3) } |
| William Mountaine | of Southwark, FRS | 15 | — | 15 | — | 6 | John Coulson (3) |
| Jacob Palmer | of London, Broker | 15 | — | 15 | — | 3 | James Dodson (3) |
| Dr Thomas Pickering | —(DD, in petition of March 29, 1760) | 15 | 20 | 35 | — | 7 | — |
| Francis Rowden | (a) *of Merton College, Oxford (b) of London, Accomptant | 15 | — | 15 | Declined to continue | — | — |
| Robert Rowden | of London, Printer | 15 | — | 15 | Declined to continue | — | — |
| Charles-Greene Say | of London, Upholder | 15 | 10 | 25 | — | 7 | John Ashton (2) |
| Francis Say | —(Druggist in Newgate St.) | 15 | — | 15 | — | 4 | John Ashton (1) |
| Joseph Sclater | of London, Clerk | 15 | 15 | 30 | — | 6 | — |
| Rev. William Sclater | MD, FRS | 15 | 20 | 35 | — | 7 | — |
| Dr John Silvester | of Christ's Hospital, London | 15 | 20 | 35 | — | 7 | — |
| Thomas Smith | of London, Clerk | 15 | — | 15 | Declined to continue | — | — |
| William Stanton | of London, Lighterman | 15 | — | 15 | Died about 1760 | 5 | — |
| John Staples | of London, Attorney | 15 | 10 | 25 | — | — | — |
| Michael Tovey | of London, Clerk | 15 | — | 15 | Declined to continue | — | — |
| Rev. James Townley | of London, Accomptant | 15 | — | 15 | Declined to continue | 3 | — |
| Henry Trafford | of London, Surgeon | 15 | — | 15 | — | — | — |
| George Vaux | —(Sail maker of Shadwell) | 15 | — | 15 | Sold | 3 | George Vaux (3) |
| Josiah Wallis | of London, Merchant | — | — | — | — | — | — |
| Paul Henry Robinson | | — | — | — | — | †2 | Charles Lucas (2) |
| | | £590 | £295 | £885 | | 146 | |

\* One of these was Robert but it is uncertain which.

† The 2 shares bought by Paul Henry Robinson were in the end forfeited because he did not assure his life with the Society as required by the Deed of Settlement.

# LIST OF HISTORICAL ARTICLES

by past and present members of the Equitable's staff

| | |
|---|---|
| J. G. ANDERSON | The birthplace and genesis of life assurance (2nd ed. ill., 1940) |
| do. | William Morgan and X-rays<br>*Trans. Faculty of Actuaries*, Vol. 17 (1945) |
| W. PALIN ELDERTON<br>(NOW SIR WILLIAM<br>ELDERTON, KBE) | Investments a hundred years ago<br>*Journal, Institute of Actuaries*, Vol. 51 (1918) |
| do. | William Morgan, FRS (1750–1833)<br>*Trans. Faculty of Actuaries*, Vol. 14 (1932) |
| do. | [Also a note with the same title in<br>*Journal, Institute of Actuaries*, Vol. 64 (1933)] |
| do. | Some family connections of William Morgan (1750–1833), FRS<br>*The Genealogists' Magazine*, Vol. 12 (1957) |
| SIR WILLIAM ELDERTON<br>and M. E. OGBORN | The mortality of adult males since the middle of the eighteenth century as shown by the experience of life assurance companies<br>*Journal, Royal Statistical Society*, Vol. 106 (1943) |
| M. E. OGBORN | The actuary in the eighteenth century<br>*Proceedings, Centenary Assembly, Institute of Actuaries*, Vol. 3 (1950) |
| do. | The professional name of actuary<br>*Journal, Institute of Actuaries*, Vol. 82 (1956) |
| M. E. OGBORN and<br>R. H. STORR-BEST | Arthur Morgan's mortality experience<br>*Journal, Institute of Actuaries*, Vol. 85 (1959) |

# INDEX

Abel Smith, Desmond, 249, 260; family, 250

accounts, 81–4; (1766–72, table) 83; Price's advice on, 103–5; publication of, 207, 238–9; first eighty-six years, 220

Actuaries' Club, 233, 235, 237, 241; and see *Institute of Actuaries*

Actuary: choice of title, 48–9, 198, 253; assistant appointed, 100; Morgan as consultant, 137, 197; list of holders, 261

Alliance Assurance Company, 173

Amicable Society for a Perpetual Assurance Office, 20, 26, 33–4

annuities: Mercer's scheme, 19; development of mathematical techniques, 22–3, by Dodson, 25–6; powers to grant, 73–4; other projects for, 91–2; Colley's deferred annuity, 74–5

Ansell, Charles, 233–5, 237

Arms, grant of, 253–4

assignments, 184

Assurance Associations, Select Committee on, 237–9

Asylum life office, 173, 209

Atlas Assurance Company, 169, 233

Babbage, Charles, 189–92, 200, 251

Baily, Francis, 151–2, 187–8, 191–2, 198–9

Bank of England, account with, 153; lends on mortgages, 172; the 'one-third bullion' rule, 174; legal advisers, Freshfields, 180

Barrett, George, 199

Batten, William, 109–10

Bayes, Thomas, 88–9

Bevan, John Henry, 249–50, 260; conversation piece including, 261 *n.*

binocular microscope, Stephenson's, 241

Blackfriars Bridge, 98–9

Boldero & Co., failure, 153

Bonham, William, 45, 55, 262

bonus: cash, 105, opposed, 109–10, 175–88: interim, 150; in stock, opposed, 175–83; and see *reversionary bonus*

boom of 1823–5, 172–3

Boswell, James, 93, 96–7, 140

Brakenridge (or Brackenridge), Rev. William, 26, 34

Bray, William, 102, 106; family, 251–2

Bridgman, Richard, senior, 31, 37, 40, 45, 262

British Equitable Assurance Company, 210

Brooke, H. J., 192

Brown, George, 178–80

Brown, Samuel, 212, 235–7

building societies, 211

Bunyon, C. J., 224–5

Burdett, Sir Francis, 196, 197

Burridge, A. F., 244, 245, 261

Bushnan, Joseph, 175–80, 188

Bye-Laws of 1816: first step, 151; the Bye-Laws, 155–9; effect of, 163–4, 203, 215–22; inequitable, 223, 226, 242; death of last pre-1817 member, 244

Cartwright, Edward, claim by, 59–60

Chamberlain family, 251

Charter Fund proprietors, see *subscribers*

charter, petition for, 32–4, refused, 35–6; provision for, in deed of settlement, 45; idea abandoned, 147

Chartists, 228

Chatham Place office, 98–9, 162, 195; freehold not bought, 106; compensation for, 240

children's endowment policies, 73, 245

City Equitable, 253

City of London, connections with, 253

claims: paid after six months, 82; generosity in settling, 148; suicides, 152–3; under whole-of-life policies, listed, 254; and see *reversionary bonus*

Colepeper, J. S., 71–3, 260

Colley case (deferred annuity), 74–5

# INDEX

Gould, Sir Charles (later Sir Charles Morgan), 75; President, 98, 99–100, 107, 260; gold cup, 112–13, 259 n.; Gainsborough portrait, 113; progress under, 116–17; career, 138–41; change of name, 140; family tree, 144

Government stocks: rise, 169, 172, 175, 202; danger of fluctuations, 204, 207, 218; price of Consols, 244; Exchequer Bills, 215

Grace, W. G., 251

Graunt, John, 22

Guardian Assurance Company, 135, 233

half-credit system, 231

Halley, Edmond, 22, 78

Halliday, Edward: conversation piece by, 260, 261 n.

Hampshire, Thomas, 161

Hardy, Peter, 212

Hardy, R. P., 244–5

Harpur Michell family, 250

Hayter, Sir George, 220

Hendriks, Augustus, 244–5

Hoare, Sir Samuel, 246

'Honest Whigs' Club, 93

house-purchase through life offices, 255–6

Hutton, Charles, 135, 136–7

Huygens, Christiaan, 22

income tax, 131–3

incorporation, limitation of liability by: refused, 32, 35; lack of, 145–6, 147; gained by registration, 244

Independent West Middlesex swindle, 231–2

inflation, and paper money, 130-2, 172, 259 n.

Institute of Actuaries, 212, 233–5, 237, 241; *Journal*, 235 n.

investments, 33; wider investment policy, 105–7; policy reconsidered, 169; mortgages *versus* Government stocks, 169–73, 183–4, 213–15, 218; policy attacked, 225; more liberal policy, 243; reversionary and life interests, 255; and see *Government stocks; mortgages*

Jellicoe, Charles, 235–7

Johnson, Sir George, 251

Kirkpatrick, George, 169, 233–4

Knight, Dr Gowin, 45, 52–3, 79

Law Life Assurance Society, 189, 233

legal opinions, reports and cases: on petition for charter, 35; on powers to alter deed, 62–3; on subscribers' claim to entrance money, 66, 70; on public subscription, 133; on income tax, 133; on loss from bank failure, 153; on changes in Bye-Laws of 1816, 176, 201, 221, 226; on majority of votes required, 201; on policy loans, 214; Windus case, 226

Lidstone, G. J., 246, 247–8, 261

life assurance: birth of, 19–21, 23–4, 26, 30–3, 47–8

Life Assurance Companies Act (1870), 239

life assurance contract, an indemnity?, 148

life assurance offices: (1796) 136–7; (1810) 151–2; (1800–26) 189; (1837) 207–8; mushroom growths, 229–39; government control, 230, 233, 239

life tables, see *mortality tables*

limited liability, 145–6, 173; and see *incorporation*

limited premium policy, 169

loans on policies: first recorded, 74; opposed, 183, 214–5

London Annuity Society, 92

London Assurance Corporation, 21, 34, 173

London Life Association, 207; Brooke's system of reducing premiums, 192

Lovelock, Edward, and his son, 161–2, 212, 227

Mackenzie, Peter, 232

magnetic variation, 78–9

Manly, H. W., 245–6, 254, 261

Manningham, Thomas, 99

Mansion House Street office, 241

Martin, Adam, 45, 62

medical examination: appointment of medical officer deferred, 102–3, 109; sub-standard lives, 192; Chief Medical Officer appointed, 251

membership: procedure on admission to, 52–3; voting rights, 151, 155, 159; and see *Bye-Laws of 1816–17; General Court*

# INDEX

Paine, Tom, 97, 196
Pascal, Blaise, 22
Pateman, W. S. D., 236
Pearson, Prof. Karl, 247
Peel, Sir Robert, 233
Pelican Life Insurance Office, 135; resists claim on William Pitt's life, 148
pelican seal, 112, 135, 253–4
pension schemes, 245, 256
Phoenix Assurance Company, 135
Pitt, William (the Younger), 130–1, 148
Pocock, John, 99–101, 261
Pollock, Sir Frederick, 242, 243, 260
Poor Laws, Committee on, 198; and see *friendly societies*
population growth, 229
Poynder, John, 177–80
premium tables: Dodson's, 21, 30–1, 33, 80–1; Simpson's method, 81; on Northampton mortality, 108–11, 116
premiums: addition for hazardous occupations and females, 33, non-appearance, 60, 73, large assurances, 105, 'sea risque', 127 and overseas residence, 213; reductions, 105, 108–9; further reductions opposed, 121, 166, 182; unpaid premiums, 125–6
Presbyterian Ministers' Fund, 259 *n.*
Presidents, list of, 260
Price, Ralph, 203, 220–1
Price, Dr Richard, 84, 261; birth and ancestry, 85–90; consulted by Edwards, 90–1; *Observations on the Expectation of Lives*, 91; *Observations on Reversionary Payments*, 92; on national debt, 92–3, 127–30; on civil liberty, 93–5; on population, 95; on social security, 95–6; American friends, and James Boswell, 96–7; and the French Revolution, 97, 259 *n.*; advice on actuarial investigations, 103–5, 108–11; presentations to, 91, 111–12; death, 97, 130; family connections, *facing* 129
probability theory, 21–2, 259 *n.*
proportionate paid-up policy, first recorded, 74–5
prospectus, first, see *Short Account*
publication of accounts, 207, 238–9

Queen's Head, Paternoster Row, meeting at the, 26, 31

Reform Bills, 228
regulations of 1816, see *Bye-Laws of* 1816
'reserved third', 123–5, 152, 159; attacks on, 166, 178, 182, 190, 200–1, 224–5; comparison with 'one-third bullion' rule, 174
reversionary bonus: origin as compensation for past overpayments, 109–10, 116; without reduction of subsequent premiums, 117–18, 120; decennial, 121–5; with interim bonus, 149–50; five-year waiting period, 151; confined to 5,000 oldest policies, 155; waiting period not to rank, 159–60; subsequent additions, 164–5, 202–3, 217–18; effect of restrictive bye-laws, 222–3, 225–6, 242; example followed by other offices, 234; quinquennial, 244–5; sums payable, including bonuses, 254–5
Reversionary Interest Society Ltd., 185, 255
Rock Life Assurance Co., 190, 197
Rogers, Samuel, 196
Royal Exchange Assurance, 21, 34, 35; the first to compete with the Equitable, 134
Royal Society: and development of the 'tools' of the actuary, 21–2, 24, 26; magnetic variation, 78–9; Bayes's theorem and Price, 88–90; life contingencies, 91, 195, 198–9; X-rays, observed by Morgan, 194–5; Copley medal, awarded to Morgan (for work on survivorships), 195; rejection of Barrett's columnar method, 199; election of Arthur Morgan (for his tabulation of mortality experience), 215

Scottish Amicable Life Assurance Society 208–9
Scottish Equitable Life Assurance Society, 210, 236
Scottish Widows Fund and Life Assurance Society, 198, 207, 210, 226
Scratchley, Arthur, and building societies, 211
'sea risque', 127

# INDEX

Walters family, 250

Warren family, 251–2

Westminster Society for Insurance of Lives and Survivorships, 134–5

White Lion, Cornhill, first assurances made at, 50

widows' annuities, see *annuities*

Willoughby of Parham, Lord, 32, 45, 53, 56, 260

Wirgman, Gabriel, 112

Witt, Johann de, 22

Wollaston, H. S. H., 218, 221, 223

X-rays, William Morgan and, 194–5

Young, Thomas, 192

GEORGE ALLEN & UNWIN LTD
*London: 40 Museum Street, W.C.1*

*Auckland: 24 Wyndham Street*
*Bombay: 15 Graham Road, Ballard Estate, Bombay 1*
*Buenos Aires: Escritorio 454–459, Florida 165*
*Calcutta: 17 Chittaranjan Avenue, Calcutta 13*
*Cape Town: 109 Long Street*
*Hong Kong: F1/12 Mirador Mansions, Kowloon*
*Ibadan: P.O. Box 62*
*Karachi: Karachi Chambers, McLeod Road*
*Madras: Mohan Mansion, 38c Mount Road, Madras 6*
*Mexico: Villalongin 32–10, Piso, Mexico 5, D.F.*
*Nairobi: P.O. Box 12446*
*New Delhi: 13–14 Asaf Ali Road, New Delhi 1*
*São Paulo: Avenida 9 de Julho 1138-Ap. 51*
*Singapore: 36c Prinsep Street, Singapore 7*
*Sydney, N.S.W.: Bradbury House, 55 York Street*
*Toronto: 91 Wellington Street West*